The Front Office Manual

Global Financial Markets series

Global Financial Markets is a series of practical guides to the latest financial market tools, techniques and strategies. Written for practitioners across a range of disciplines it provides comprehensive but practical coverage of key topics in finance covering strategy, markets, financial products, tools and techniques and their implementation. This series will appeal to a broad readership, from new entrants to experienced practitioners across the financial services industry, including areas such as institutional investment; financial derivatives; investment strategy; private banking; risk management; corporate finance and M&A; financial accounting and governance; and many more.

Titles include:

Daniel Capocci
THE COMPLETE GUIDE TO HEDGE FUNDS AND HEDGE FUND STRATEGIES

Guy Fraser-Sampson
INTELLIGENT INVESTING
A Guide to the Practical and Behavioural Aspects of Investment Strategy

Michael Hünseler
CREDIT PORTFOLIO MANAGEMENT
A Practitioner's Guide to the Active Management of Credit Risks

Gianluca Oricchio
PRIVATE COMPANY VALUATION
How Credit Risk Reshaped Equity Markets and Corporate Finance Valuation Tools

Andrew Sutherland and Jason Court
THE FRONT OFFICE MANUAL
The Definitive Guide to Trading, Structuring and Sales

Michael C. S. Wong and Wilson F. C. Chan (*editors*)
INVESTING IN ASIAN OFFSHORE CURRENCY MARKETS
The Shift from Dollars to Renminbi

Global Financial Markets series
Series Standing Order ISBN: 978-1-137-32734-5

You can receive future titles in this series as they are published by placing a standing order. Please contact your bookseller or, in case of difficulty, write to us at the address below with your name and address, the title of the series and the ISBN quoted above.

Customer Services Department, Macmillan Distribution Ltd, Houndmills, Basingstoke, Hampshire RG21 6XS, England

---

The Front Office Manual

The Definitive Guide to Trading, Structuring and Sales

Andrew Sutherland

and

Jason Court

First published 2013 by
PALGRAVE MACMILLAN

Palgrave Macmillan in the UK is an imprint of Macmillan Publishers Limited,
registered in England, company number 785998, of Houndmills, Basingstoke,
Hampshire RG21 6XS.

Palgrave Macmillan in the US is a division of St Martin's Press LLC,
175 Fifth Avenue, New York, NY 10010.

Palgrave Macmillan is the global academic imprint of the above companies
and has companies and representatives throughout the world.

Palgrave® and Macmillan® are registered trademarks in the United States,
the United Kingdom, Europe and other countries

ISBN: 978–1–137–03068–9

This book is printed on paper suitable for recycling and made from fully
managed and sustained forest sources. Logging, pulping and manufacturing
processes are expected to conform to the environmental regulations of the
country of origin.

A catalogue record for this book is available from the British Library.

A catalog record for this book is available from the Library of Congress.

Contents

List of Figures

List of Tables

Preface

We set about the task of writing a book, simply, to be the book *we* wished we had been given when we started our careers.

Working in finance is often very hard. There are long hours and huge responsibilities – and little time outside of work to improve one's skills. In many companies, what little formal training is available is patchy, simplistic and often irrelevant. There is nowhere to start, to get a foundation in the hard facts needed to understand the business – one has to just pick up bits and pieces of knowledge along the way.

This book won't solve the problem, of course. It's just a modest collection, another snapshot of facts and details, scratching the surface of a huge world of knowledge. What we hope it is, however, is a useful collection of information, information which until now has been scattered across many different sources, and often hidden behind abstruse language.

Language is an important part of the presentation of this book. We hope to express ideas in plain English. The concepts are hard enough as it is – hiding them behind jargon is unnecessary. In many cases, we've made a big effort to translate into readable prose ideas presented, until now, in the language of quantitative finance.

We're assuming readers have a background in mathematics, at least to secondary school calculus. There are no real derivations, or long tangents into mathematical explanations, but some ideas are most clearly expressed in equations. When we use equations, we try to explain all the terms as clearly as possible.

The areas we're concentrating on are those that we know are (a) major markets for banks and investors, (b) have, to some degree, been underreported so far and (c) require time and focus from employees of financial institutions.

The last point is the key – this book is for people who work in finance. We want to create a resource which is helpful to everyone who works in or around the front office. This means not only traders, assistants and employees who work on the trading desk, but also risk-managers, programmers in IT departments, department heads, spreadsheet designers … everyone, in short, who is required to understand some part of this complex world.

We concentrate a lot on over-the-counter business. This is not because it is more interesting (in terms of risk and volume, securities trading is often riskier), but because of the second point mentioned above: this area is less written about. There are countless tomes, for instance, on bond trading and bond mathematics (of which this book only covers some aspects) – but there are very few sources on, for instance, yield curves and their relation to trading.

We hope you enjoy the book and find it useful.

Acknowledgements

We'd like to thank everyone who helped us with the immense task of putting this book together – our families, colleagues and friends. Special thanks to Chandranth Gunjal, whose great knowledge of collateral and financing issues was very helpful; Vladimir Kvasov, who gave invaluable insight into foreign exchange trading issues; Don Smith at ICAP for very helpful background material on the interest rate markets; Piotr Karasinski for his help and teaching, over many years at Citi; Dean Garwood for his background on equity trading issues; Mike Tester for all his knowledge and advice.

1
The Structure of an Investment Bank

1.1 Introduction

Most people think of banks as institutions which take deposits from customers and lend money. This book isn't about these banks – it's about *investment banks*. While some of the larger investment banks may take deposits and lend money (through their consumer divisions) the primary aim of investment banking is something completely different.

Investment banks are special kinds of businesses, which do a number of unique things:

- *Core* investment banking is the business of helping companies issue stocks or bonds to raise money. This traditional role revolves around a small number of large deals, each producing considerable profit for the bank.
- *Sales and trading* is the business of buying and selling investment products to other professionals in the marketplace. (The definition of these 'investment products', and how they are managed, will take up much of this book.)
- *Analysis and research* goes along with sales – most banks provide market analysis (of a supposedly neutral type) to encourage clients to trade with them.
- Other functions may include wealth management services (wealthy individuals are good sales and trading clients as well), investment advisory services, or any number of services aimed at helping institutional customers do business with them.

This book primarily will look at the sales and trading functions, and the tasks performed by departments that support sales and trading.

While investment banks all have subtly different organizations, the basic structure is similar throughout the industry.

1

Core functions within a bank are broken down (roughly) into two types.

1. *Front-office* functions face the customer, or the market, and revolve around creating business – of a profitable sort, hopefully.
2. *Back-office* functions are supporting the business, and providing the backbone needed to make everything work.

On another level, we can divide the functions into *production* versus *control*:

- *Producer* functions are those which revolve around producing a profit for the bank.
- *Controller* functions revolve around making sure the producers do the right thing, keeping risks in line and making sure regulations are followed.

We can lay out the major types of role in a simple chart as shown in Figure 1.1.

We'll look at each of these functions during the course of this chapter. In brief, however, here are some summaries:

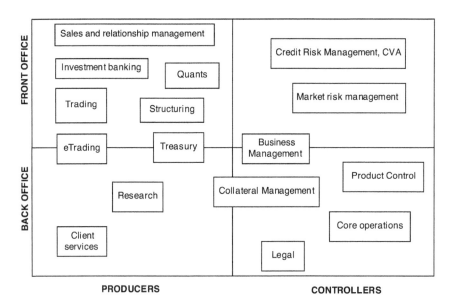

Figure 1.1   Divisions of an investment bank

- *Sales and relationship management.* Sales people are the ones in touch with individual clients – often corporations, hedge funds, investment and pension funds, or other financial institutions. Their role is to encourage trading with the bank – they send in requests to the trading desk, arrange deals and even book trades.
- *Investment banking.* This is the 'traditional' banking department, in charge of closing deals to issue new stocks, bonds or arrange loans to customers.
- *Trading.* The trading desk is at the heart of any investment bank. Divided into departments, usually by asset class, traders perform a multitude of functions on a daily basis:
  - *Making markets.* Often the desk is obligated to offer prices to buy and sell investment products, such as those arranged by investment bankers.
  - *Hedging risk.* Traders go to the market to enter into positions such that the bank's risk is minimized, within certain limits.
  - *Proprietary trading.* More popular in less risk-averse times, 'prop' trading is essentially taking speculative positions with the bank's money.
  - *Supporting sales.* Traders need to offer customers of the sales team prices on whatever products they want (often a stressful requirement).
- *Quants.* A 'quant' within the front office is a mathematician, working to ensure the trading processes and models are appropriate for the products being sold. This usually, but not always, involves derivatives trading.
- *Structuring.* A structurer is someone who builds more complex trades out of simpler building blocks supplied by the trading desk, for sale to customers.
- *Treasury.* Overseeing the balance sheet of the bank, Treasury is often involved in trading as well: buying and selling in the short-term money market, and funding the activities of the whole organization.
- *Research.* A largely self-contained department, research provides investment ideas and opinions to institutional clients.
- *Client services.* This department supports client requests for help in making or receiving payments, reports, valuations – anything a client of the bank may wish to know.
- *Credit Risk Management.* This control function ensures that traders don't over-extend credit lines to vulnerable customers, and monitors the collateral that customers are keeping with the bank. This may also include credit value adjustment (CVA), which provides credit 'insurance' of a sort to allow trading with risky customers.

- *Market risk management.* The Market Risk department ensures that trading positions stay within pre-set limits, and that the bank is not taking undue overall risk.
- *Product Control.* Product Control will provide an independent accounting function to the trading desk – reporting official profit and loss (P&L), and ensuring that traders trade only allowed products.
- *Operations.* – will do the actual work of making payments, receiving confirmation of trades, and other inter-bank functions.
- *Legal.* The Legal department supports the entire business – much like Operations – providing advice, documentation and support for each aspect of the bank's work.
- *Collateral Management.* Closely aligned with Credit Risk Management, Collateral Management is involved in ensuring counterparties have adequate collateral with the bank to support their trades.

It's worth noting that all of these departments (with a few exceptions) do most of their work via computer systems. Each department will have its own IT department to develop systems to do the work, support the systems, and extend them to enter new markets or to do new roles.

1.2   Front office versus back office

Traditionally, banks are set up with distinct front office and back office divides. The structure enables control of activities, and ensures that P&L (as well as risks to the bank) are ratified by more than one area.

As trades are placed on the book, the trader will monitor risk and generate estimate of P&L, but crucially, separate functions have responsibility for controlling and producing official measures.

This means that Product Control will have the job of saying how much money the trading desk has actually made. Risk controllers will have the job of saying how much (overall) the traders can trade of any one asset. Operations has the job of actually moving the money in and out of the bank. Segregation of duties, in theory, allows the bank to function in a well-ordered fashion. (When we read about rogue traders, many of the situations occur when the segregation between front and back office breaks down or is deliberately circumvented.)

Over the years, some banks have introduced a so-called *middle office*. This consists of departments, once considered to be more back office in their nature, which have moved closer to the front office – often sharing desks on the trading floor. Examples include (for instance) Client Service Teams (client facing operations departments), or Product Control. The definition of 'middle office' is different in different organizations.

1.3 The basic front to back process

The basic business process for banking can be rationalized into a series of sub-processes.

- The generation of trades and client management
- Trade and book management
- Risk management and valuation
- Settlement and mitigation of settlement risk
- General control processes

1.4 The generation of trades

Within large investment banks there are likely to be a series of legal entities, each with different benefits and restrictions. For example there may be a US broker dealer entity, and a series of banking entities. In very few banks does all business flow through a single legal entity.

Within all these entities, however, a few will be key to the trading process, and trades will flow in through a number of channels.

- Trades can come from exchanges. Some banks will make markets (in bonds, stocks, or derivatives) on exchanges, and trades will flow in electronically. For instance, if a bank has helped a client company issue stock, it is required to buy and sell the stock on an exchange (i.e. be a market maker) for a period of time after issuance.
- Trades can come from individual clients via the sales channels. Sales people will call the trading desk, or execute trades on electronic systems on behalf of clients.
- Trades can be the result of risk management on the inter-bank market. Banks are constantly buying and selling to each other in an effort to reduce their own risk, or boost profits.

The trading process can be very different depending on where the business is derived. If the bank is a member of an exchange, or has e-Commerce pricing platforms, the trades generated have a reasonably high degree of automation. Setting up on an exchange or setting up and onboarding clients to an eChannel may be initially expensive, but once done, the trading activity is largely rule based and requires manual intervention in exceptional cases only (like when a trade is for a large amount).

Dealing with financial institutions and major corporate entities as well as central banks is often by voice, usually with either a dedicated sales desk or a market maker directly. For captive business (i.e. long-standing customers), relationship managers will handle a lot of the business – cross selling products, arranging credit lines, and making introductions to specialist sales teams.

1.5 Structure versus flow

Trades can be divided into two broad types: *structured trades* and *flow* business. In general, structured trades are:

- More complex, consisting of a combination of two or more components combined into a single trade.
- More low volume. Structured trades are not only complex to assemble, but also complex to book, risk-manage, and most importantly, complex to sell.
- More high-margin. Structured trades generate more profit per-trade than simple, flow trades.

In contrast, flow business (such as trading stocks, bonds or currencies) generates little profit per-trade, but each trade is cheap to manage, and volume can become enormous.

In the aftermath of the 2007 banking crisis, structured trades have taken a bit of a beating. It was, after all, structured credit deals which started much of the drama leading to the collapse of Lehman Brothers. Appetite for highly structured products has tapered off a bit, and many banks have refocused on flow trading as a profit centre.

What types of structured trades exist?

The most popular form of structure is the so-called *structured note*. A structured note is nothing more than a bond, which can be bought and sold like any other investment. Notes are often listed (nominally) on a minor stock exchange somewhere. Unlike a bond, however, rather than paying a fixed rate of interest, a structured note will usually return to the holder some amount based on an embedded derivative trade. So for example, if the embedded derivative is a call option on XYZ corporation – the note-holder will make money if the stock price of XYZ rises before the note expires.

Notes are popular, mainly because it is impractical (and sometimes illegal) to sell derivatives to individual investors. Wealth management companies like to sell notes to their customers – the customer gets returns which are uncorrelated to, say, the stock market, and the wealth manager gets a hefty commission.

Along with structured notes, structured *deposits* are popular in Asia, where the note structure is not as legally convenient. A structured deposit can be sold by a bank, like a standard deposit, and it can offer the same returns as a structured note.

Structured one-off deals with clients represent another type of complexity. These are trades specifically crafted to help individual clients. Examples might include, say, a client of the bank who issues a bond in a foreign country (say, the United States). If the client is based in Europe, they'll want to make payments on the bond in Euros – and will need a variety of swaps to be arranged to ensure that they are not exposed to exchange rate or interest rate risk during the life of the bond. This sort of structure is very common, and a normal part of the work of any bank on a customer's behalf.

1.6　Vanilla versus exotic trades

As part of the structure/flow continuum, the world of derivatives is divided into 'vanilla' products (the simplest derivatives) and 'exotic' products. Prior to 2007, the trend was for more and more exotic products to be seen as vanilla, and for trading volumes in these exotic products to rise year after year.

Post-crisis, this trend has reversed.

One reason is the lack of appetite in the market for the increased risk posed by more exotic trades. Another reason is that the market structure itself has changed. As we'll see in the chapters on the yield curve (Chapters 3–5), the focus on funding costs has led to a great deal more complexity creeping into the pricing and risk management of vanilla trades. As some have said: 'vanilla is the new exotic'.

1.7　Over-the-counter versus securitized trades

Over-the-counter (OTC) trades are individual trades between a bank and a customer. Each one is, really, a separate contract. In contrast, when you trade in a 'security', the asset (like a structured note, for instance) is tied up in one nice legal bundle, which can then be sold to thousands of people, under the aegis of its own special branch of the law.

OTC trades are harder to manage by their very nature – each one must be separately booked into a trading system, and selling to more than one client means re-entering the whole thing each time.

A securities trade, by contrast, just needs a few details: the name of the security, the name of the customer, how much they bought (and at what price).

As banks move into a more regulated, more risk-conscious environment – more and more OTC trades are starting to look like securities trades. This is because, for simple, vanilla OTC deals, banks are being forced to use clearing-houses. A clearing house functions like a securities exchange for OTC deals: when a bank trades with a customer, they both agree to use the clearing house as an intermediary. The clearing house will manage credit, collateral and payments – the bank and the customer will be insulated from the risk that either will fail to meet their obligations.

1.8   New products

All of this ties in to the process, within a bank, of introducing new products.

Structuring new products, particularly structured notes or leveraged products, requires dialogue between structurers, sales and trading teams, to identify which product is most likely to have broad appeal to the bank's list of clients. The interaction is further complicated as the legal department will have to get involved with the creation of term sheets (and contracts). Often a 'new business committee', with representatives of all actors in the process, will have the final say in agreeing product launch.

Sales and Structurers will often run a deal pipeline, where new trades pitched to clients are logged, with a percentage likelihood of completion associated with them, plus a view of where the client and the product are in any approval workflow.

1.9   Trading and profit in a bank – the role of the trader

Where do banks make their money? A list of profit-making activities might look like this:

- Fees and profits from classic investment banking: arranging new issues of stocks, bonds or loans and/or advising clients on complex corporate re-structuring.
- Trading profits from buying and selling products in foreign exchange (FX), bond markets, stock markets or markets in derivatives.
- *Inception* gains from selling complex derivatives. (Inception gain is the profit from the initial sale – it stands apart from the smaller gains in daily market-making).
- Inception gains from issuing structured notes, structured deposits or other investment products.

We'll focus primarily on the second category – pure trading.

There are many different types of trading activities in many products. Simpler products which rely on volume will be traded in large size, or grouped into large positions. Here, traders will look to cover positions arising from banks client or broking activities or other financial institutions and even central banks. Market prices will be made as two-way prices with generally tight spreads. Where trading is with smaller clients, the sales desk will often spread the price wider, or quote a bid or offer not a two-way price. This enables the bank to lock in profit.

The trader is accountable for managing the risk associated with their book. This is monitored and ultimately controlled by the risk management department. Traders are also accountable for trading only with clients that have gone through the client on boarding process and are known to them, in products which the client has the necessary credit lines in place, and in products appropriate for the market knowledge of that client, although it is possible to trade on an 'execution only' bases which to some degree absolves the trader from the clients decision to trade in a product.

Traders are regulated and generally will have passed an exam and be registered with a Board like the Securities and Exchange Commission or the UK's Financial Conduct Authority. Some may have been 'grandfathered' in before the exam was mandatory, but all should be registered.

Traders are responsible for estimating and explaining their daily P&T figures, although these numbers are not posted to the bank's books and official P&L is subject to a separate control process. Just as with market risk, trader may employ different curve structures, pricing algorithms and market data intraday, as it may provide them with more competitive pricing. Official P&L and risk numbers will always be generated from official valuation models, market data and market data environments, and the P&L control process will, therefore, rarely tie up with the trader estimate.

Often, books will need short-term funding from a central Treasury function. These funding activities are internal to the company and provide general liquidity to the book. The trader, being within a profit centre, will be charged by Treasury for the cost of funding positions and this cost is deducted from the trader's P&L. Traders are seldom allowed to go directly to the market to fund positions. It should be noted that some trading books will have long cash positions, and these positions may be 'lent' back to the group's Treasury function. Similarly, securities and equities held may also be used to generate funding via 'buy sellback' or Repo agreements with the market.

Traders generally have dedicated support over and above groups of quants and other functions they may share. Some organizations employ desk support, clerical staff who will input or check the trader's input into bank's systems, for example. Almost all will have a business manager or chief operating officer (COO)who will manage the trading interactions with other departments, ensuring the process is well run, that the desk is free to conduct business efficiently, and facilitating the new business process with support groups to ensure new products can be launched in a timely manner.

It is worth mentioning briefly the new challenges to trading which have arisen from increased electronic trading. Algorithmic (Algo) trading, for example, uses computer algorithms to generate trades and orders, automatically and systematically, based on movements in, for example, price or timing. Algo trading systems can be run by banks themselves (to automate the trading process a bit) or by customers, such as hedge funds.

Hedge fund Algo systems can produce a high number of trades and can dramatically add to market volatility, and put stress on a bank's trading systems. In addition, Algo traders are notorious for exploiting even the slightest error in a bank's trading systems. If a system is off, even a small amount, in the price it offers, Algo customers will pounce. Bank systems usually limit the size of a trade that will be accepted before a human intervenes – but customers, knowing this, may 'machine-gun' the system with hundreds of trades just under the order limit size.

1.10   Different types of trading activity

Trading covers a multitude of different roles. The basic, broad categories include:

- Market making
- Sales trading
- Proprietary trading
- Treasury

Each of these roles differs, and each type of trader has different goals.

Market Makers are traders who are obliged to quote a two-way price in the market: they must offer to both buy *and* sell the assets they're trading – regardless of whether they want to or not. The Market Maker will charge a spread between the bid and offer prices – but the prices quoted will reflect their actual trading book position (Figure 1.2).

For example, if a trader has a long position in an equity, the price will usually be skewed downwards – to reflect the fact they want the market to buy from them. While Market Makers have the advantage of a spread, it is worth noting that in certain very liquid markets, such as FX, these spreads are very tight, and the trader will often try and keep the book flat, taking profit or realizing losses quickly. Where very large trades are undertaken, for example with a Central Bank, the trader is usually informed of the size of the deal being quoted for, and generally will quote a wider spread while the desk will simultaneously try and get multiple quotes from other Market Makers in smaller size in an attempt to flatten the book before the market moves.

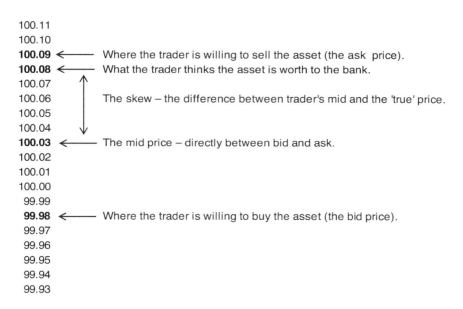

Figure 1.2 An example of spread and skew in market making

Sales traders' role is primarily to price trading arising from the Bank's sales network, or e-Commerce platforms. Spreads are generally much wider, even in very liquid markets, and are set by notional size and client categorization. Sales traders will generally have a view of the market, but also have the advantage of understanding what the Bank's client flows are. So a large Banking group with a Retail Banking arm will tend to be long certain currencies, for example, and prices quoted will reflect that. Volume and turnover are important for sales trading, and there will be an emphasis on retaining and rolling client positions. Sales traders are not, generally, supposed to take bets on the market – and will generally be required to fully hedge every position they take. (That said, in derivatives especially, it's never possible to completely hedge – so risky positions are allowed within strict limits.)

Proprietary trading takes positions on the Bank's own account. These positions are not derived from market or client activity – the traders are actively taking risky positions in an attempt to create profit. Proprietary trading will often take a long-term view of a market, either in terms of value or volatility, and will look to exploit any arbitrage opportunities. Owing to the nature of the trading activity, there are strict 'Chinese Walls' which need to be in place between the Proprietary Desks and the rest of the Bank's trading and other corporate activities such as Advisory and Mergers and Acquisitions.

Proprietary trading has been put under the spotlight recently by the Volcker Rule, which is part of the Dodd Frank Act that aims to reform banking practice in the wake of the Financial Crisis of 2007–2009. It defines proprietary trading as:

> engaging as principal for the trading book of the covered banking entity in any purchase or sale of one or more covered financial positions. Proprietary trading does not include acting solely as agent, broker, or custodian for an affiliated third party.

It is worth making a short note on the distinction between the trading book and the banking book. This is basically an accounting distinction which has an impact defined under Basel II.[1] The *trading book* is for assets which are not expected to be held to maturity – in other words, positions which will be actively traded and, therefore, will be marked to market every day. *Banking book* assets are to be held to maturity. The actual impact is the capital charge on the less liquid banking book is higher than that of the more liquid, marked to market, and actively hedged trading book.

Similarly, a 'covered position' as defined by the Volcker Rule is a security, including an option on a security; a derivative, including an option on a derivative; a contract of sale of a commodity for future delivery, or option on a contract of sale of a commodity for future delivery.

So as we can see, while Volcker does not prohibit all proprietary trading activity, it has curtailed it by product, with simple products, such as loans, Government bond trading, FX, commodities still allowed to be traded on the Bank's own trading account.

Banks will have a centralized *Treasury*. This performs a variety of roles, but its impact on trading activities is mostly relegated to funding positions. Put simply, Treasury will 'borrow' funds from cash rich trading activities, such sales relating to note issuance, and will 'lend' to desks requiring short-term funding. The Treasury should see the net position across the bank as a whole and can go to the market to fund that position. Treasury will 'fund' the banks internal desk based on its own funding rate. Of course there are many options available for banks to fund positions, and some desks will provide specialist funding, such as Bond Repos and stock borrow loans.

It is also worth making a short note on the distinction between the trading book and the banking book. This is basically an accounting distinction which has an impact defined under Basel II. The *trading book* is for assets which are not expected to be held to maturity – in other words, positions which will be actively traded and, therefore, will be marked to market every day. *Banking book* assets are to be held to maturity. The actual impact is the capital charge on the less liquid banking book is higher than that of the more liquid, marked to market, and actively hedged trading book

1.11 Risk management and valuation

Traders are often put into the awkward position of defending their own numbers – or risk being seen as sloppy, or worse.

At any point in time, a trader will have to have a good approximation of the risk run across the portfolio, and the profit or loss being made on a position. Traders, however, cannot be the official source of that information for the bank. It would be far too easy for manipulation of these numbers if the group accountable for creating profit were to be the group controlling the risk associated with their own endeavours and booking the P&L generation from these efforts into the Bank's balance sheet.

So while traders are 'responsible' for managing their own risk, and knowing their P&L, they are never the final arbiter. Their activities are, in fact, tightly controlled.

Control over trading is delegated to a number of independent groups. If we start by considering how these numbers are generated, there are a variety of parameters that require control.

On a trading desk, what needs controlling?

- The actual trading position. Traders are generally only allowed to trade specific products to specific limits in specific currencies.
- The valuation methodology the firm is prepared to accept as 'official'. The models used may be different to the ones used by the trading desk day-to-day. (This is particularly an issue in the case of derivatives, where different mathematical models determine how much something is 'worth'.)
- Market data is quite important: to find out how much something is worth, you need to know how much the market thinks it is worth. Control departments will oversee things such as the composition of the instruments in yield curves, FX rates, stock prices, or options volatilities. All of these need to have defined rate sources and cut off times, and the data 'snapped' needs to be verified.
- Limits need to be set and monitored – around how big positions can be (and how much risk can be generated), how much business can be done with certain clients, even things such as country and large exposure limits. All of these too need to be independently set and verified.

With these things controlled, we have the basis of an official valuation of a portfolio, and official risk numbers. These official numbers rely on processes which run at the end of the day, so generation of official figures is usually done systematically in overnight batch processes. The numbers can be decomposed into 'buckets' (or divisions) which explain either how the P&L has been created, or how sensitive a portfolio is to different risk elements. The official numbers can be compared with the trader's view of the world and adjustments for errors arising from mis-bookings, for example, can be made. Any such errors must be rectified systematically, front to back, and will be reflected in the following days official figures. It is generally accepted practice to allow for non-persisted adjustments to be made, especially to P&L, in the interim.

Nowadays, the Board and senior officials are responsible for defining the risk framework and associated controls. They need to convince the regulators that they have robust processes and systems to control their framework.

Trading businesses within the bank have different levels of product complexity and liquidity – so will run differing levels of risk. Generally, however, official valuation models will be set to assess the value of the portfolio at risk; stress testing and a measure of the sensitivity of a portfolio and its associated hedges to risk factors will be required – applying a series of standard 'shocks' (up and down movements) to market data, yield curves and volatility surfaces as well as applying historical and hypothetical shocks to simulate extreme potential market conditions; concentration of risk will be monitored; some view of instrument or market liquidity will be taken.

All of these risk measurements are required to be run systematically and monitored by the Board, or Senior Management in a Risk Board, on a daily basis. Valuation models and methodologies must be seen be in use in a practical sense within the organization, for example to calculate exposures versus real trading limits.

1.12   Explaining P&L

It's all very well to say that you've made a profit. It's much better if you can explain *how* you made it. This is not always straightforward.

The daily P&L process begins with discussions over differences in the headline P&L number between trading and product control – both of whom will have their own views. The sources of any differences need to be analysed. Often they will be timing issues related to market data snapshots or late trade booking or amendment. Sometimes they will arise from known issues in representation of a trade, particularly a structured one, in the firm's official systems. They may also reflect differences between trader curves and valuation models and those officially sanctioned by the risk monitors. Occasionally differences will relate to mis-booking of trades.

Once the major differences have been identified, trades requiring amendment will be amended and re-booked in the trading systems to flow down into the systems of record (and be corrected the next evening when the official P&L is run). In parallel, non-persisted adjustments will be made by Product Control to correct the P&L.

The headline P&L number is then analysed further. This process, sometimes called 'P&L Attribution', or 'P&L Explained', means breaking down the source of each gain or loss.

The most obvious change to P&L is new trades added to the portfolio, as is changes in price of the existing portfolio (including maturing trades or trades sold off the book). However, just as risk numbers are sensitive to a variety of factors, so is P&L. Options are sensitive to time. Products may have exposures to fluctuations in interest rates or FX rates, products that accrue (e.g. bonds or equities) or amortize will also see daily changes, and volatility and changes to market liquidity will also impact P&L. We'll see more of this subject in Chapter 13 on Risk.

1.13   The role of Product Control

Product Control is in charge of the process of P&L Attribution.

To do this well, however, they need a number of tools. They need to be able to oversee the process of re-valuing the books based on 'official' rates – which means overseeing the process of generating these rates, and running the official end-of-day pricing and risk numbers on the bank's systems.

All of this is quite complex, and requires a lot of systems to be in place and running smoothly on a day-to-day basis. Frequently the end-of-day numbers, as well as being the official P&L for the bank, are used by the trading desk at the start of the day to get their position. If the end-of-day numbers are not available (as they sometimes aren't) there can be quite a lot of trouble.

Product Control will construct a trial balance based on the prior day's activity. The object of a trial balance is to reconcile all debit and credit ledger accounts, thus ensuring no errors in posting to the general ledger.

Product Control will often undertake a periodic 'off market rate check' function, where rates used for revaluation purposes by trading are compared against the market, and movements in the rates themselves within the period are checked to ensure they are within acceptable and expected general parameters. This control also ensures that trades have been executed and re-valued at fair market rates for the client.

As products become more complex, so do the valuation models to support the accurate pricing of them. Because products have evolved from more basic types, and also owing to the more structured packaging of groups of products, for example, a note may have a basket of equities, and option, and a FX leg associated with it, many of the trading and risk systems simply cannot accurately value them. The P&L will, therefore match, but be incorrect in the system and the ledger. In these instances, the trade will be valued off-line (e.g. in a spreadsheet) using the correct and officially sanctioned model. Product Control is responsible for independently checking the valuation. The difference between the mark-to-market (MTM) calculated in the trading system and fed to the ledger, and the correct, validated MTM is posted to the balance sheet as a valuation reserve. Product Control will also ensure that the valuation reserves match the differences between incorrect and correct MTM and have been posted correctly.

1.14   Sales and distribution

For all sell-side[2] institutions, the sales teams are vital to the operation. They may be organized to sell specific products, to target particular client segments, geographically, or to support certain specific trading channels such as e-Commerce.

The sales team is a point with many connections. Let's consider some of them.

The most obvious is with the client. A sales desk will have a client list, with sales people either sharing clients or having a one-to-one relationship. This is usually determined by the kind of client the desk covers. For an organization with small commercial firms, often the number of clients and the smaller size and volume of trading will lead to a sharing of customers around the team. For large and specialist relationships, a sales person may own a specific set of client relationships. Where an organization has a retail base, the sales function is often more of a distribution function: sales will distribute quotations to branches, and deal with a branch office as intermediary, rather than directly with the client. In these cases, the branch will know the customer and this is more efficient than having a central sales desk having to complete all the regulatory and credit checks. (High net worth individuals, however, will probably have direct relationships.) Retail business will usually be netted into larger positions at average rates for the sales trader, who will then execute in the market.

Management Information and Customer Relationship Management are vital for a sales team when dealing with clients. They will usually have position maturity diaries for clients, which enable them to actively contact them in an attempt to keep funds with the bank. They will know what the client's business is, and also have a record of what kind of levels the client may be interested in trading at in the future. They will diarize calls with the clients and synchronize diaries with relationship managers to visit client sites. Very few organizations have managed to convert Management Information into Business Intelligence. Those that have a distinct advantage, as their relationship with the client can become much more proactive. Clearly, managing highly productive interactions with customers becomes harder the more of them a sales desk has to service.

The relationship with the client relies on two further interactions, those between the relationship manager and with the credit department.

For smaller clients, the credit lines are usually managed by via the relationship manager, who will look at all of the client's requirements from the bank. Clients are often categorized by size and geography and discussions will include general banking facilities, such as overdrafts, and loans or deposits, specialist trade financing such as documentary credits, as well as the trading activities the client wishes to undertake. The relationship between relationship managers and sales desks is key. Often a relationship manager will ask sales teams to price more competitively in certain instances in order to keep the client 'sticky' in the face of competition. The sales teams, on their part, are able to discuss new opportunities with the relationship manager, maybe based on new product offerings, and are able to target clients more effectively with their help.

For large clients and institutions, credit lines will be in place, pre-authorized and managed via the Credit Risk Management function. Recently, these credit checks have been incorporated into the trade workflow and in some cases are automated pre-check checks in real time. For more esoteric products, the credit risk calculations and the facility may be negotiated along with the trade term sheet and managed as a 'one off' credit line alongside the clients major credit facilities.

Over the past couple of decades, banks have invested heavily in e-Commerce platforms. Initially these were seen as a threat from the sales perspective, as roll-over activity and new trading activity could be done, within credit facilities, without their intervention. However, while making trading of certain products such as FX easier for the client, it has actually allowed the sales teams to spend more time looking at data around how the client is trading, and what cross selling opportunities there are, while reducing the amount of time spent on small trade execution. A good sales team in an organization with good e-Commerce platforms have the tools to enhance the client relationship.

Even with e-Commerce platforms, however, there are still many instances where clients will get on the phone to their sales desk. E-Commerce can't cover everything, and usually clients are limited in what they can trade on any electronic platform. Any deviation from the pre-agreed (or technically allowed) trading menu will lead to a discussion over the phone.

1.15   Structuring

Trading is a fast-moving part of the business – there's not always time to stop and design solutions to specific problems.

Structurers help with this by concentrating on designing things such as structured notes (mentioned previously), or other, complex deals with customers which require special attention.

Structures are almost always simple combinations of products the bank already sells – put together in a form which makes them attractive to customers.

For example – suppose a customer wants to arrange to borrow money today in US dollars – but only pay a fixed lump-sum in Euros in two years' time. The bank could arrange a series of swaps and FX transactions easily to make this happen – and a structurer could work with the sales team to put together a proposal. Each part of the structure (the FX trades, the swap, the loan) might normally have a fee associated with it, perhaps in the form of an increased interest rate. The structurer could work to reduce the individual fees to make the overall package profitable for the bank, while still being attractive to the customer.

Once finished, the structuring desk will put together a term sheet, or proposal, for the customer. They'll also work with the trading desk to get up-to-date prices, and generally serve as a technical resource and go-between.

1.16   Quantitative analysts

In addition to structurers, the quants will also provide technical assistance to the trading desk to help design and price complex products. Where the structuring team can make products that are simple, linear combinations of existing products – the quants are generally in charge of products where the pay-outs are non-linear, inter-dependent or otherwise more complex.

Quants are primarily responsible for the generation of *pricing and risk models*. Later parts of this book will go into more detail on exactly how this works in practice – but it's important to understand what exactly a pricing model is.

Most pricing models are involved in the pricing of derivatives. A pricing model will give the value of a trade – based on certain assumptions. Usually, these assumptions are:

- You can hedge the risk from the trade, in a market that's both transparent and liquid.

- You, in fact, *have* hedged the risk from the trade.
- You re-assess and re-hedge the risk on a regular basis.

If these criteria are met, then a good quant model, with inputs of current liquid asset prices, will give an estimate of the value of a derivative instrument which depends on those assets.

Quants are responsible for creating models for the trading desk; separate teams of quants will be involved in checking the work of the trading desk quants. These quants (doing so-called *model validation*) will re-assess the trading desk models using their own research and development methods.

Traders are at liberty to use whatever models they want during the trading day – official pricing and risk management models and curve construction, applied to the official books and records of the bank, will usually be older, more established models, agreed by the firm's internal pricing committee. This more conservative approach is usually taken to ensure external reporting is easily explainable and in line with other market competitors. Occasionally, different desks may price the same product using different intraday models, depending on how the product is used in their portfolio. The common 'official' model, therefore, also ensures consistent books and records reporting.

1.17 Support functions around the trading desk

Within the front office, there are a series of support functions. They are designed to maximize trading activities, either by focusing on process improvement, reducing the administrative overhead or the traders, providing ancillary services to make client relationships 'stickier', or making product pricing more competitive.

Most trading desks will have a business manager or COO. This role is vital in ensuring the smooth running of current and future trading activities, and ensuring compliance with firm or regulatory directives. The business manager will regularly meet and direct the support functions, including IT. For current business, they will manage the risks and efficiencies of the supporting functions, often through regular front office and back office (FOBO) meetings and by reviewing key performance indicators (KPI) and key risk indicators (KRI) information. They are uniquely placed in order to keep the support functions in order, but also to ensure trading are doing what they should be in terms of timeliness of execution, and procedural aspects such as curve marking at the end-of-day.

The COO will ensure that the impact of upcoming regulatory or firm's best practice are understood by all, including trading, and that all associated projects and process changes are understood, appropriate and delivered on time. For new business, they will coordinate all groups front to back, ensuring that impacts are understood, risk and caveats to trading activity are appropriate, and the appropriate approvals are in place. They will also coordinate activities with sales, structuring, trading, risk management and legal with the client and ensure the appropriate documentation is agreed and signed off, such as term sheets, netting and credit agreements.

Desks may also have trading assistants. Their role can be vague. Initially they would be responsible for inputting deal tickets into the Bank's trading and risk management systems, however most firms nowadays expect traders to do this themselves. Trading assistants often maintain spreadsheets, or do repetitive tasks that don't need trader focus.

1.18 Research

Almost all banks will have an economist or a research department. Their dual role is to enhance the client relationship and differentiate the bank from its rivals; and to provide impartial reading of the market for the bank's own trading operations. They will review key economic data due out with the trading floor which may affect the market, usually giving the market expectation for a figure, and announcing the actual numbers as they are released with an associated observations. They will provide in-depth, independent research into the financial performance and expectations of companies, indices and markets, and tend to be organized by specialism in either a market or a sector.

Their output is produced in written or online format. The firm's chief economist will often appear on news and financial channels on television. The content is designed to help sales teams discuss specific market segments or macro-economic factors with their clients. These conversations will increase client awareness of the risks their business or trading activity may be running and provide sales teams with an opportunity to sell hedge instruments to clients.

1.19 General control processes

As we have seen, control and segregation of duties is key to managing risk and ensuring profitability in an investment bank. Organizations are large, and departments are often set up as product silos.[3] Communication both internal and external is vital. Some communications and control processes are externally mandated by regulation, others internally mandated by bank committees, and some just evolve as generally accepted best practice.

Most organizations have seen organic growth into evolving markets. This evolution may be geographical, in terms of trading in emerging economies where the range of instruments available to trade will grow over time from simple FX and money markets; it may be an evolution of complexity, where client needs require banks to innovate and specifically tailor financial products at very specialized areas of business; or it may be driven by technology, for example Algo trading, or even benchmarking and averaging or large trade time series information into single rates to be applied to huge volumes of trades.

Many organizations deal with product innovation through vehicles like New Product Committees. These require structurers, sales, traders and relationship managers to articulate clearly what the product profile is, who the target audience for the product are, and what benefits there will be in trading it. All the areas that will then need to manage, control or support the new activity, will be asked to write up their process and any concerns or caveats they want to place on the new business. Compliance and regulatory issues, such as which entity the business will be conducted in, will also be set out, models will be reviewed to ensure official systems and control functions are able to accurately value the product and assess market risk, credit impact will be discussed as will any management of settlement and confirmations, as well as how the product will be booked to the balance sheet and shown on regulatory returns.

For existing business, some organizations also apply this 'front to back' approach with regular FOBO meetings. These meetings allow business and trading management to review, usually monthly, metrics set out designed to measure the control environment. These metrics are based on pre-defined KRIs. They tend to cover things like the age of unresolved account breaks, number of unmatched confirmations or non-affirmed trades, balance sheet utilization, liquidity costs, system outages, and so on. The meeting allows the back office to discuss issues with the current trading set up, and which traders enter trades late or without the correct client information, and so on. It also allows the business and trading management to monitor the performance of the front office through pre-defined KPIs, monitoring month on month or year on year profit numbers for example, or the success or a new product, and performance of a client sector or sales team.

External reporting is continually evolving and can be an onerous undertaking, as regulators tend to issue guidelines to banks but rarely direct them as to how the reporting needs to be physically implemented, instead leaving it to the bank to define best practice.

The increase of regulation has been noticeable over the past two decades. Often regulatory changes lead to re-structuring within the banking organization itself. This can be a costly process. Just understanding the nuances of the regulation, and then ensuring the information can be reported, can be a large undertaking. Often the consolidation of data is a major issue relying on manual processes and complex data translation and enrichment. Some examples of current regulation include:

- *Capital requirements.* The amount of capital a bank has to hold versus the amount lent. This is set by the Bank for International Settlement's Capital Accords, starting with Basel I in 1988. The most recent evolution, Basel III will require banks to hold six per cent of Tier I (shareholders' equity and disclosed reserves) capital of risk-weighted assets (RWA). Basel III also states that banks must hold enough high-quality, liquid assets to cover the next 30 days of its net cash outflows. These changes are designed to ensure there are adequate assets available to a bank to cover the general default risk of their portfolio.
- *Reserve requirements.* The amount of client deposits that must be retained by the bank as a ratio of the total held. The remaining amount can, therefore, be used by the bank to lend.
- *Financial disclosure and reporting requirements.* Regulations like the US Sarbanes-Oxley Act of 2002 add extra emphasis, among other things, on banks proving the independence of their financial auditing process and the need for banks to show they have no conflicts of interest.
- *Anti-money laundering and Anti-terrorism.* Banks needs to prove that they know who their clients actually are and the source of their clients' money. This makes client onboarding more lengthy and has also resulted in additional training programmes for bank staff.
- *Large exposure reporting.* Large exposures against a single client or institution, or in a certain position have to be reported. This is to protect the bank's capital against a single point of default risk.

Finally, departments such as HR and Compliance help with managing the reputational risk of an organization. While rogue traders may damage a firm's image, more common events which can change public and client perception of an organization are disputes for wrongful dismissal, general redundancies and outsourcing policies, mis-selling of products, and any manipulation which shows the bank as acting in its own interests and not those of its customers.

In summary, banks require a control structure to manage market risk, settlement risk, operational risk, and reputational risk. Some of these risks are managed by specific functions in the organization, and others through FOBO coordination and collaboration.

1.20   Risk management

Management of the risk arising from a Bank's trading activities is a key part of the process. The process itself is not solely limited to the risk management function, traders, relationship managers, product controllers, financial controllers, regulators and operations are all involved in managing aspects of risks. Operational and reputational risks can all be exacerbated by poor market and Credit Risk Management and are, therefore, intrinsically linked. This section will focus solely on the risk management function, however, namely the control and management of the bank's exposure to market and credit events based on the assets and liabilities, options and future commitments they have on their books.

The risk management landscape has changed dramatically in the past 30 years.. Once, firms did a lot of risk management (such as it was) on simple spread-sheets – now complex, expensive risk management systems are essential. Market risk 'worst-case' scenarios are more realistic, and focus on more extreme cases than ever before. Estimation of different types of risk is seen as important (such as liquidity risk, and risk of sudden market jumps). Credit Risk Management has become more sophisticated, granular, and focuses not just on clients, but on entire countries and sectors. Margining – a once small part of the risk management function – has come to play a central role in both risk and valuation across all asset classes.

1.21   Trading and market risk management

Trading and market risk measures the effect on the value of a position held by the trader when changes occur in the market. For example, a trading book may change in value due to changes in FX rates or interest rates, changes to volatility of the market, or even the time to maturity of the instrument.

The role of risk management is to identify and assess market risks. They must establish the appropriate models and methodologies to be used, establish what risk scenarios and measures are appropriate, and define the process for generation and calculation of these values. Risk management is also responsible for setting risk limits, position limits and loss control limits.

Trading books are marked to market every day. These marks are reviewed and ratified as part of the role of trading and market risk management (as we talked about, in the P&L process earlier). Because positions may have exposures to other market factors, FX rates, and instruments making up the yield curve will also have 'official' rate snaps, again verified as part of the daily risk and P&L process.

Over the past decades there has been significant investment in risk management systems. These allow traders to manage intraday market risk, and equally allow trading and market risk managers to run complex risk scenarios. However, even with this level of investment, the more complex and structured a product, the more likely it is, still, to be risk managed on spread-sheets. This has led to a series of operational risk issues, generally arising from lack of automated controls over data, specifically trade data, market data environments and valuation models. Part of the control process is always to move as many trades as possible onto high-volume, controlled, uniformly understood computer systems.

1.22 Credit Risk Management

Credit risk arises because of the potential for another bank, counterparty or other institution to default on its obligations. This may mean the failure to provide funds in settlement, the failure to deliver an instrument or product, or the failure to meet an event under the lifecycle of an instrument. Credit risk can be at a counterparty or individual level; be a market wide event; or can be a default at a sovereign level. Credit Risk Management therefore needs to monitor exposures versus pre-agreed limits at a counterparty level, a trading or banking book level, and as a total exposure across the entire operation.

Over the years, the emphasis on managing risk has been shifting from market risk to credit risk. In the past, credit risk was largely seen as the management of client credit facilities. With the rise of credit default swaps and options, as long as a book seemed to be hedged, little additional attention was paid to it. While credit risk managers would often highlight that they required the same sort of tools and systems trading and market risk managers had access to, the level of investment was simply not the same. Customer credit facilities were often the domain of the relationship manager, and sales teams would often treat them more as a guideline than a hard and fast limit. When trades were executed, the majority of institutions were unable to check limits pre-trade in real time. Meanwhile, most of the systems budget was spent on sophisticated trading and market risk platforms.

Nowadays, credit risk plays a much more central role. Traditionally, systems inside a bank would show, for each customer, the allowed 'credit limits' that the bank would be allowed to trade within. These limits, based on the amount of risk involved in a trade (and how much money the customer would owe the bank) were flexible. While still in place, these systems are now augmented by a heavy reliance on collateral, a much more stringent measurement of risk, and the use of third-party clearing-houses to serve as risk-reducing intermediaries.

1.23   CVA

Some banks have also introduced another concept – the *CVA* (*credit value adjustment*) desk. Standing between the trading desk and the customer, the CVA desk will, in effect, underwrite customer trading – for a fee.

The insurance metaphor is apt, in fact. The trading desk that wants to trade with a credit-risky customer can, essentially, buy insurance against the customer's default. The cost of this insurance is then bundled into the trade.

This makes the trader's role simpler as well. Rather than having to price credit-risky customers' trades using special credit-risky models (as was sometimes the case), trading desks can use the same risk-free models to get values for everyone's trades – and then add the cost of CVA on top.

The CVA desk will then have to work closely (very closely) with the credit risk department to ensure that their exposure hedging is effective. CVA desks can use a combination of methods to hedge against counterparty default. Credit default swaps (which pay a premium on a customer's default) are very popular (although overuse can drive up customers borrowing costs, and systemic risks abound). Diversification, like a traditional insurer, can play a role: with many customers, one can allow one or two to default and the fees from the others will cover the loss.

1.24   Back-office functions: settlement and mitigation of settlement risk

The bank's Operations department is pivotal to its success for many reasons. Nearly all trading activity results in cash movements, whether it be a premium payable on an option, a periodic cash-flow (such as a dividend, coupon or swap payment), or physical payment for an asset bought or liability received onto the book.

The more efficient the operation is, the more profitable the business.

Product complexity can greatly challenge the operating efficiency and increase the bank's operational risk profile, but even the control of simple cash movements can be challenging depending on volume or netting, for example. Management of the bank's accounts held with other firms (their Nostro accounts) is often time consuming and usually a whole department will be dedicated to following up un-reconciled or missing items from the accounts. Nowadays, banks tend to rationalize the number of accounts they hold with other firms, but this simplification also adds its own control issues, as many different product areas will use the same account, and the effort required in chasing up discrepancies is multiplied.

As industries move to centralized clearing of products and more exchange trading, the role of operations shifts, as trading activity tends to be *pre-matched*. The complexity moves to managing margin payments and collateral holdings.

Operations will also be involved in a series of trade lifecycle events. These will range from manual confirmation generation for certain products, confirmation or affirmation and trade matching, event fixing, such as fixing non-deliverable rates or swap reference points, trade or portfolio novations, managing expiry events; and cancellations, queries and amendments.

Many of these terms are idiosyncratic to the operations world – a little explication of some common back-office processes might be helpful.

- *Novation.* Novation is the process of changing the counterparty on a trade. A trade with customer A may be novated if customer A transfers the obligation to customer B (for a fee, perhaps).
- *Matching.* Trades come to the back office from two sources: the trading desk and third-party customers. Matching is the process of lining up these trades into matching pairs – each trading desk trade corresponds, typically, with one customer trade.
- *Confirmation.* In the old days, OTC trades were individually confirmed by fax. These days, electronic systems do most of the work, but for complex, one-off trades the old ways persist.
- *Affirmation.* A short-form of confirmation, affirmation consists of 'affirming' to a third party(such as a clearing house) that trades 'alleged' against the bank do, in fact, correspond to matching trades at the bank.
- *Allocation.* Large trades are often done in blocks, sometimes against a single 'block' counterparty. Allocation is the process of breaking the large trade down into smaller trades, each of which may, in reality, settle against a different counterparty.

Settlement means making payments – moving actual cash or (in some cases) ownership of physical things (such as precious metals). The primary role of Operations is to ensure settlement occurs accurately, in accordance with Standard Settlement Instructions, in a timely manner, and in accordance with the legal documentation associated with the trade. Where this does not occur, Operations are also accountable for resolving errors.

Settlement can be, as mentioned, as cash payment or physical transfer. Nowadays, most physical settlement is actually electronic, where ownership of a security or a commodity, for example, is updated by the repository. In addition, some instruments which would have traditionally be settled physically, are now traded as 'contracts for difference' and cash settled at maturity.

The timing of settlement varies by product, and market or region, and the time the trade is executed.

The bank will hold Standard Settlement Instructions (SSIs) for counterparties, and will deliver cash to their nominated accounts. Banks themselves will nominate their own account they wish to receive cash into. (An account a bank holds with another institution is called a 'Nostro', and an account held at the bank by another institution is known as a 'Vostro'.)

Often, trades will be executed at a 'parent' level and then allocated across a variety of client accounts or entities. Operations are required to book the allocations to the correct settlement accounts.

Executed trades will have a legal confirmation associated with them. For complex structured products, a term sheet will be drawn up and agreed with the client pre-trade, and the terms in that document will be used to manually create a confirmation. Confirmations need to be matched and it is the role of Operations to manage the confirmation process and resolve any queries and error associated with it. For many markets, confirmations are standard and automated, and may even be dispensed with, replaced by an affirmation of a trade instruction. This is particularly true of trading on exchanges or through central counterparties. The role of Operations has changed, therefore, to be more concerned with reconciliations of trades alleged by exchanges and affirmed by trading, and the internal trade capture and risk management systems in the bank.

Cash settles over bank accounts. Within Operations, the Nostro Control group will monitor bank statements to ensure that all credits and debits have been passed and will follow up on any 'breaks' which will occur if the bank itself has not posted the correct funds on settlement date, or funds have remained unclaimed by the counterparty. Most Nostro accounts are not interest bearing, so they are run with close to flat balances. A large Nostro break can, therefore, either result in an overdraft charge, or result in a large balance that could have been invested overnight or used elsewhere within the group as funding. Nostro accounts are usually single currency. Operations will also monitor 'reciprocity'. In other words, they will use specific accounts in a currency held with banks which tend to use their Vostro account most. Often the bank will have negotiated preferential overdraft terms with other banks based on the understanding that a certain amount of settlement transactions will occur over that bank account.

1.25 Client Services and Client Valuations

Other middle office functions designed around the client experience include teams such as Client Services and Client Valuations.

Client Services teams are important for certain trading activities, especially where trades are not necessarily transacted with the bank. For example, a prime broker will generally have a team dedicated to ensuring all trades given up or given in to the bank have been received, matched or affirmed. They will also need to ensure that client collateral and margin activity is managed, and will have to resolve queries arising from clients. Owing to the nature of the business, that is, high-volume low P&L, and the highly automated nature of most modern day prime brokerages, queries may be rare, but will generally be impactful and time sensitive. Client Services will also be expected to field questions on any official reporting to the client from the bank as well as talking to other banks or brokers. They will also have to liaise with the client about roll-over activity, so in reality they are almost a mix of sales, Client Valuations and operations all in one.

Producing statements for clients with the correct current market valuation is straight forward for simple products, and these activities, if not automated, will generally be done in the back office. However, for structured and exotic products, where pricing is more complex and where trades are made up of different trade legs with potentially different product types, automating a valuation from the back office will only lead to a misstatement of the current revaluation. In these instances, a Client Valuation group may be formed in the middle office to produce periodic valuations for clients or to field client queries on the value of their holdings. The staff in these groups will be specialist and familiar with the products, and will sit close enough to trading to get price updates as required.

1.26   Finance and regulatory reporting

Banks are required to disclose their finances. Regulators will set out the financial reporting standard and banks are required to produce annual financial statements which have been independently audited. Furthermore, the Bank's Board has to affirm that the financial statements have been produced according to the standards, and must set out what internal controls and processes have been followed to ensure that is the case. The frequency of financial reporting is often more than annual; usually they are required to produce quarterly disclosure statements.

The Board sets out how the bank will implement the standards set down by the Regulator, and the Finance department's role is to ensure these are being followed in its day-to-day activities.

The main daily control activity is the creation of the *trial balance.* Finance will list all of the ledgers and sub-ledgers based on its chart of accounts, and will ensure all credit and debit entries sum to zero. Once the trial balance has been completed, and the sum of credit values and debit values are shown to be equal, Finance will create a balance sheet and a P&L statement. The trial balance does have limitations. It is reconciliation at a balance level, and cannot capture if individual ledger entries have been posted incorrectly (e.g. if a fee has been incorrectly booked). That error will be captured by reconciliations in Operations, as the cash paid or received on the Nostro will differ from the expected amount incorrectly booked in the Bank's systems.

The Bank's Board also has to prove to Regulators that it is adhering to other standards and is complying with its Banking Licence. The main areas that the bank needs to satisfy the Regulator over are:

- *Prudential* – The minimization of risk, especially to client deposits, but for all of the Bank's creditors.
- *Systemic* – Ensuring that risk is adequately managed, especially where adverse market conditions occur.
- *Compliance* – Ensuring banks cannot be used as vehicles for money laundering and that the origins of funds held with the bank and the end client is known.
- *Capital requirement* – Set out in the various Basel Accords, covering the relationship between the assets held (and their relative quality) against capital.
- *Reserve requirement* – Some Regulators will stipulate the amount of reserves a bank needs to hold with the Central Bank. This has largely been replaced by the Capital Requirement rules, although the Bank of England still has operational reserve requirements while the FED tends to stipulate the reserve as a percentage of the proportion of deposits.
- *Liquidity* – Maintaining the balance between short-term assets and liabilities and the relative 'stickiness' of funds.

The Bank's Regulatory Reporting department will be responsible for producing these reports, usually as snapshots. The Regulation will differ by jurisdiction and by product. Regulation is constantly evolving in reaction to market events – and it's obvious that since 2007 or so the rate of regulatory change has accelerated dramatically.

1.27 Collateral Management

Collateral is designed to mitigate credit risk. Originally, loans would be backed by collateral, which would be legally the property of the lender in the event of a default on the loan. The most obvious example of a collateralized loan is a mortgage, where the bank has legal title over the asset bought by the loan (the property) in the even the borrower cannot repay it.

Collateral is taken by banks for a variety of trading activities, but mostly for derivative exposures and OTC trades. Margining at exchanges or for Prime Brokerage activities will also result in collateral being pledged.

Because collateral involves a legal pledge, collateral agreements are nego-tiated before trading can begin between the bank and its counterparty in the relevant instruments. Often the ISDA[4] Credit Support Annex (CSA) template is used as a standard template. The collateral pledged has to be of sufficient quality for the bank to accept it. Generally collateral is posted as cash or Government Securities, and in acceptable liquid currencies, although there are a wide range of instruments that may be considered, although not all of them will have the same 'value' in terms of quality.

Pledging collateral can achieve multiple goals. It can free up existing credit lines which may be close to limits; allow access to more exotic or risky markets; provide a negotiating tool when agreeing credit terms; reduce capital exposure by netting; increase liquidity.

The process of Collateral Management starts with the valuation of cli-ent liabilities to the bank. The initial trade will create an initial margin amount (IA) which will be called from the client. The positions are then market to market periodically, and changes in the margin calculation will be assessed against the CSA. Margin is usually called in steps. The varia-tion margin is calculated and if it has increased enough it will trigger a further margin call. It should be noted that clients can also ask for col-lateral pledged to be returned to them if the MTM moves in the opposite direction.

Collateral Management are then responsible for ensure the margin pay-ments are made and the collateral balances adjusted accordingly. They will resolve disputes, and also check that the collateral posted is valid under the CSA.

Collateral Management are also responsible for valuing the collateral held. (In the case of Government Bonds, they are also required to pay the coupon back to the client.)

2
Interest Rate Swaps

2.1 An overview of the product

Interest rate swaps (IRS) are incredibly popular. They have come from humble beginnings (only a few decades ago) and grown to be an irrevocable part of the fabric of our financial system. They are bought and sold around the world by banks, individuals, hedge funds – so much so, that the total outstanding *notional* amount of swaps amounts to hundreds of trillions of dollars.[1] As we'll see, *notional* amount is just that – this isn't real money. Notional amounts are rarely transferred between parties – they are just used to compute interest payments. But still, the amount of risk involved in enormous.

Because it is a *swap*, the IRS agreement means that two parties are involved, and each one swaps, literally, payments with each other. The typical IRS will include one party making payments on a fixed interest rate for the life of the swap, and the other making floating-rate payments based on a public, published floating-rate index.

An IRS is an *over-the-counter* (OTC) instrument. Each OTC trade is a separate legal contract between the parties – there is no underlying thing being transferred. This is in contrast, for instance, to the purchase or sale of stocks, bonds or futures – where one party is (contractually) selling some bit of a fungible security instrument to another. If I wish to back out of a stock purchase – I simply sell the stock. If I wish to back out of a swap trade, I must cancel the contract (often at a cost), or do another, new trade in the opposite direction (if possible).

Rather than buying or selling IRSs, we refer to buying *payers* (where we pay the fixed rate) or buying *receivers* (where we receive the fixed rate).

Figure 2.1 shows the hypothetical payments on a four-period vanilla IRS which is half-way through its life. The floating payments in the past have been determined, and fixed, while the floating-rate payments in the future are still unknown.

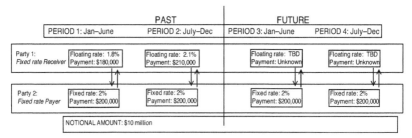

Figure 2.1   An example of payments and rate-fixings in an interest rate swap

At the end of each period, the party that pays the fixed rate pays a fixed amount. This amount rarely changes much (unless, for instance, if the one payment period is shorter or longer than the others).

At the end of each period, the party that pays the floating-rate pays an amount that changes based on the level of the floating *index*. What is a floating-rate index? Obviously, it is an interest rate – an interest rate that changes on a daily basis. Beyond this, it can be just about anything – within certain parameters.

Firstly, an index must be published every (business) day in a manner that can be referred to in legal contracts. So, for instance, UK Sterling 3-month LIBOR might be referenced as the rate published on the Bloomberg page

---

The ISDA Master Agreement

The institution most involved in swap dealing internationally is ISDA – the International Swap Dealers Association. The most important document between two parties, indeed more important than any single OTC agreement, is the ISDA master agreement. Almost universally, before anybody can trade a swap, they must sign an ISDA master agreement with the bank they're dealing with.

The ISDA master agreement basically eliminates the boilerplate associated with a contractually based trade – such as an IRS. Once the ISDA (as it's sometimes referred to) is in place, one can trade with minimal paperwork. The ISDA master agreement will determine all the contractual details – such as how to resolve disputes, what law will govern disputes (useful if the two parties are multi-national), and, perhaps most importantly, what terms will govern the payment and (potentially) re-payment of collateral to the customer's account. (Collateral is covered under the 'Credit Support Annex', or CSA)

BTMM under the heading 'LIBOR', or the Reuters page LIBOR01.

Most importantly, an index must mean something to those buying the swap. It's not very useful to have a swap based on LIBOR if nobody's real-world interest rate exposure has anything to do with LIBOR. To this day, even with all the negative press LIBOR has received, a great many parties have interest rate exposure linked to the rate. Even home mortgages can be LIBOR linked.

Table 2.1 Some popular float rate indices used in interest rate swaps

Currency	Rate	What is it?	Bloomberg/Reuters
CAD	BA	'Bankers Acceptance' rate (IDA)	BTMM CA / CDOR
CAD	LIBOR	BBA LIBOR	BTMM CA / CADLIBOR
EUR	EURIBOR ACT/365	EURIBOR in non-standard ACT/365 basis	EBF / EURIBOR365=
EUR	EURIBOR	Standard EURIBOR	EBF / EURIBOR01
EUR	EONIA	Euro overnight-index average rate	BTMM EU / EONIA=
JPY	LIBOR	JPY LIBOR	BTMM JN / LIBOR01
JPY	TIBOR	Tokyo inter-bank offered rate	BTMM JN / TIBM (under 'average')
GBP	LIBOR	GBP LIBOR	BTMM UK / LIBOR01
GBP	SONIA	Sterling O/N index average	SONIO/N <Index> Q /SONIA1
USD	CD	Certificate of deposit rate	NDX H15 / H15FED1
USD	CP	Commerical paper rate	NDX H15 / H15FED1
USD	FF	Fed Funds rate	NDX H15 / H15FED1
USD	LIBOR	USD LIBOR	BTMM / LIBOR01
USD	PRIME	Prime commercial lending rate	NDX H15 / H15FED1

In addition to LIBOR, there are a number of global benchmark rates which can form the floating side of a swap. Table 2.1 is a list of a few popular rates as listed by ISDA. Of all these rates, LIBOR is by far the most popular, but customers can easily request other rates if desired. In some currencies (such as Canadian Dollars and Australian Dollars) the BA rates are widely used as well.

2.2 Technical aspects of the swap

It's important to understand the technical underpinnings of the swap trans-action. Unlike more simple contracts – not all the details of the swap trans-action are known when it is traded. Specifically – we don't know the floating rates at each point in the transaction (except for the first period). Because of this, as time goes on, the floating rate of the swap will be periodically set (in so-called *rate-setting* events). Each rate setting will happen when the floating rate index is published (such as LIBOR – as it appears, for instance, on the Reuters page LIBOR01). Once that occurs, the swap transaction will immedi-ately change into a trade that's got more certainty, and less risk attached to it.

A good way to visualize the events associated with a swap is to lay out a timeline. Figure 2.2 presents all the events which are typically associated with the floating side of a swap. Keeping track of the swap requires managing all the important dates – which means, for each period tracking the four dates for the floating leg (reset date, start date, end date and payment date), and three dates for the fixed leg (start and end dates, and payment date).

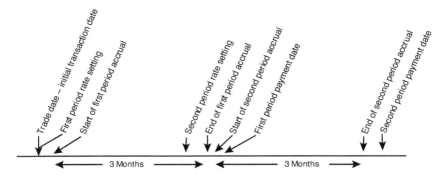

Figure 2.2 Interest rate swap floating leg – important dates and events

Since the fixed and floating-rate may be on different schedules, this usually means keeping separate lists of dates for each part of the swap. (The fixed rate, for instance, may be on a semi-annual frequency, whereas the floating-rate may be quarterly.)

Each floating-rate will have a certain time delay between the rate-setting and the start of the accrual period. This period (sometimes referred to as the number of *spot days*, or the rate-setting delay) varies for each floating period. For most LIBOR rates the delay is two business days, except for UK Sterling LIBOR, where there is no delay. (In addition Canadian dollar CDOR also has no delay, nor does Australian BBSW.)

2.3   How much is a swap worth?

When a swap is traded, the vast majority are traded at *par* – that is, they are traded with a fixed rate level adjusted such that the overall value of the swap is zero.

How does one know what the 'overall value' is, however? In Chapter 4 on the yield curve, we'll go into some detail on the methodology behind actually arriving at a value for the floating side of a swap. Suffice to say that, given the right tools, one can arrive at an expected market price for a series of floating payments. Given that – the value of a swap is simply the sum of all the floating payments *minus* the sum of all the fixed payments:

$$\text{Swap value} = f_1 D_1 + f_2 D_2 + \cdots + f_n D_n - (F_1 D_1 + F_2 D_2 + \cdots + F_n D_n)$$

Here, the *f*s are floating payments, and the *F*s are fixed payments – the *D*s are *discount factors*. Like the floating payments, discount factors are derived from our yield curve model. (The discount factors tell us what the present value of the future payment will be.)

The value of the floating side is determined by the tools we use to value it (our yield curve model, that is). The value of the fixed side is largely determined by our fixed rate. (In the example above, each of the *F*s is probably the same – because the fixed rate is probably the same throughout the swap, and each of the periods is probably similar to the others in length.) A swap dealer will choose the fixed rate to ensure the swap has zero value before offering it for sale.

Obviously, if you are paying the fixed rate, you'll want to pay as little as possible. Dealers will typically offer receiver swaps at a lower rate than payer swaps – the difference between the two being the bid-ask spread. As such, in the eyes of the bank that is selling the swap, its value is not exactly zero – rather its slightly positive, to represent the small profit made by selling at a fixed rate slightly off the middle of the market.

What happens is that the yield curve model used will help determine the fixed rate at *mid-market* – the spread will be added afterwards to get the rates at which to offer payer and receiver swaps. In addition, dealers will typically *skew* their bids as well, to account for their estimates of what different customers will want, and which direction the market is going. Thus, the value of the swap will become the positive value of both spread and skew.

2.4   Counting the days

During each period of the swap, interest is paid on the notional amount, on both the fixed and floating sides. But how is the amount to pay actually computed?

The formula for the amount to pay, for either the fixed or floating side, can be broken down as:

Amount = Basis factor × Rate

The basis factor is a number based on the number of days in the period. So, for instance, if you had a swap which has quarterly payments, the basis factor for each period might be something close to 0.25 (one-quarter of a year). (The rate, in all cases, is expressed in annual terms.)

In the quarterly case, we say 'something close to 0.25' – but often not exactly. The formula used to arrive at the basis factor varies according to the day-count convention used by the swap. The day-count convention varies according to the type of rate (fixed or floating), the type of swap and the currency.

Floating-rate day-count bases (often called *money* or *money market* bases) are typically governed by the currency underlying the swap, as well as the type of rate used. For LIBOR swaps, typical money bases are:

- Actual/360, or ACT/360. This is computed by taking the actual number of calendar days in the period and dividing by 360. Note that this means, for a 10 per cent rate of interest, say, the effective rate paid over a whole year will be 10 per cent times (365/360), or around 10.14 per cent. For this reason, rates quoted in ACT/360 may appear somewhat lower than financially equivalent rates in other bases. Most markets use ACT/360 as their money market basis, except for those that use...
- Actual/365, or ACT/365, or ACT/365 Fixed. Computed like ACT/360, except dividing by 365 instead of 360. This is the default money basis for Sterling (GBP) swaps, Canadian domestic swaps, Hong Kong Dollar swaps, New Zealand, Polish and South African swaps.

There are others (such as Brazil's wonderful BD/252 convention, which requires counting the business days in each period and dividing by 252), but these two bases account for 99.9 per cent of cases usually seen.

On the fixed side, the standard conventions are:

- 30/360, or 30/360 US. This rule assumes each month is 30 days in length, and the year has 360 days. If we are computing the basis between two dates, D1 and D2, formula would be:

$$\text{Basis} = \frac{Y_2 - Y_1 \times 360 + M_2 - M_1 \times 30 + (D_2 - D_1)}{360}$$

(Here, date D1 is in year Y1, month M1, day-of-month D1, and so on for date D2.) If D2 is the last day of the month, and D1 is also the last day of the month (or the 30th), then D2 is changed to 30. Whatever the case, whenever D1 is 31, it is changed to 30.

This basis is often called the *bond-basis*, and is the standard for US Dollar Swaps.

- 30/360 ISDA. As above, but D1 and D2 are adjusted in a more simple manner: if either day is the last day of the month, it is changed to 30. (Sometimes called the German basis).
- 30E/360, or 'special German' basis. Even simpler than the above: D1 and D2 are only changed if they reach 31, in which case they are rolled back to 30. This is the standard rule for EURIBOR swaps.
- Actual/365, as with the floating side. This basis is often used for fixed rates as well, such as in Sterling, GBP swaps.

See Chapter 3 on yield curves for a list of the default bases and frequencies for swaps in major currencies.

It's common to see quotations against different bases in the same currency. For instance, in the US market you can easily find brokers quoting swaps such as:

- 3M LIBOR/SB (the most common). The floating side is quarterly, the fixed side is semi-annual with the bond-basis (30/360 US).
- 3M LIBOR/QM. Three-month LIBOR swapped with quarterly fixed payments based on the money market basis (ACT/360).
- 6M LIBOR/AB. Six-month LIBOR swapped against annual bond-basis payments.

2.5   Adjusting the days

Swap schedules are computed using a simple procedure called a *marching convention*. The basic overview of schedule construction is something like this:

- *Find the effective date.* A swap is agreed to on the trade date, which is often the date on which the agreement becomes legally binding: the so-called effective date.
- *Find the start of the first period.* From the effective date, we compute the start of the first accrual period by adding the given number of spot days for the appropriate index. For instance, a EURIBOR swap entered into on a Monday might have its first accrual period start of Wednesday.
- *Mark the roll day.* The roll day will be the day of the month on which the schedule will 'roll'. This is often the same as the start of the first period. If the first period starts on Wednesday the 15th of March, the roll day will be the 15th.
- *Advance a given number of months.* If the swap is quarterly, we'd add three months to the start of the period. This date becomes the *unadjusted* end-of-period date.
- *Adjust the date.* If the end of a period is on a weekend or holiday (as defined by the holiday calendar or calendars agreed to in the swap) move the date according to the given marching convention. The possible conventions are:
  - *Modified following.* This is by far the most common marching convention. If a date falls on a holiday or weekend, it is moved to the next *good business day*, unless that takes it into the next month, in which case it is moved backwards to the previous good business day.
    - For instance, if the end of the period is Saturday the 29th of June, the next good business day might be Monday July 1st. Because this is in the next month, we adjust the date backwards to Friday June 28th.
  - *Following.* Using the *following* business day convention, we would just move the date to the next good business day.

- *Preceding.* Under this convention, we move the date to the prior good business day.
- *Start the next period from the unadjusted date.* We always use the *roll day* (which can, in some computer systems, be specified explicitly) to mark the beginning and end of periods, without reference to holidays or weekends.

Using this procedure, we may end up with payment periods which do not completely match the underlying rate – a 3-month LIBOR contract may span a floating period which is 1 or 2 days short of 3 months – but overall the procedure is quite good.

Not all swaps will accrue from the adjusted dates. It is possible to have variations whereby we use the unadjusted dates to compute the interest due. Either leg can have interest computed between adjusted or unadjusted dates. The default, however, in all markets is for both sides of the swap to use adjusted dates when computing interest payments. Asking a broker to arrange a swap with unadjusted dates might make sense if one wanted to hedge bond payments, for instance – since bonds compute interest based on unadjusted dates.

2.6 Holidays

Adjusted dates are arrived at with reference to a calendar of holidays. The process of finding, and adjusting for holidays is actually fairly involved.

Holidays are usually defined with regard to trading centres. LIBOR fixings, the most popular swap basis, are determined by the British Bankers' Association, based in London. As such, all LIBOR swaps will reference London holidays. In addition, they must mention the holiday calendar of the centre with which they trade. So a US Dollar swap, for instance, will reference both London and New York holidays. A holiday in either centre will cause the dates to be adjusted.

EURIBOR swaps only reference so-called TARGET holidays. TARGET (now TARGET2) is the pan-European financial payment system. TARGET is quite easy to deal with, having minimal holidays each year: New Year's Day, Good Friday, Easter Monday, May 1st, Christmas and Boxing Day.

2.7 Special features – stubs

'Stubs' are payment periods which depart from the normal schedule. A stub period is usually on either the front or back of a schedule, and can be either longer or shorter than a normal period. For instance, a semi-annual swap can have a 3-month front stub period, which would be (on the floating side) fixed with the 3-month LIBOR (or other index) tenor, rather than the 6-month LIBOR.

Stubs are useful in hedging bond payments, since many bonds will also feature stub coupon periods, either at the front or back.

2.8   Special features – IMM² Dates

Interest rate futures are another popular way to hedge floating-rate payments. The bridge between interest rate futures and swaps is the so-called IMM swap.

Interest rate futures (as explained in more detail in the yield curve chapters) are daily-settled exchange-traded contracts based on the three-month LIBOR rate. Since they are exchange-traded, however, these futures contracts are for fixed periods of time, and start on fixed dates. These dates are the IMM Dates – the third Wednesday of the month. Since they are three-month contracts, the months they start on are March, June, September and December. These contract months often get a one-letter abbreviation: H (March), M (June), U (September) and Z (December).

The IMM Dates never fall on a holiday. Perhaps this is why Wednesday was chosen?

It's quite easy to get IMM swaps in any major currency. They behave just like normal swaps, except the roll dates are IMM days. The rate-setting day, then, for these swaps will typically be two business days prior to the Wednesday (i.e. Monday), or, if this is a holiday, the preceding Friday.

In Australia, New Zealand and Canada, the popular floating indices include BA rates and CDOR – which have their own futures contracts which don't follow normal IMM conventions. AUD BA IMM swaps, therefore, will start (with no reset delay) on the Thursday prior to the second Friday of the month. Canadian CDOR IMM swaps will roll on the Monday prior to the third Wednesday (again no reset delay is present). New Zealand IMM dates are stranger still: the first Wednesday after the ninth day of the month.

2.9   Special features – amortization

Up until now, the notional amount that we've based the swap upon has been constant. One fairly common variation is to base payments on a variable notional – either amortizing (decreasing) or accreting over time.

Most amortizations and accretion schedules can be calculated easily. The starting amount and ending amount will be known, as will the period, and the schedule is, therefore, linear. For instance, if we start with a vanilla 5-year swap with a notional of $100 million which will amortize to zero over the life of the swap, we can see that we will have 20 quarterly payments which will each reduce by $5 million.

Technically, on the fixed side of the swap, the amortization amount is paid to the fixed rate receiver after each period. This reflects the fact that the notional is being 'returned', much like a home mortgage will have its outstanding balanced repaid on a regular basis. Since the notional amount applies to both sides of the swap, however, the equal and opposite re-payment on the floating side will cancel this out. We can safely ignore the 'notional return' payment. Even so, many structurers in banks will use amortizing swap legs by themselves, without a floating side, in specially constructed trades. In these cases, having the notional return be explicit is quite useful.

Besides being linear, amortization can be based on the fixed rate. Each period, for instance, could reduce the notional by the amount of the fixed payment.

Basing amortization on the floating-rate results in something called an *index amortizing swap* (or IAS). A form IAS was popular in the 1990s in the United States, where it was a hedge against certain risks in the mortgage bond market. Whatever form they take – they are notoriously difficult to value, since their notional amounts go up and down based on (unknown) interest rate fluctuations.

2.10   Special features – compounding

The notional on each side of the swap need not always be the same.

The floating side of the swap can (and often does) have *compounding* notional. This means that each floating payment, instead of being given to the floating-rate receiver, is added back to the notional. The entire notional amount, then, is paid to the other side at the end.

From an economic standpoint, this compounding makes no difference to us. If we assume that the floating-rate is the rate at which we discount our cash-flows (for the purpose of computing present value) then we should be indifferent – we can receive the payments at the end of each period, or at the end of the swap on a compounded basis.

The fixed side can also compound, if desired, resulting in a single, large fixed payment at the end. Rather than explicitly compounding, however, one can just stipulate a lump-sum payment to be subtracted from the final floating side compounded payment. Since the fixed side is *fixed*, there's no need to enter into the complex mechanics of computing each hypothetical period. In fact, a compounding swap such as this is a good way to hedge against the risks associated with paying or receiving large lump-sums in the future.

For example – suppose we are due to pay $100 million in 5 years' time. We determine that, given our rate of funding (which we'll assume is LIBOR) we can invest $90 million in cash today to cover our obligation. But what if rates go up or down? If rates go down, for instance, we could see our liability increase, since the return on our $90 million will get smaller.

However, in this example – the $90 million invested at LIBOR is exactly like the compounded floating leg of a swap. We can invest our $90 million, and agree to pay the floating leg of a compounding swap. This will give us a fixed lump-sum of $100 million in 5 years – exactly enough to cover our obligation! A perfect hedge.

2.11   Special features – accruals in arrears

While calculation of accrued days is always the same, it is possible to fix LIBOR and apply the rate retrospectively. We have already seen that at inception, for example, we fix our LIBOR rate, and on the first fixing date in 3 months' time, we apply that rate to the accrued days and calculate the floating-rate cash-flow. If we were to apply LIBOR-in-arrears, we would not fix the rate at inception. Instead, on the first fixing date in 3 months' time, we would fix LIBOR and apply that rate to the prior 3-month accrued days.

If we look at a simplified schedule as a comparison we see that:

	Vanilla	Arrears
Inception	Fix floating r_0	
End-of-period 1	Fix floating r_1	Fix floating r_1
	Accrual calculation using r_0	Accrual calculation using r_1
End-of-period 2	Fix floating r_2	Fix floating r_2
	Accrual calculation using r_1	Accrual calculation using r_2
Maturity	No fix required	Fix floating r_3
	Accrual calculation using r_2	Accrual calculation using r_3

Arrears swaps are typically priced differently than normal, fixed-in-advance swaps, due to the fact that the rate is being used in a manner it was not designed for. In any case where the floating-rate is not applied to the period which it was meant to be applied to (such as a 6-month rate applied to a 3-month period, or a USD LIBOR rate applied to EUR notional) complex pricing effects rear their heads. Suffice to say – in these cases, the simple, easy-to-value trade becomes (to some extent) a complex derivative, and special care must be taken.

2.12   Basis swaps

One common variety of swap is the so-called *basis swap*. A basis swap, generally, is any swap where both sides are based on floating rates. This means that the only thing being exchanged is the *basis* on which payments are made.

Basis swaps can be on different frequencies: one common type of basis swap is to swap, for instance, 3-month LIBOR against 6-month LIBOR.

Basis swaps can be across currencies. The most common type of cross-currency basis swap involves swapping three-month LIBOR payments between parties (for more details see the Chapter 7 on cross-currency trades).

Basis swaps, finally, can be between different types of rates. Another common swap, for instance, is the LIBOR/overnight index swap (OIS), where one party pays LIBOR and the other pays the overnight rate – either compounded or averaged. (This is an area of difficulty, actually. If the overnight rate is averaged, it will not match, payment-wise, the standard OIS as described below. Many LIBOR/ON swaps will use averaging rather than compounding.)

2.13   Non-deliverable swaps

We briefly mentioned cross-currency swaps as a kind of basis swap. We will discuss foreign exchange (FX) in Chapter 6. The chapter will also include material about local markets which are restricted by exchange control.

By way of introducing the subject, we can say that currency control is a mechanism of restricting flows of currency in and out of a country, by either restricting whether a currency can be transferred out of a country; who has access to the markets; whether the exchange rates are pegged, or managed in some way.

In some cases, there are two currencies, one deliverable (or partially deliverable), and one non-deliverable. A good example of this is China, where CNY can only be delivered on-shore to residents of China, and CNH which is deliverable in Hong Kong via certain controlled Banks.

Non-deliverable swaps are designed to provide a relatively liquid alternative way of hedging or speculating on such markets. They differ from deliverable currency swaps because, while rates are still observed and fixed, all payer/receiver cash-flows are usually netted into a single USD cash-flow.

2.14   Overnight-index swap

The overnight-index swap (OIS) is an increasingly popular form, based not on LIBOR, but on one of the overnight interest rates. Since it is impractical to make daily payments, the overnight-index is usually compounded – so the final payment made at the end of the period corresponds to what would be returned if the notional were invested at the overnight rate for the entire period.

One issue with this is that the OIS fixes at the *end* of each floating period. (Unlike LIBOR-in-arrears, however, this is unproblematic, since we're using the overnight rates in a financially accurate way.)

The mechanics of compounding are simple enough: each published rate is applied to for a given number of days, and compounded with all the preceding rates. The overall floating-rate is then:

$$r = \frac{360}{n}\left(-1 + \prod_{i=d_1}^{d_n}\left(\frac{r_i\,(d_{i+1} - d_i)}{360} + 1\right)\right)$$

Here d_1 is the starting business day of a given period, d_{n+1} is the ending day, and each r is the published overnight-index rate for a given day. Notice that we apply each rate for a given number of days – if two business days are separated by a weekend, we'll multiply the rate by three before applying it. In jurisdictions like the United Kingdom, we'd use 365 in the above formula, rather than 360.

The indices commonly used for OISs include those mentioned in Table 2.1: EONIA for Euros, SONIA for UK Sterling and Fed Funds for the United States.

Two features make OIS attractive – especially for banks. Firstly, they represent a more realistic view of funding costs. Banks are much more able, willing, and likely to borrow from each other on an overnight basis (minimizing counter-party risk) than they are to do so on a term basis. If one looks at the inter-bank lending market, the vast majority of transactions are done on an overnight basis, typically through the treasury department of a bank. The second feature is tied to this – OISs are based on real transactions, not on hypothetical ones as in the case of LIBOR. The OIS rate is published *after-the-fact* in most cases, and based on actual bank transactions. EONIA, for instance, is the weighted average of all unsecured lending trades which the ECB is aware of via the Euro-area settlement systems. LIBOR, by contrast, is the average of a number of 'guesses' banks make about what they think rates might be.

2.15 Using swaps for hedging exposures

There are many uses for swaps. Much of the swap market is taken up by inter-bank trading – since banks find swaps useful as a way to buy and sell longer term interest rate risk. Banks can use swaps to hedge a wide variety of obligations they may find themselves under; since swaps can ensure that the bank will be insulated against movements in interest rates. In addition, more interestingly, swaps form an important part of the toolkit of trades banks can recommend to clients. Below are a few examples of how bank customers can use swaps.

Case study A: Hedging a variable rate exposure

Often, corporations will have loan facilities with banks. These come in many forms, but are most likely to be revolving facilities or long maturity loans charged at a margin over Libor. In periods of low interest rates, the fair fixed rate of a swap may be attractive enough for the corporation's financial director to consider locking in exposure at a fixed rate. This has the advantage of allowing the corporation to account for future loan payments with certainty.

There are, however, some factors for the corporation to consider. The swap itself will take up some of their credit facility with the bank. However, as the swap does not need to be with their lending bank, this allows them to negotiate credit lines with whomever they wish. If the corporation does not have enough headroom on their credit facility but has cash and wants to add certainty to future interest payments, they may consider buying an interest rate cap.

The corporation will aim to match their liabilities schedule with a swap leg. They may therefore need the swap notional to amortize, and will certainly require the floating leg fixing points to match their loan in respect of both timing and rate basis. Under the swap they will receive the floating cash-flows and pay the fixed. While there may be no margin on the floating cash-flow leg on their swap, when all cash-flows are netted, the corporation will end up with a fixed rate payment with the margin on their original loan added, as we can see in Figure 2.3.

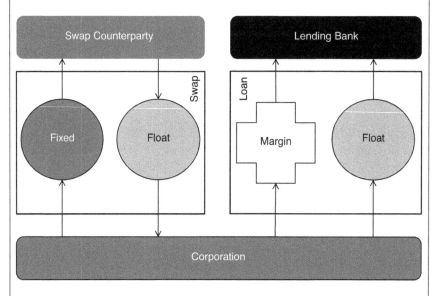

Figure 2.3   Using a swap to hedge floating-rate loan payments

Case study B: Swapping fixed rate exposure for variable rates

A corporation may raise funds by issuing debt. In this example, they have issued a fixed rate corporate bond paying interest semi-annually. The rate that they pay is effectively a reflection of their credit rating.

If the corporation prefers to manage variable rate exposure, they will enter the swap market and look to receive fixed and pay floating. While the schedule of the fixed rate cash-flows on the swap will need to match the bond coupons, they can swap was any variable rate, so they may end up with mis-matched cash-flow periods. The swap itself also needs to match the bond structure, in this example a bullet schedule (Figure 2.4).

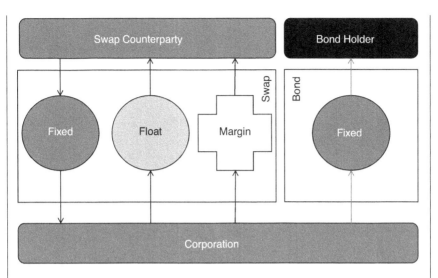

Figure 2.4   Using a swap to convert fixed payments into floating

The fair fixed rate of a swap can change if a margin is added to the floating-rate, so the corporate may choose to match their fixed bond coupon rate exactly and pay a variable rate plus a margin. They may instead merely fix at the fair rate and receive a fixed rate that doesn't match their bond coupon. In this example we will assume that the fair fixed rate is to be adjusted to match the bond coupon and the variable cash-flows have an additional margin, expressed in basis points over, say, LIBOR.

Case study C: Minimizing exchange risk

A US corporation manufactures in the United States. It has an existing loan facility with its US bankers. Over time, the Firm has become more and more successful selling its product into the European Union. As a result, it finds itself with USD interest rate risk, and EUR receivables creating FX risk.

The corporation can swap the USD loan nominal into a EUR position which it can service using its EUR receipts. Under the swap, it can receive USD floating to service its USD loan.

While cross-currency swaps generally involve an exchange of principal, this does not have to be the case. The corporate has the option, therefore, of either physically exchanging USD funds raised in the United States for a physical EUR position which can be invested, or entering into a swap with no nominal exchange. At the swap maturity, the principal cash-flows are either reversed at the same FX rate, or in the latter case, not exchanged at all. Either way, FX risk is eliminated. However it is worth noting, that just as with any other hedge, eliminating risk also means eliminating opportunity gain.

In our example we will assume a physical notional exchange at the beginning and end of the swap (Figure 2.5).

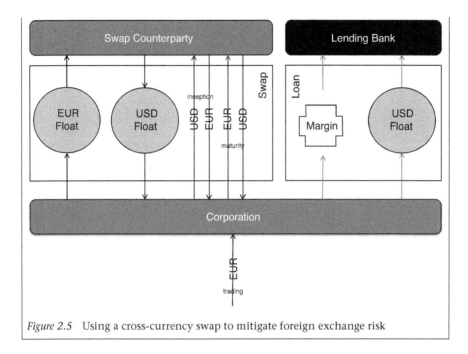

Figure 2.5   Using a cross-currency swap to mitigate foreign exchange risk

2.16   Management of the swap lifecycle

This section describes, quite briefly, what may happen in a large bank that deals with swaps.

Swaps are managed by traders. Traders sell swap to counterparties, book trades into their primary trading systems, and oversee automated trading and market-making operations.

Automated trading can consist of automated market-making (setting up a digital store-front to buy and sell swaps, via Bloomberg, for instance) or algorithmic trading. Automated market-making was slow to take off (driven by fear of lower margins, some claim) it is now gaining a firm foothold, pushed onwards by the regulators and consumers alike.

Once a swap has been traded, a wide variety of banking departments become involved, as explained below.

2.17   Operations

Swap operations have changed a huge amount in the past decade. With automation taking over, many of the manual processes have gone completely.

That said, some processes still need to produce reporting that people will see. One of these is the operational reconciliation that usually happens at the end of each day, between what a bank (or institution) thinks it has traded and what the outside world says it has traded.

In many cases, the 'outside world' is represented by a post-trade processing provider, such as MarkitServ. The important processes that must be taken care of by such a provider include:

- *Matching*. Matching means taking trades from one party (such as Bank A) and finding the trades from the counterparty (Hedge-Fund B) that match. If Bank A says it sold a 10Y EUR Receiver to Hedge-Fund B with 10 million notional, the matching process must look for a trade which matches those details from Hedge-Fund B.

Hedge-Fund B can see, often, on-line that Bank A has *alleged* a trade against it. Hedge-Fund B can then *affirm* the trade, which will trigger matching to be complete.

- *Confirmation*. In the old days, every OTC transaction triggered a fax sent to the counterparty, detailing the trade and acting as legal documentation. The receipt of the confirmation could then be affirmed. These days, the on-line matching process with affirmation largely fills the same function.

Generally the payer of the fixed cash-flow on the swap, is responsible for entering the swap trade into MarkitServ. The other side merely checks and confirms the trade online. Where a broker is involved they will enter the trade and both counterparties on the swap will check and confirm it. (For internal, inter-desk swap trades in a bank, the fixed rate payer will enter the trade into the bank's systems and the other desk will check it.)

A check will be undertaken to ensure no swaps trades have been left in systems at a 'pending' status.

Paper confirmations are rare nowadays, but where they are issued, they are reconciled T+1. The Federal Reserve have set a series of targets for paper confirms, and banks need to report any unchecked or unmatched confirmations to them for age brackets T+1, T+7 and T+31.

Each day, operations are required to track fixing events. Fixings may be in the form of a published reference rate, in which case the timing of the fixing and the fixing source will be part of the swap's term sheet and referenced in the trade confirmation.

It is worth noting that for cross-currency swaps, once the swap trade has been completed, it is 'torn' into two halves and the trader responsible for each currency will manage their half independently. This is unless there are FX fixing events during the swap's life, in which case these events need to be managed together.

Swap settlements are all done electronically, via the SWIFT network.

2.18   Product control and the profit and loss process

One of the roles of product control is to reconcile the trader's estimated profit and loss (the so-called flash P&L) with the bank's official P&L numbers.

The trader's P&L estimation is often driven by risk variables. The trader will have their risk report in front of them, saying, for instance, that every 0.01 prer cent move in the 10Y swap rate will make them gain $100,000. If they see the rate change by 0.03 per cent (3 basis points) over the course of a day, they'll claim a P&L at the end of the day of $300,000.

While the trader completes a P&L estimation based on risk variables, an 'actual – actual' P&L number will be created at the end of each day. The 'actual – actual' number is derived by looking at the net present value of all cash-flows based on the official yield curve, plus any cash balances and reserves minus yesterday's values. Any differences need to be explained by looking in detail at the risk factors in the trader's flash.

The trader will expect product control (or the so-called middle office) to ensure there are no outstanding confirmations or disputes and that payables and receivables have been reconciled. If there are any trade or cash disputes, these will impact the trader's ability to manage the correct risk and will also lead to mis-statements of P&L.

2.19   Risk management

Risk is as important to the bank as profit. Calculating and publishing risk numbers helps the bank explain its position, and justify its use of capital in the trading arena.

During the day, risk is managed by the traders. Each trader looks at the risk based on their swap yield curve, and buys or sells accordingly. However, at the end of the day, official risk numbers need to be published.

Official risk is usually based on a *different* yield curve – the official, end-of-day curve based on official, end-of-day rates. These rates are collected by a specialized department, and built into end-of-day curves which are used to re-value the banks positions and re-calculate risk.

End-of-day rates are not just a snapshot at a given time – they often must be 'cleaned' (to remove erroneous data), possibly they are averaged over a period of time, or averaged between rate providers. The structure and com-position of the end-of-day yield curve would have been already agreed and ratified by the bank's own committee responsible for approving pricing models. (It is worth noting that intraday the trader may well be pricing and managing risk using different yield curve constructions and interpolation methods.)

2.20   Changes to swap clearing

Since the 1970s and 1980s, as the swap market grew, the volume of associated confirmation paperwork started to negatively impact swaps operations. At its height, the 'paperwork crisis' led to exchanges closing on Wednesdays, extending settlement to T+5 and shortening trading hours, all just to catch up on the backlog. In the United States, the Depository Trust Company (DTC) and National Securities Clearing Corporation (NSCC) were formed, and these entities eventually combined in 1999 to form the DTCC.

In Europe, the London Clearing House, established originally back in 1888, developed from a commodities clearer to include swaps clearing, merging with the Paris based Clearnet in 2003 to form LCH.Clearnet.

These Clearers allowed for the reduction of paper confirmations primarily by multilateral netting. It allowed firms to net all their individual trades against an individual counterparty into one, as the Clearer became the central counterparty. The Clearing House also assumes the counterparty risk involved when two parties trade. In effect, the Clearer becomes the legal counterparty to the trade, taking on the settlement and credit risk of the trades. This rationalises collateral and margin flows also. Initial and variation margin is collected by the Clearer from its members, based on their exposures, and, in the event of a credit failure, this margin is used to fulfil their obligations.

To understand the mechanics of how the central counterparty works, let us consider what happens to a swaps trade executed via LCH.Clearnet. Both swap counterparties, or their broker, will enter the swap into MarkitServ (formally swapswire). Once they are matched in the system, and assuming the counterparts are members of LCH.Clearnet, they are cleared via the clearing house.

The original swap trade is covered by their bilateral International Swaps and Derivatives Association (ISDA) Master Agreement. This is replaced by two contracts on the same economic terms as the original trade, and standard Clearing House terms between the Clearing House and each participant. At this point, the Clearing House assumes the counterparty risk against each of the swap counterparts.

All of the swap lifecycle events are now determined by the Clearer, including fixing rates. All settlement amounts, coupon payables or receipts are then netted for each counterparty daily by individual currency. Margin payments, both initial and variation, may also be netted into this one daily payment per currency. The Clearer will also mark member positions to market daily, and provide all of the reporting required by operations departments for reconciliations.

2.21   Tri-Optima

An amusing innovation in the past few years has arisen to address the challenge of trade volumes. As mentioned, since swaps are OTC instruments, they
are rarely resold. (Reselling of OTC instruments is possible, with transfer of
legal obligations through a process called *novation*, but this is onerous and
time consuming.) Instead of selling existing swaps, traders will move in and
out of positions by taking on more and more swap trades. The only way they
ever disappear is by maturing. Over time, bank computer systems quickly
become overwhelmed.

One way to reduce this came from the Tri-Optima organization: a group
of swap dealers would submit, confidentially, a list of their swap trades will
all the other members of the group. Tri-Optima would then 'compress' the
trades, keeping their mark-to-market value, and retaining their risk exposure
to within certain parameters, and come up with an 'unwind proposal'
consisting of, perhaps, a smaller set of trades and some cash adjustment. In
recent years this has extended to clearing houses, with (according to them)
about 80 trillion dollars of notional reduction in 2012.

3
An Introduction to the Interest Rate Yield Curve

3.1 What is a yield curve?

The term 'yield curve' can mean several things. The most common use of the term is in the bond market, where it refers to a chart made by the yields (i.e. effective annual rates of return) of government-issued securities. Here, the 'curve' is just a line drawn between points – a graph of yield versus time to maturity.

The bond yield curve can tell you many things about how bonds are priced, and how the returns of other investments compare to benchmark investments in the bond market. From a practitioner's point of view the bond yield curve is quite simple to create, requiring only access to bond rates and a spreadsheet.

In the interest rate market, you can make similar curves, by charting the rates charged by banks for deposits, forward rate agreements (FRAs) or swaps. The most basic form is the swap yield curve – a simple chart of swap rates (similar to the bond yield curve) versus time to maturity.

Bond market yield curves and interest rate yield curves end up being almost entirely different in the way they are used. In the bond market, the yield curve is merely a chart, an instrument to gauge whether a particular bond lies above or below the curve made by the other bonds. Traders use these curves as an indicator to see how the market is moving, and make trades based around the curve's dynamics.

In a simple graph, the interest rate curve can appear very similar to the bond market curve. In fact, in some markets (like the United States) the interest rate curve can be computed by adding a 'spread' to the bond yields (see Figure 3.1).

The interest rate curve, however, can also be decomposed much further than the bond curve. This is because there is a lively market, not just for the instruments that make up the curve (like swaps, and deposits, for instance) but also for bits and pieces of the curve. For instance, using FRAs

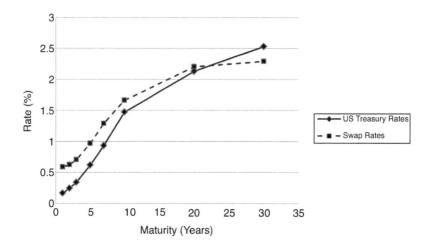

Figure 3.1   US Treasury bond yields and swap rates

it is possible to trade short pieces of the curve in the future. (FRAs are investigated in more detail in the next chapter.) This facility means that the curve itself must be able to be interpreted mathematically in a much more complete, subtle way.

The way that interest rate curves are constructed has changed greatly in the past few years. Most of this chapter will be devoted to discussing the breakdown of the simple relationships between interest rates of different sorts. Before delving too deeply into the (admittedly somewhat complex) story of this breakdown, it is useful to talk about the classic and simple methods of constructing interest rate curves.

3.2   LIBOR and the interest rate curve

Traditionally, interest rates were traded between banks on the basis that banks had good credit, in fact, the best credit. We saw in the credit crisis of 2007–2008 that this is not always true. We'll examine over the latter part of this chapter the implications of this. However it will be useful, first, to look at the traditional old-fashioned model of interest rates.

A note on arbitrage-free pricing

Buying something (product A, say) and then reselling it immediately for a profit is called *arbitrage*. Arbitrage also includes buying product A, and selling product B, where B is exactly financially equivalent to A. In the world of interest rates, this once meant being able to know that rates agreed in the future (using FRAs, or Interest Rate Futures for instance) could be combined with deposit instruments, for instance, to extend them into the future.

The intuition behind this is very simple. In the traditional model, deposits are *fungible*. That is to say, it should make no difference from a financial point of view whether I deposit money for 6 months directly, or deposit money for, say, 3 months, then (using a FRA) lock-in the rate for another 3-month deposit, starting 3 months in the future.

That is to say, these alternatives were once equivalent:

Alternative 1: Deposit $1 million at 1 per cent for 6 months.
Alternative 2: Deposit $1 million at 0.9 per cent for 3 months.

Agree rate of 1.1 per cent for 3 months, starting in 3 months.

Arbitrage-free pricing is two things. It is an *observation:* financial markets are arbitrage-free, and where small arbitrage opportunities appear, the market quickly adjusts as market participants buy and sell to make the difference disappear. It is also a *proscription:* we must design our models around the assumption that there are no-arbitrage opportunities in the market. Briefly put: if we know A and B, and we know A + B *should be equivalent to* C, then we must assume that C = A + B.

The breakdown of certain arbitrage relationships in the interest rate market has changed the way we analyse many instruments. We'll see that the two alternatives above have diverged considerably, with many ramifications for banks and other market participants.

It is very well to know deposit instruments, and deposit rates, but it is important to know how they can be used in financial calculations. Deposit rates long formed the basis for computing the so-called *risk-free rate of return* for any period in the future.

The risk-free rate is used in many calculations, in many areas, from equity derivatives pricing to computing the value of a company.

London Interbank Offered Rate (LIBOR) was often assumed to be 'risk-free'. One may ask why, since many banks that participate are hardly risk-free institutions. The definition is, admittedly, rather circular. If an institution is able to trade (borrow and lend money) at LIBOR, then they are risk-free. As soon as an institution gets into trouble, it will find its credit rating cut, and it will no longer be able to trade at LIBOR. But what of the trades done, say, last month, when it was trading at LIBOR? They arc still on the books. This is an inconvenient detail.

Working with LIBOR rates, we'll be able to build a risk-free *yield curve model*, which will tell us the risk-free rate to any time in the future.

What is a 'yield curve model'? This is a good question. The short answer is: it's a function. A function that takes inputs, and provides some outputs. The inputs are the data from the market (deposit rates, in this case), and the outputs are information (the risk-free rate) that will help us make decisions.

In a practical sense, this can all be done in a spreadsheet. Admittedly, some of the fancier features of a yield curve model might be better suited to a proper computer system, but the basics can be modelled quite well using something like an Excel. We'll try to provide some examples as we go along, showing how the yield curve model we develop can be actually implemented.

3.3   An introduction to discounting

What is the value of money?

When a bank is due to receive, say, 1 million dollars from a customer (perhaps repaying a loan) in 1 month's time, they must report that amount on their balance sheet.

They will not report $1 million exactly, however. Because the money is not paid yet, the customer can deposit some amount of money *today* (say, perhaps, $999,000) and be guaranteed $1,000,000 in 1 month, which they can use to pay the bank.

So, in other words, $1,000,000 in 1 month is equal to $999,000 today. The bank is *required* to report the value of the payment as being worth $999,000. The bank has *discounted* its future cash-flow.

One of the most useful things to do in any financial application (spreadsheet or complex risk-management system) is to determine the value of a cash flow received in the future. To do this, one needs to discount the cash-flow back to the present. A basic yield curve model should be able to provide the ability to do this for any arbitrary date in the future.

Discounting is a way of saying that since any amount on the books today could be deposited and earn interest, we value money today more than we value money in the future.

If money today can be deposited for 1 year at 5 per cent, then we should 'value' a payment of $1,000 in 1 year as being the same as whatever amount would give us $1,000 in 1 year.

We'll call that amount X, where $X \times \left(1 + 5\% \times \dfrac{365}{360} \right) = 1000$

We see from this that $X = 1000 \times \left(\dfrac{1}{1 + 5\% \times \dfrac{365}{360}} \right)$ or $X = 1000 \times 0.951751$

The amount at the end (0.951751) is the *discount factor* – this is the amount we need to multiply any cash-flow to be received in 1 year's time by to see what its value is today.

So we'd need $951.75 today to make a payment of $1,000 in 1 year.

There are discount factors for every date in the future. For an amount to be received (or paid) in around 1 year or less, we can use deposit instruments to estimate these discount factors.

3.4 Using deposit rates to build a very simple yield curve model

Traditionally, as mentioned, deposit rates were used to build yield curve models, based on the idea that deposits are fungible, and exchangeable. Let's examine how this is done, given that it's a good introduction to the process, and it is an approach still valid in many markets, and for many types of applications.

Suppose we have the following deposit rates (again using USD deposits as the example):

Start date: June 20, 2012 (a Wednesday)
Spot date: June 22, 2012 (a Friday)
Overnight rate: 0.30 per cent
One week rate: 0.315 per cent
Two week rate: 0.325 per cent
One month rate: 0.381 per cent
Two month rate: 0.393 per cent
Three month rate: 0.415 per cent
Six month rate: 0.46 per cent
One year rate : 0.56 per cent

As mentioned, the 'spot' date is a special date on which most deposits begin. In many currencies, this will be two business days from today, although some (such as Pounds Sterling) have contracts that start right away.

The first step in building a yield curve model is to determine the ending date for each deposit. In this case, it means:

- Adding 7 days to the starting date for each week, in the case of the 1 and 2 week rates.
- Adding 1 month for each month.
- If the resulting date is a holiday, moving to the next valid business day.

In the case of monthly rates, not allowing weekends or holidays to force a jump past the end of the month. End-of-month holidays almost always cause a jump backwards (see the section on swaps for more information on this).

This gives us explicit dates for each instrument we're using in our yield curve:

Rate Name	Start Date	End Date	Days	Rate (%)
Overnight	Weds, 20 June	Thurs, 21 June	1	0.3
One week	Friday, 22 June	Friday, 29 June	7	0.315
Two weeks	Friday, 22 June	Friday, 6 July	14	0.325
One month	Friday, 22 June	Monday, 23 July	31	0.381
Two months	Friday, 22 June	Wednesday, 22 Aug	61	0.393
Three months	Friday, 22 June	Monday, 24 Sep	94	0.415
Six months	Friday, 22 June	Monday, 24 Dec	185	0.46
One year	Friday, 22 June	Monday, 24 June	367	0.56

After determining the end date, we can easily interpolate the deposit rates between points, if we wish.

In this case, 'interpolating' means finding the rate between the two rates we know. We can find the rate based on a straight line between the two surrounding rates.

Suppose we wanted to find the deposit rate that made the most sense for 10th August. To start with we find the two rates which are nearest to 10th August: 23rd July and 22nd August. We take these two rates (0.381% and 0.393%) and find the point on the line between them that corresponds to 10th August. Figure 3.2 shows how this works.

Simple geometry gives us:

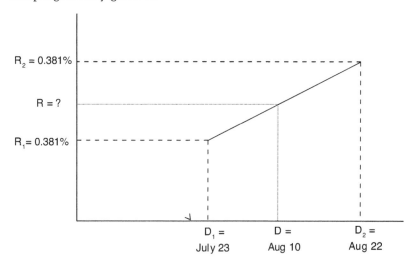

Figure 3.2   Linear interpolation

$$R = \frac{D - D_1}{D_2 - D_1} * (R_2 - R_1) + R_1$$

In other words,

$$R = \left(\frac{18}{30}\right)(.393 - .381) + 0.381 = 0.3882\%$$

This approach works well, and can give a generalized 'deposit rate' to any time in the future.

LIBOR rate sources

If you have access to Reuters or Bloomberg, getting LIBOR rates is fairly straightforward.

Using Reuters, for end-of-day LIBOR fixings (the most useful in all applications except perhaps interest rate trading) simply go to the LIBOR page (LIBOR01 or LIBOR02). This shows the major LIBOR BBA fixings. EURIBOR01 shows EURIBOR fixings. (The corresponding Bloomberg page is BBAM for LIBOR, EBF for EURIBOR.)

For real-time deposit rates, supply a Reuters code (RIC) in the form {Currency}{Term}D=. For instance, EUR3MD= gives the 3-month Euro deposit rate (as averaged and reported by Reuters).

Free sources abound, and while they may not give up-to-the-minute reporting of rates, are perfectly adequate. Euribor fixings are readily available at the source (http://euribor-ebf.eu/). The Bloomberg web site for instance gives LIBOR fixings for major currencies: http://www.bloomberg. com/quote/US0003M:IND shows the latest 3-month USD LIBOR fixing (reported with 'at least' a 15 minute delay, of course). Replace the 'US' with JY, BP, CD, AU or NZ for Japanese, British, Canadian, Australian or New Zealand currency fixings, respectively. The '3M' can become 6M, 1M or 'O+N' (for overnight).

We can now easily build a function to give us the 'hypothetical' deposit rate for any date in the future, given current rates. But are these rates realistic? Could you go to a bank with these 'interpolated' rates and expect a quote that's similar? The answer is: probably, you'd get pretty close. Banks will use their own interpolation scheme, and the will charge a premium for customized cash-flow dates (i.e. dates falling between the canonical 1-, 2- and 3-month periods), but the rates will not be far off.

Once we have the deposit rate for any time in the future, we just need to add another function to compute the discount factor, and we have a generic way of accounting for payments or receipts on our balance sheet.

This is not, however, the most exact approach. Admittedly, precise exactness does not matter for most applications. A first-order approximation of the deposit rate to a point in the future may be acceptable, say, when discounting cash flows, or approximating calculations not directly involving interest rates. A general model, however, should give exact rates taking into account such details as the delay between today and the spot date, and also building into the model the fact that we may eventually want more than just deposit rates.

How do we turn this into a general model?

3.5 The zero coupon curve

The term 'Zero Coupon' is taken from the bond market. Like deposits, bonds are loan agreements, paying interest on so-called 'coupon dates'. A zero coupon bond is, therefore, a bond that pays no interest until maturity.

Such a bond, however, *will* return the loan amount (the *face value*) at maturity. The face value is determined when the bond is issued. The bond is then sold on the market.

How much would someone pay for a zero coupon bond? Well, it would depend on what else they could do with their money. If the alternative,

Table 3.1 Types of compounding

Compounding rule	Payout after 1 year
No compounding	$1 + \text{Rate}$
Semi-annual compounding	$\left(1 + \dfrac{\text{Rate}}{2}\right)^{2}$
Monthly compounding	$\left(1 + \dfrac{\text{Rate}}{12}\right)^{12}$
Continuous compounding	e^{Rate}

Note: Compounding refers to how often the interest is added to the principal when computing returns. Deposits are generally NOT compounded: the interest is computed once, at the end. However some instruments do have compounding: below are examples of return calculations for different compounding rules for a 1-year investment of $1.

for instance, is a LIBOR deposit, then they should get the same return, ideally. So a zero coupon bond would be worth the face value times the LIBOR-based discount factor to maturity.

Zero coupon rate (ZCR) is usually just a short-hand way to say 'interest rate that applies to a point in time'. Not very complex, but we should keep in mind that ZCRs are usually represented in *continuously compounded* form. Table 3.1 shows the types of compounding

In general, the continuously compounded return is given by e^{rt}, where r is the continuously compounded ZCR and t is the time to maturity. Time can be measured using any basis we choose as long as we are consistent.

Typically, to make things easy, financial applications measure time as (Number of Days)/365, which is a simple and intuitive computation to make. The divisor here is arbitrary – it just must be consistent!

Notice that the equation to find the discount factor, given the ZCR, is also quite simple: $D_t = e^{-rt}$.

Converting our deposit rates into ZCRs will be a big advantage in building our application:

- Since ZCRs are continuously compounded, they will allow us to extend our yield curve model beyond the 1-year limit of most deposits.
- ZCRs are a simple form to work with, requiring less mathematical programming.
- It's far more mathematically sensible to interpolate ZCRs, rather than deposit or (as we'll see later) swap rates.

Our goal, therefore, should be to use other financial instruments (such as FRAs and interest rate swaps) to extend our yield curve, and create a general model that will extend for 10, 20 or 30 years into the future.

This is, in fact, what many practitioners still do. The general approach is as follows:

- Determine the ZCRs for a set of deposit rates, generally out to 6 or 9 months in the future. Add these rates to our *rate table*.
- For a set of interest rate futures (or FRAs):
  - Determine the ZCR at the start of each new instrument by interpolating the rate in the rate table.
  - Determine the ZCR at the maturity by taking into account the simple interest rate paid over the instrument's period.
- For a set of interest rate swap quotations:
  - Determine the implied LIBOR rates that we can from the rate table.

- Solve for the unknown LIBOR rates, to make the swap's value zero. (Note that all swaps are quoted so that they trade at *par*, that is, zero net value).

The aspects of the procedure are explained in detail in the next chapter. The general approach, however, is to assume that all rates are fungible, and we can use a *single curve* to both figure out LIBOR rates in the future, and discount all our cash flows.

3.6   Issues with the classic yield curve

We can easily add the zero coupon approach to our deposit curve. This is the classic method to extend a yield curve. However, it will be useful first to examine the motivation behind this approach, and look at other alternatives.

As mentioned, the no-arbitrage relationship between different tenors of deposits *no longer holds*. Let's look at what this means from a practical point of view.

On a day in January, 2012, the Euro interest rate market stood as follows: 3 month deposits were quoted at 1.06 per cent, 6 month deposits were quoted at 1.42 per cent, and 3x6 FRAs were quoted at 0.933 per cent. All of these quotes were available at the same time, in mid-afternoon.

An investor could invest 1 Euro for 3 months, and then (using the FRA) lock-in another, subsequent 3 month deposit rate. Since, in this example, each period of time was exactly 91 days, the return would be:

$$\left(1 + 0.0106 \times \frac{91}{360}\right)\left(1 + 0.00933 \times \frac{91}{360}\right) = 1.005044$$

This return (1.005044) is equivalent to a 6 month rate of 1.00 per cent. *But the quoted 6 month rate is 1.42 per cent – larger by 42 basis points.*

There will always be small differences between different investment strategies, even under the no-arbitrage conditions. This is because of a number of factors:

- Quoted rates might be stale or old.
- Rates might not be sampled at exactly the same time.
- Rates might not be available in meaningful size.
- The difference between the bid and ask rate might be significant.

Bid, ask and mid: which rates to use?

Rates are always quoted in two forms: bid and ask. The bid is typically (but not always) below the ask. In the case of deposits, the bid will be the best rate an investor can get to deposit money, and the ask will be the best rate they can get to borrow money.

When building yield curves, we typically use the mid-rates. These are simply the average of the bids and asks. The reason we use mid is that we are agnostic as to the direction of our investments: we want to build a yield curve that can be used to value and compare both assets and liabilities.

In the example above, the greatest source of variation is the difference between the bid and ask rates quoted.

Both deposit rates had a difference of 20 basis points (0.2%) between the bid and the ask. The FRA had a bid-ask spread of five basis points.

Using the best deposit rates imaginable (i.e. using the ASK instead of the bid) would give us an imagined 6 month return of 1.13 per cent, *still 29 basis points less than the 6 month deposit's bid.*

Why is this? Can't banks see the arbitrage opportunity?

The answer, of course, is that there is no-arbitrage opportunity. Banks are in a very tight position, and they don't have the ability to do large-scale unsecured lending any more. A deposit is, in essence, an unsecured loan after all. In addition, banks are unwilling to make long-term commitments, not only because they are unsure about their counterparty's credit rating, *but because they're not sure of their own position.* What if regulations change? What if there's another crisis and they need cash? No one has confidence in the long term to the extent necessary to tie up money without compensation.

The result is that we've come to see that the different types of deposit (1 month, 3 month, 6 month, 12 month) represent completely different assets. They cannot be compared (at least not in the major currencies, in a dependable way).

3.7 Where do we go from here?

The first thing is to ask: what do we want to achieve? We were seeking, originally, to gain an insight into the interest rate market by using rates to estimate the present value of assets and liabilities on the balance sheet. We were doing that by using time-deposit instruments, arguing that they represented the best view we had of the 'risk-free rate' to a point in time. As we've seen, they don't always provide that.

There is one rate that does the best job of removing the uncertainty around depositing cash for long periods of time: the *overnight deposit*. This is a type of deposit (like any other) where the term is, as stated, overnight. (Overnight can mean, of course, over a weekend too.) Overnight deposits are as close as we can come to a termless term deposit.

The overnight deposit is the instrument with the smallest amount of time-uncertainty, and thus the instrument that will give us the best indication of the 'real' level of rates. The problem is that it is overnight! It gives no indication of the level of rates in 1 week, let alone 1 month or 1 year.

Until 2007, overnight deposits existed as just another type of deposit, related to the other deposits in an explainable fashion. After 2007, this relation broke down.

In Figure 3.3, we see the difference (or spread) between the 3 month deposit rate (in Euros, EURIBOR) and the Euro overnight rate (EONIA). This data shows that the difference between the rates has always been *variable*, but that since the crisis of 2007 the spread has widened and become more volatile.

This spread has gained notoriety in the last few years. While the LIBOR-EONIA spread is interesting, there are better ways of looking at the evolution of the rate universe.

One question to ask is: what is the effect of *compounding* the overnight rate? If a bank were to take 1,000,000 Euros, and invest it overnight

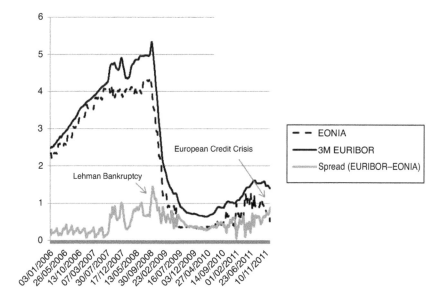

Figure 3.3   Evolution of the spread between EONIA and 3M EURIBOR

repeatedly for 3 months, would the return equal the 3 month EURIBOR return? Well, before 2007, you could execute a *swap* to guarantee just that. The EONIA overnight index swap is available in many terms, and it was (and is) possible to agree to exchange *compounded overnight interest* for a fixed return up front.

The overnight index swap is called, in short, an *OIS Swap*. It is a simple deal between banks where one party agrees to pay a fixed rate of interest over a period (on a notional principal amount of money) in exchange for the *compounded overnight rate* applied to the same notional (Table 3.2).

Overnight index swap rates are typically lower than the corresponding LIBOR rate for the same term. In a typical example (again, January 2012) EURIBOR fixed at 1.1245 per cent, while EONIA swaps were quoted at 0.348 per cent, over 77 basis points apart.

Table 3.2 Overnight index swaps in brief

Term	Anywhere from 1 week to 2 years
Party A pays	A fixed rate of interest for the term of the swap, paid on a *notional amount* of money (agreed up front).
Party B pays	The accrued interest assuming the notional amount is re-invested nightly for the term of the swap at the Overnight Index Average Rate.
Settlement	The final payment is made *net*, and in actuality only the difference between the two amounts is paid to party A or party B. Payment may be 2 days after maturity, due to the index lag.
How is interest computed?	On both sides (the overnight and the 'term' side) interest is computed by multiplying the rate by the number of days involved (overnight is often 1 day, but three over weekends) and dividing by 360. (SONIA, the UK Sterling average rate, uses 365 on both sides.)
What is the Overnight Index?	In America, it is *Effective Fed Funds*. This rate is an average, computed by the Federal Reserve, and released the next day (see http://www.federalreserve.gov/releases/h15/current/). In Europe, this is called EONIA, and it is compiled by the European Banking Federation (http://www.euribor-ebf.eu). In the United Kingdom, SONIA is appropriate rate.
What happens if the swap extends past 1 year?	Interest is paid in two parts on swaps past 1 year. Strangely, the *second* part of the swap is made into an even 12 month term, ending at the swaps maturity. The first part (the *stub*) will be of an odd number of months. So, for instance, an 18 month swap will consist of a 6 month swap period (settling after 6 months), followed by a 12 month period (settling at maturity).

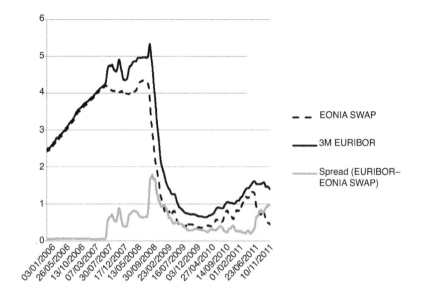

Figure 3.4   Evolution of the spread between 3M OIS and 3M EURIBOR

But was this always the case? Figure 3.4 shows that, prior to 2007, the standard interpretation was that the OIS rate was largely *equivalent to a deposit rate* (plus or minus a few basis points). There was little, if any, variation between the rates.

In 2007, we see that a spread suddenly appeared, and has remained in place, narrowing somewhat by 2009, but widening again in 2011.

This is a dramatic illustration of a true paradigm shift. In August 2007, the spread widened from a mere five basis points (where it had been for years) to over 50. From a financial perspective, this was just a symptom of a deep malaise which would affect the world for years to come. From a purely technical viewpoint, this meant re-thinking the way we viewed interest rates.

Looking at Figure 3.4, we can see that, prior to 2007, we could have used *either* deposit rates or OIS rates in our yield curve models, and achieved much the same results.

After 2007, which should we use? Which makes the most sense, from a financial point of view?

Many argue that, if you want to use the yield curve as a tool for *discounting*, the OIS rate is the best rate to use. This is because it represents, better than any other yardstick, the *true cost of funding* – especially, as we'll see, if trades are collateralized with cash.

Overnight index swaps can take the place of deposit rates in our yield curve model, and give a good estimate of the actual *cost* of holding assets or liabilities on the balance sheet of a bank. Since banks funding is largely overnight, this will be a good estimate from a financial point of view.

In the next chapter, we'll look more closely at the mechanics of how to construct an OIS curve. But, first, there is another, important aspect of discounting which bears discussion.

3.8   Credit effects

Since 2007, there has also been a great deal of emphasis put on the credit-worthiness of the counterparties to a deal. When dealing with counterparties which might default (and this includes just about every counterparty these days), it is essential to factor in credit quality.

What does this mean? Well, in most trading environments, credit questions are handled in one of a number of ways:

- Trades may be *collateralized* in a two-way agreement between a bank and a counterparty. This agreement is often formalized in a Credit Support Annex (CSA), which is an addendum to the International Swaps and Derivatives Association (ISDA) Master Agreement between bank and customer. CSAs typically require that when a customer may owe the bank money at some time in the future, they place collateral with the bank to cover any potential default. The collateral would still be owned by the customer, but would be under the bank's custodianship.
- Trades may be *cleared*. This is the case with trades done via an exchange, or may also be affect trades which are covered by clearing agreements. This means the trade will also be collateralized, with collateral held by the *clearing house*. Clearing houses are a sort of central counterparty, which are intended to reduce the effect of individual firm's bankruptcy on the financial system.
- Trades may be uncollateralized, but managed via a Credit Value Adjustment process (CVA). Many banks have a dedicated CVA team, or desk, which effectively purchase insurance against default in return for a fee (paid to the desk, by the customer in the end).
- Trades may be uncollateralized and have credit effects modelled explicitly. This is by far the most difficult approach for the trading desk, as it requires each trade type to be modelled both for underlying economics and for credit effects.

For those who simply wish to value cash flows against the balance sheet, it is fortunate news that trades in the first three categories require little change to the discounting approaches we've discussed already. Discounting cash flows at LIBOR (or OIS) will still be valid, given that the added uncertainty around default has been taken care of (either by the presence of collateral, or by some sort of insurance).

For the case of uncollateralized, unmanaged deals (the last category) ... the story is much more complex. Essentially, one is faced with either modelling the credit spread of the counterparty explicitly (a non-trivial task), purchasing credit default insurance (i.e. behaving like the CVA desk), or simply estimating the 'spread' to add to account for the risk involved.

The value of an uncollateralized trade can be broken down into two parts. Suppose we transact an interest rate swap with a risky counterparty. We're not sure what might happen to this counterparty in the future – so to protect ourselves in case of default, we purchase default insurance.

In our example, let's say the interest rate swap requires the counterparty to pay us 5 per cent per annum on a notional of 1,000,000. In addition, the default insurance costs 0.2 per cent (20 basis points) per annum, for the life of the swap. We add this to the customer cost – requiring them to pay 5.2 per cent in total.

It's useful to break down the payment structure. In a typical deal:

$$\text{Credit Adjusted Value} = \text{Value}\,(\text{priced at LIBOR/OIS}) + \text{Cost of Credit Protection}$$

With this relationship, we see the benefit of externalizing the credit protection cost. We can retain our analytic capability, and set the calculation of credit protection as a separate task.

4
The Mechanics of Simple Yield Curve Construction

4.1 The yield curve model

In the previous chapter we discussed a number of issues relating to the yield curve market. This chapter will go into more detail on how one actually constructs a yield curve model, and how that model can be used to estimate value, analyse and compute risk measures.

Before jumping in, however, it is useful to ask a number of questions. First, simply, is to ask *why do we need a yield curve model?* There are several possible reasons, including:

- To find the *present value* of assets or liabilities on our balance sheet, relating to cash-flows that may be in the future.
- To help find the expected *future value* of financial assets, such as stocks, or even currencies.
- To find the present value of trades which are based wholly or partially on the level of interest rates.

This third category – the valuation of interest rate trades – is the most complex. Before examining the implications of these needs, however, we should also ask the straightforward question: *how are we going to use our yield curve?*

- We could use the curve for trading. We'd need to update the curve intra-day, and we'd need to reflect the latest market prices in real-time. The curve would need the highest degree of accuracy.
- We could use the curve for intra-day risk estimation or portfolio valuation. This might mean that we'd like real-time market prices, but we are happy with a more tractable, less super-accurate curve than the traders use.

- We could use the curve for risk estimation or reporting, as above. However, we're happy to do the analysis based on rates that are updated once per day (or less often).

A great many yield curves that we use fall into the third category, and may be the simplest, most tractable curves to build.

Things are not as simple as they were in pre-2007. At that time, one yield curve model could serve all applications. A trader would use the same model as a market-risk analyst, and it would be easily explainable to both. Now, we are confronted with a situation where the needs of the trading desk have become much more complex, and much harder to implement.

We'll look first at the classic single-curve. This somewhat mirrors the approach used pre-2007, and still holds some interest today, even if as simply a stepping stone towards understanding the full-blown array of curves typically used in different applications.

4.2   The classic single-curve

The classic curve has been around for decades. Used traditionally as the basis for much trading, it serves as a tool to estimate discount factors or forward interest rates in any currency.

When we say *single curve,* it should be emphasized that we mean *a single curve that is used for both discounting and estimating future levels of interest rates.* Even if you are using the curve only for discounting, you are also implicitly using it to estimate forward rates, because when constructing the curve, the future level of rates is needed to estimate discount factors! (This relationship will be explained in more detail in the next sections).

A simple way to visualize this is to think of an interest rate swap (IRS). An IRS, in simple terms, requires on party to pay a fixed amount each period (every 3 months, for instance) in return for receiving an amount based on LIBOR (3-month LIBOR, in our example) plus or minus a spread. To determine what the swap is worth, one needs to subtract one side from the other: one needs to subtract the present value of the fixed payments, for instance, from the present value of the floating payments. The most straightforward way to do this is to use a yield curve model to estimate the discount factors for each payment date, and also to estimate the level of forward interest rates .

Table 4.1 shows that we're using the same yield curve model to discount *all* the payments in the swap. However, the only time we need to use it to estimate the level of interest rates in the future is when we are

Table 4.1 Example: Estimating the value of an interest rate swap with two payment periods

Period	Rate	Payment	Discounted payment (using discount factor from yield curve model)
First fixed period	1.0% Fixed for 6 months	5,000	4,975
First floating period	0.99% Floating rate fixed via LIBOR fixing.	4,950	4,925
Second fixed period	1% Fixed for 6 months	5,000	4,950
Second floating period	1.02% Floating rate estimated from yield curve model	5,100	5,049
Total value (Fixed-Float)			−49

looking at *floating rates which have not yet been fixed.* In the world of IRSs, we can see that the first floating period is nearly always determined in advance, since the day of fixing is usually the same day the swap is agreed.

It should not be underemphasized that the classic single-curve is not really very useful for serious estimation post-2007. This is because, as mentioned earlier, it is making assumptions about the operation of the markets that are no longer valid. Nonetheless, it is useful to understand how it is put together, simply because it forms such a core part of the fabric of modern finance.

Table 4.2 is a summary of the rate sources that would be used in a single-curve in the classic formulation. The single-curve can exist both as a real-time, intra-day tool and as a snapshot-driven end-of-day model. The main difference between the two lies in the source of rates: if using a curve that is updated once per day (or less frequently) one must be careful to ensure that the inputs to the curve model are carefully chosen. The 'snapshot' version of the curve must have rates which are sampled at the same time as each other, and (ideally) examined and produced carefully by a dedicated department (Table 4.2).

The intra-day single-curve, as mentioned, is largely irrelevant for meaningful estimation these days. The end-of-day curve, could potentially still have uses however. One could imagine using the end-of-day curve for, for example, estimating market-risk on a portfolio of swap products, for regulatory or internal control purposes. It is much less likely that the intra-day version would be used by the trading desk to price and risk-manage the swap portfolio.

Table 4.2 The single-curve in a nutshell

What can it do?	It is a model which can produce estimates of discount factors or forward interest rates to any time in the (reasonable) future.
Shorter interest rate source	LIBOR-based deposit Instruments (out to between 3- and 6 months, depending on the term of the other instruments).
Medium-term interest rate source	Interest rate futures for the appropriate market, and/or FRA quotations from a broker.
Long-term interest rate source	Interest rate swap rates for the appropriate market. Care should be taken to ensure the LIBOR instrument referenced by the swap matches the term of the futures and/or FRAs, and that the deposit instruments do not exceed this term.
Main uses in modern markets	Of diminishing utility, but still used widely in many systems for discounting or even pricing interest rate products. Not recommended for any new systems, and can badly misprice trades.

4.3   The basic discounting curve

The basic discounting curve should be the one on which we can reliably estimate the *present value* of any future cash-flows. This says, in essence, that the curve should replicate in some form the funding of our organization. This will enable us to be able to accurately state that the present value we're estimating is a reflection of what we could invest today (at our funding rate) to get the future value we're seeing. Since most banks are funded using overnight deposits, the curve should be built around the overnight deposit (or loan) rates.

Put another way, there is no meaningful information to be gained by using LIBOR rates for discounting. LIBOR is not used for any sort of lending in reality. The post-2007 world has seen a great expansion in the amount of *secured* lending at the expense of unsecured (LIBOR) lending. This means that if a counterparty owes us money, we must demand collateral from them as security. The secured lending market is huge; but how do we measure the interest rates?

If a customer, say XYZ corporation, is expected to pay us $100 in 1 year's time, we might demand collateral from that customer to cover the eventuality that they won't be able to pay. Supposing we discount the payment to today, we might estimate it to be worth $99. In that case, we might rationally demand $99 in collateral from the client.

Why would the client give us collateral? The bank, after all, is supposed to be lending money, isn't it? Indeed, but we are now breaking the relationship between the *structured product* and the *loan*. A loan, an unsecured obligation by the customer, is thought of completely separately from the product itself. If the $100 is the expected payment, for instance, on an IRS agreement, the value could change drastically (and daily) depending on the interest rate markets. The customer might be agreeing to pay collateral now, because they are hoping that the swap agreement will save them money overall.

Once we have collateral from the client ($99) we can see that if the client defaults today, we can recover our $100 in the future by *re-investing the collateral* at the appropriate interest rate. What is that rate? For banks, this is the overnight deposit rate, the rate which they get for holding cash at the relevant central bank.

Overnight rates, as mentioned in the previous chapter, are not only available on an overnight basis. Using overnight index swaps (OISs) we can estimate funding levels into the future. In addition, we can go even further out by adding LIBOR-overnight swaps to the mix. The result is a curve which reflects the market's opinion on the level of overnight funding for as long as 10 years into the future.

We can use these overnight rates to build an *overnight* version of the yield curve model. The overnight discount curve, built from these rates, is the most appropriate yield curve model to use in cases where we want to estimate the present value of future cash-flows (Table 4.3).

As mentioned, the OIS curve is useful for estimating the value of future cash-flows from customers who have cash collateral. What if the collateral they have with the bank is in some other form, however? And what if they have no collateral, and are in effect asking for a variable loan agreement? We'll touch on these issues more in later sections.

Table 4.3 The basic overnight discount curve in a nutshell

What can it do?	Give us estimates of *discount factors:* allow us to estimate how we should view the present value of future cash-flows.
Shorter interest rate source	Overnight Index Swap rates, generally supplied out to 2 years by brokerage houses.
Long-term interest rate source	LIBOR interest rate swaps coupled with LIBOR-overnight swap spreads. (See discussion on building these curves for more details). In addition, major currencies (USD and EUR) have some quotes of vanilla OIS swaps out to 10 years.
Main uses in modern markets	Discounting future cash-flows with higher degree of accuracy. Can be used in conjunction with the forward rate curve to build more appropriate swap and interest rate product pricing and risk systems.

4.4   The forward rate curve

As we saw in the example of swap pricing, we need to be able to estimate both discount factors and forward interest rate levels in order to arrive at a value estimate for the swap as a whole. The OIS discounting curve, while useful, tells us nothing about LIBOR. And, as irrelevant as LIBOR may be, it is still the bedrock of the IRS market.

The forward rate curve is used to estimate the level of interest rates that can be locked-in at futures dates. As mentioned earlier, the level of future rates was once implied by the level of current rates in a simple relationship. In terms of deposit rate calculations, for instance, if we deposit money for 3 months, then again for 3 months, we could once replicate a 6-month deposit. We saw, however, that the relationship no longer holds up.

What we are left with is a world in which each *tenor*, or period, of deposit exists as its own market. Thus, we can build a curve using the 3-month deposit rate, coupled with 3-month interest rate futures, and swaps based on 3-month LIBOR. This will give a consistent view of rates based on the '3-month' marketplace. Similarly, we can do the same with 6-month rates (using 6-month FRAs instead of futures, since there are no 6-month futures). Markets also exist in many cases for 1- and 12-month rates. So the forward rate curve will not be one curve. It will be several curves, each representing its own market.

One important thing to recognize is that the forward curve must be built in conjunction with the overnight discounting curve. This is because, when building the longer-dated part of the curve incorporating swaps,

Table 4.4   The forward rate curve in a nutshell (1-, 3-, 6- or 12-month variety)

How often is it updated?	Intra-day using rates from brokers, or daily using cleaned, snapshot rates.
Shorter interest rate source	Deposit rates, as with the classic single-curve. Note that deposit rates should be of no tenor longer than the tenor of the curve. So the 3-month variety could have 1-, 2- and 3-month deposits, but not 6-month deposits.
Medium-term interest rate source	Interest rate futures (for 3-month curves) or FRAs (for any curve). FRAs must match the tenor of the curve.
Long-term interest rate source	Interest rate swap rates, of the appropriate tenor. Brokers can supply rates against 'threes' or 'sixes' for most currencies, alternatively the most liquid tenor can be combined with a basis swap to convert to a new tenor.
Main uses in modern markets	Pricing interest rate deals, estimating risk in interest rates to a higher degree of accuracy than the single-curve.

we must be able to price the swap correctly. This means discounting the cash-flows, which must be done on the discounting curve (Table 4.4).

4.5 A note on rates

All of the curves we have considered have both an intra-day and end-of-day version. The intra-day versions are simple to construct using rates from a reputable broker, or using aggregate rates from a market data provider such as Reuters.

End-of-day rates, useful for less frequent analysis, or for posting official numbers on a daily or monthly basis, are both important and harder to get. Ideally, a bank or institution should have a department set up to collect, analyse and distribute end-of-day rates. The typical process might entail something like:

- For all rates we're interested in, sample them periodically for some time (perhaps 10 minutes, perhaps longer) prior to the snapshot time.
- From the sample, remove some of the highest and lowest outlying rates.
- Take the average as the 'closing' rates.
- Take steps to adjust for global effects. For instance, users of the rates may wish to look at products which are not actively traded at the snapshot time. These users may wish to have alternate snapshot times, or adjust their expectations.

4.6 Building the classic single-curve

The classic single-curve makes a key assumption: you can discount payments in the future from the same curve on which you estimate forward rates. This assumption makes curve building easy and efficient, and until 2007 was the market standard.

To construct the single-curve, we're making the assumption that you're either using a computer language, or you're skilled with Excel. This book makes no assumption about programming skill – so we're going to describe the procedures in English, but in sufficient detail to implement in any language or system.

The approach used is fairly straightforward. What we get at the end is a *model*: a system or spreadsheet which will give us answers to at least two simple questions:

- What is the discount factor from today to time T in the future?
- What is the implied interest rate between times T_1 and T_2 in the future?

The classic single-curve is the only model that can answer both questions. As mentioned, it is no longer used by traders for accurate pricing of interest rate products, However, it is very useful to understand how it's built.

The process of construction is iterative. First we collect all the *input rates* we'll need: levels of deposit rates, futures prices, FRA rates if desired, and swap rates out to the end of our curve. We'll then use them, one by one, to extend our curve model.

The first step, therefore, if we want to illustrate the process, can be to build a table showing each instrument we'll use, the starting date for each instrument, the ending date, and what market data we have for it. We'll work with the example below, showing fictitious rates for the Euro interest rate market (Table 4.5).

Notice that we've used FRA instruments to cover the period between 6 months (the last deposit) and 2 years (the first swap). We could use interest rate futures (which are liquid, widely traded instruments) but we chose not to. This is because interest rate futures are 3-month contracts, while the Euro-based swap market is based on 6-month EURIBOR. As mentioned earlier, mixing three and 6-month contracts would result in meaningless information. *Even in the single-curve setting, it is essential to use only one flavour of LIBOR.*

That said, we are using different flavours of LIBOR in the short end of the curve. This is potentially defensible, in that our view of LIBOR rates prior to 6 months is arbitrary. In fact, our view of LIBOR rates (not of the 6-month variety) is arbitrary as well. Building a single-curve in the classic fashion, and extracting meaningful information from it is difficult.

Table 4.5   Market data for an interest rate curve

Interest rate curve example: today's date being 16 January 2013				
Instrument type	Term or code	Starting date	Ending date	Market rate (%)
Deposit	Overnight	16 Jan 2013	17 Jan 2013	0.3
Deposit	1 Week	18 Jan 2013	25 Jan 2013	0.35
Deposit	1 Month	18 Jan 2013	18 Feb 2013	0.5
Deposit	2 Months	18 Jan 2013	18 Mar 2013	0.75
Deposit	3 Months	18 Jan 2013	18 Apr 2013	0.9
Deposit	6 Months	18 Jan 2013	18 Jul 2013	1.1
FRA	6 × 12	18 Jul 2013	20 Jan 2014	1.2
FRA	12 × 18	20 Jan 2014	18 Jul 2014	1.24
Swap	2 Years	18 Jan 2013	18 Jan 2015	1.25
Swap	3 Years	18 Jan 2013	18 Jan 2016	1.3
Swap	5 Years	18 Jan 2013	18 Jan 2018	1.65
Swap	7 Years	18 Jan 2013	18 Jan 2020	1.95
Swap	10 Years	18 Jan 2013	18 Jan 2023	2.3

The purpose of this exercise, however, is to review the process, so we can refine it later when we examine the discounting and single-LIBOR forward curves. We'll build the single-curve first by iteratively adding each instrument (Deposit, FRA, Future (for illustration) and Swap) in turn.

We'll review how each instrument operates as we add it to the model. The important thing is to realize how we deal with each instrument.

4.7 Introducing the ZCR table

As mentioned previously, it is better to have a consistent way to measure the information we're collecting than to use ad-hoc methods based around market conventions. The first step in our yield curve construction is to settle on a way to *normalize* the input data: this means convert it all into a common format which is easy to do computations with.

In this example we will use the zero coupon rate (ZCR). This is by no means the only, or even the best, way to normalize our data. It is however, the most tractable and easy to work with, and all other numbers we could possibly want can be derived from the ZCR.

What this means in practice is that we will add another column to our table to store this rate.

Recalling the ZCR formula – the zero coupon rate is simply an easy concise way to represent interest rates. In a basic formulation of the yield curve, you can get the discount factor to any point in time simply by finding the appropriate ZCR (or interpolating between two adjacent ZCRs), then computing

$$\text{Discount factor} = e^{-ZCR \times T}$$

Here T is the time, measured in some common standard way. (The most common way to measure time is to take the difference between two dates, measured in days, and divide by 365. There is no requirement to be an exact count of years, merely to be internally consistent in all calculations.) The method of interpolating is open to much debate. In a later section we'll look at different methods. First, however, let's look at the relationship between the ZCR and forward rates.

Suppose we have two ZCRs, to two times in the future, T_1 and T_2. Using simple math, we can see that the forward interest rates between these two times must satisfy the equation

$$e^{ZCR_1 T_1} e^{f_{1,2}(T_2 - T_1)} = e^{ZCR_2 T_2}$$

That is to say, assuming the yield curve does not allow arbitrage, any sum invested to time T_1, then reinvested at the prevailing interest rate to time T_2, should be equivalent to an investment directly to time T_2 Using a very little algebra gets us the level of the expected forward interest rate:

$$f_{1,2} = (ZCR_2 T_2 - ZCR_1 T_1) / (T_2 - T_1)$$

Very simple. But this does not tell us anything about the level of the forward rate *between* these two times – simply the level over the whole period. We may be interested in breaking down the period between T_1 and T_2 into daily increments, for instance. This would give us a much finer grained view of what's going on. If we did this for n days, we could say:

$$f_{1,2} (T_2 - T_1) = \sum_{i=1}^{n} f_i(t_i - t_{i-1})$$

This may look abstruse, but what it's saying is very simple. The left side represents the forward interest rate for a period (between T_1 and T_2), multiplied by the length of that period. The right side breaks the period down into n days, and says, for each day, add up the forward rate for that day times the period between that day and the next.

We can see from this that the levels of each small, daily forward rate could be *anything*, as long as their compounded sum is equal to the overall rate for the period. This means, quite simply, that even if we have the hard requirement that the ZCRs we compute are *fixed points*, between these fixed points the rates can satisfy any number of shapes. We'll look more at this in later sections.

4.8 Populating the ZCR table from deposits

The first step in building the curve model is to populate our ZCR table from the deposit instruments we've collected. In the first case, this is simple. For the overnight rate, we have 1 day of interest to pay, at a rate of 30 basis points. The simple formula for the ZCR from deposits is:

$$ZCR_t = \ln\left(1 + \frac{r_q d}{D}\right) / t$$

Here, r_q represents the *quoted rate* for the deposit (0.3%). Here d stands for the number of days of interest we're paying (probably one for overnight, but possibly three for weekends), D is the number of days in the rate's day-count basis (as mentioned, usually 360 but possibly 365 in some regimes such as UK Sterling). The time t is measured by us (in our spreadsheet, or program) in our internal measure, which as mentioned is probably the number of days divided by 365.

A few issues arise immediately. The first is from where do we measure time? Deposits (except overnight) measure time from the spot date, whereas we exist today, about 2 days before spot. We must remember that in the ZCR equation, we measure days for most deposit instruments from spot. This means that the ZCR's time must also be from spot.

There is also the small issue that we don't have interest rates for every day. Even if we do have an overnight rate, there is no rate for the next day (given that the spot date is 2 days away). We can gloss over this, however, if we wish, by simply assuming that the overnight ZCR also applies to the next day (such small assumptions make no great difference in the grand scheme of things).

In some cases we may have no overnight rate, or no generally useful rate applying from today to spot. In these cases some assumptions must be made, such as that the shortest rate applies to the today-spot period.

We put this all together in a simple process to get the final ZCR which we use for each time in the deposit table:

1. Compute the overnight ZCR from today to the next business day: assume that it also holds to the spot date.
2. Compute the other ZCRs from spot to the term of the deposit.
3. Adjust the other ZCRs to hold from today. This is done by computing, for instance, $ZCR_{total} = (ZCR_{overnight} t_{overnight} + ZCR_{1Month} t_{1Month}) / t_{1Month\text{-plus-spot}}$ for the 1-month point.

Table 4.6 gives us the resulting ZCRs for all the major deposit tenors.

Table 4.6 Market data for an interest rate curve, with ZCR

Interest rate curve example: today's date being 16 January 2013 T$_2$					
Instrument type	Term or code	Starting date	Ending date	Market rate (%)	ZCR (%)
Deposit	Overnight	16 Jan 2013	17 Jan 2013	0.3	0.3
Deposit	1 Week	18 Jan 2013	25 Jan 2013	0.35	0.34
Deposit	1 Month	18 Jan 2013	18 Feb 2013	0.5	0.49
Deposit	2 Months	18 Jan 2013	18 Mar 2013	0.75	0.73
Deposit	3 Months	18 Jan 2013	18 Apr 2013	0.9	0.89
Deposit	6 Months	18 Jan 2013	18 Jul 2013	1.1	1.08

Table 4.7   Basis, spot days and fixing sources for major floating indices

Currency	Spot days	Basis	Typical fixing source	Holidays
EUR	2	360	EURIBOR (European Banking Federation, EBF)	TARGET
GBP	0	365	BBA LIBOR	London
USD	2	360	BBA LIBOR	London + NY
JPY	2	360	BBA LIBOR	London + Tokyo
AUD	2	360	BBA LIBOR	London + Sydney
CAD	2	360	BBA LIBOR	London + Toronto
CHF	2	360	BBA LIBOR	London + Zurich

4.9   Deposit basis, spot days and holidays

Table 4.7 shows briefly some of the basic rules around spot days and basis for some major currencies. Generally, the only currencies that use anything other than 360 as the day-count basis are Sterling, Hong Kong Dollars (which uses 366 on leap years), Thai Baht and Singapore Dollars.

4.10   Extending the ZCR table with futures

Interest rate futures are a generally accepted standard method of trading 3-month interest rates, as explained in previous chapters. The quotation convention is that the rate being traded is 100 minus the quoted price.

So a future whose price is 98.05 would refer to an interest rate of 1.95 per cent

Reviewing the date conventions around futures, we recall that each future starts on the *third Wednesday of March, June, September or December*, the so-called IMM Dates. Historically these have been tagged with letter codes (to match exchange parlance), where H is March, M is June, U is September and Z is December.

So, in a first approximation, we can see that futures are nothing more than deposits which happen to start quite a long time in the future.

To extend the ZCR table with futures, we follow the simple steps:

1. Using linear interpolation (see previous chapter), find the ZCR to the start of the contract period.
2. Apply the formula we used for deposits to find the ZCR within the contract.
3. As before, find the ZCR to the end of the contract to put in our table, for instance $ZCR_{total} = (ZCR_{to-start}t_{to-start} + ZCR_{future}t_{future}) / t_{to-end}$.

Note that we'll only have to interpolate the ZCR to the start of the first future. After this, the ZCR to the start of the next futures contract will be the same as the ZCR to the end of the previous future. (Futures are based on 3-month deposits, and are spaced 3 months apart. Since the dates on which futures begin are arbitrary Wednesdays, however, and the deposits last for exactly 3 months, the alignment may not be perfect. It is however pretty close.)

Futures convexity

There are some complexities that come into play when you wish to have a more advanced view of the yield curve. One of these is *convexity*.

Futures, since they are traded on margin, end up getting settled every day, even if the referenced rate is far in the future. If I purchase a futures contract trading at 99.0, and it then jumps to 99.1, I will find $0.1 worth of 'variation margin' in my account. In addition, I can then sell the contract to someone else, and take the $0.1 profit immediately.

So the rate is effectively not a true 'interest rate', but something traded now which references the interest rate in the future. The only hedge for this is an interest rate agreement in the future, but this will pay out also *in the future.* The difference is that *if rates go up, the value of the future payment goes down due to discounting.* The futures contract, however, will pay the same whether rates go up or down. So the futures contract price is not a perfect guide to future interest rates.

The convexity *adjustment*, a mathematical correction to the interest rate based on the *volatility* of interest rates, is typically small (1–2 basis points for futures expiring in less than 2 years). Given the other problems with the curve (such as its imperfect representation of economics), it is best to ignore the convexity adjustment until the other problems are addressed. We'll discuss the convexity adjustment in more detail in the section on second-order corrections.

Overlapping contracts

One thing that should be obvious when constructing a ZCR table with futures: they often overlap the deposits! This means you may get the situation where you will have futures contracts and deposits both contributing ZCRs applying to the same period.

In this case, it's usually best to choose one instrument type (such as futures) as being dominant. In other words, when choosing ZCRs to interpolate, it can be better to prefer those originating from futures. Whichever we choose, however, we can run into difficulties replicating the prices of instruments we've already used. If we effectively *erase* some information from the curve when we insert a ZCR from a futures contract, we might want to re-adjust the remaining information in the curve to ensure we can still recover prices or rates properly.

Alternatively, when inserting the first futures contract into the curve, we can retain the deposit rates, and 'trim' the first futures contract. This means we create a trimmed contract, with the ZCR needed to complete the futures contract at the right rate, for the small piece of the contract not covered by deposits. This approach is simpler (in that we will get the correct rate for both the deposit and the futures contract from the curve) but may lead to blips in the curve if the period to the end of the contract is very short.

It is often best to ignore the first future contact as it approaches expiration. As futures become closer and closer to the spot date, they become less and less liquid, fewer people trade them, and they become less reliable. In addition, the short end of the curve is tricky, and moving too quickly into futures can make the forward rates unstable in some cases. Since all of the first eight or so futures contracts are quite liquid (in USD and EUR at least), and have many people trading them, it is best to set a rule that the first futures contract will 'roll off' at about, say, 3 weeks to expiration.

Futures can overlap each other. This is because futures are contracts based on 3-month LIBOR, and so the period on which interest is calculated extends exactly 3 months from the starting date, which is an IMM date. The next futures contract, however, starts on *the next IMM date*, which may not be exactly 3 months in the future. If there is a gap of a few days between futures contracts, our curve model should deal with it fairly well. We can simply assume, in the case of a gap, that the last internal interest rate holds also for a somewhat longer period. In the case of *overlap*, however, where one futures contract starts before the other has ended, it may be best to shorten the prior futures contract period somewhat before inserting the next contract into the curve.

When dealing with two overlapping futures contracts, the second-to-last ZCR in the curve model must be moved (backwards) to the start of the last contract. As we move it, we can interpolate the value of this ZCR to the appropriate value for that date. However, when we then use the curve model to recover the rate for the first contract, we will get the wrong result! This is because we had depended on the ZCR applying for a longer period in the first contract. The solution is to re-calculate the ZCR at the end of the first contract.

Our goal, in re-computing the ZCR for an overlapping futures contract, is to create a yield curve that can price the futures contracts we used to build it. So, if we move a ZCR point backwards, we must adjust it to ensure we re-price things correctly. The adjustment formula, using linear interpolation of ZCRs, is:

$$ZCR_{new} = \frac{ZCR_{original}\, T_{original} - ZCR_i\, (T_{original} - T_{new})}{T_{new}}$$

Here, ZCR_{new} is the new ZCR to the start of the second contract, $ZCR_{original}$ is the original ZCR to the end of the first contract (which will be removed from the table), and ZCR_i is the *internal rate of return* on the second contract. The internal rate of return is simply the ZCR that applies from the start to the end of the second contract:

$$\ln\left(1 + r \times \frac{days}{360}\right)/t$$

Rolling futures off the curve

As futures roll forward (and then roll off) the curve will change shape and character. This is one of the features, and dis-advantages, of futures-based curves. This means that each day, small differences in the curve shape may become noticeable. In addition, when the first future rolls off, there will be a sudden, larger change in the curve's composition. These changes may seem small, but when large amounts are being measured on the curve, the sudden jumps can result in large swings in profit or loss.

A more stable way to build curves is to eschew the strange world of futures, and use a more stable, deposit-like set of instruments: FRAs.

4.11 Extending the ZCR table with FRAs

To briefly review: FRAs, Forward Rate Agreements, exist alongside interest rate futures as a key method of trading interest rates in the future. FRAs, unlike futures, are over-the-counter (OTC) arrangements. The March 2015 Eurodollar future is a standard contract, and exists day after day. In contrast, FRAs are re-created daily, and exist as on-off, customized contracts. FRAs are like deposits: they are quoted by brokers for periods starting, say, 3 months from today, and lasting, say, 6 months.

The standard notation for FRAs is to name them after the number of months in which they are contracted to start, followed by the number of months until they expire. For example, '3 × 6' means a FRA starting in 3 months and ending in 6 months.

FRAs are settled in cash at the start of the period – the settlement being the difference between the agreed rate and the actual LIBOR rate multiplied by the *notional amount*. In this sense a FRA differs from a deposit in that it is settled at a different time. For this reason, when dealing with

Table 4.8 Extending a curve table with FRAs

Interest rate curve example: today's date being 16 January 2013

Instrument type	Term or code	Starting date	Ending date	Market rate (%)	ZCR (%)
FRA	6 × 12	18 Jul 2013	20 Jan 2014	1.2	1.14
FRA	12 × 18	20 Jan 2014	18 Jul 2014	1.24	1.17

FRAs one could (as with futures) apply a convexity adjustment, but in practice the adjustment would be vanishingly small for FRAs of less than 2 years.

The approach to implementing FRAs within the yield curve is identical to that used for futures. FRAs are quoted directly as a rate, so the procedure becomes simply:

1. Using linear interpolation, find the ZCR to the start of the FRA. FRAs will start a certain number of calendar months from the current spot date: a 3×6 FRA will start 3 months from spot, and continue until 6 months from spot.
2. Apply the formula we used for deposits to find the ZCR within the contract.
3. As before, find the ZCR to the end of the contract to put in our table, for instance

$$ZCR_{total} = \frac{ZCR_{to\text{-}start}\, t_{to\text{-}start} + ZCR_{FRA}\, t_{FRA}}{t_{to\text{-}end}}$$

Using FRAs may provide stability, but FRAs are sometimes not the most liquid instruments for trading interest rates. That said, in major currencies, FRA quotes from major brokers will match the rates seen in the futures markets quite closely. Given the other uncertainties around curve building, in the interest of stability and simplicity it is often better to use FRAs rather than futures.

Another advantage of FRAs, of course, is that they exist in a variety of tenors. There are both three and 6-month FRAs quoted from brokers, and either can be used to mix with swaps or deposits of the same tenor.

Following from our example before, we can extend the ZCR table with FRAs by following the recipe shown in Table 4.8.

4.12 Introduction to swaps in the yield curve

Depending on the market, futures and FRAs can be used to extend the yield curve out to a maximum maturity of between 18 months and 2 years. Beyond this, longer term instruments are needed. (It should be noted that futures *are* available out to 9 years in some currencies, such as US dollars. Liquidity in these contracts falls off rapidly, however, and the most traded contracts are the first eight 3-month ones.)

IRSs are by far the most traded long-term 'derivatives' in existence. Swaps are derivatives in the sense that they are instruments *based upon* interest rates; they do not represent a way to directly trade rates. For that reason, to extract the interest rates from within a quoted swap, we must de-compose the swap itself.

Swaps are quoted by brokers. When quoting swaps, the *rate* at which we can swap a fixed rate of interest for a floating rate is given. The *value* of the swap is therefore zero: all of the payments of a fixed rate of interest will equal all the payments of floating rates. (Another way to say that is that the swaps are quoted at *par*.)

Suppose we were to value a swap transaction, using the requirement that fixed and floating payments are the same. Suppose also that we have a yield curve model that can give us discount factors to any point in time. We should be able to say:

$$\sum_{i=1}^{n} F B_i D_i = \sum_{i=1}^{m} f_i b_i D_i$$

Here, F is the fixed rate of the swap and f_i represents a floating rate for a period. D_i is the discount factor at the end of a given period. The final term, B or b represents the so-called *basis factor*.

The basis factor is simply the day-count for each period: on the floating side, this is simply the number of days in the period divided by 360 (or 365). The fixed-side basis factor is more complex (see the section on IRSs), but is also essentially a constant which can be easily computed.

Note that the number of periods on the fixed-side does not have to equal the number of periods on the floating side: frequently the floating side will have twice as many periods. The standard US dollar swap convention is to have semi-annual fixed payments, but quarterly floating payments. In the Euro and British Pound markets, the convention is annual fixed payments, but semi-annual floating payments.

A key insight, used in the single-curve world, is as follows. Suppose we borrow one unit of money and pay it back in N years. We should be able to do that, as long as we pay interest on a regular basis. In the simplest case, suppose we pay interest every few months, *at the same frequency as a swap schedule*. We should be able to equate these sides: one unit value today is equal to future payments for N years, plus the return of principal:

$$1 = \left(\sum_{i=1}^{m} f_i b_i D_i \right) + 1 \times D_m$$

Rearranging a bit yields:

$$\sum_{i=1}^{m} f_i b_i D_i = 1 - D_m$$

Elegantly, this shows us that there is a much simpler way of representing the floating side of the swap in the single-curve world. We can re-write the swap formula itself now, and come up with a simple way of expressing the fixed rate, if we wish:

$$F = \frac{1 - D_m}{\sum_{i=1}^{n} B_i D_i}$$

We now have a way to get the implied swap rate from any yield curve model, simply by looking at discount factors.

This also helps answer the next question: how do we use swaps to extend the yield curve model? Obviously, since we only have one new piece of data available for each swap (the swap rate), we can only infer one new piece of data for our yield curve. Therefore we must assemble the curve so that only the last discount factor in the equation above is unknown.

4.13   Extending the ZCR table with swaps the simple way

Assuming that D_m is unknown, the swap equation re-arranges easily to become:

$$D_m = \frac{1 - F \sum_{i=1}^{n-1} B_i D_i}{1 + F B_n}$$

This equation allows us to easily use a swap rate to extend the curve, assuming we know the discount factors to each of the periods before.

We can then easily convert to ZCR notation for each term, using the identity

$$ZCR_T = \frac{-\ln(D_m)}{T}$$

A question arises, however. What if we are missing more than one discount factor? This happens when we have a fixed frequency which is semi-annual and only annual quotations, or when we skip years in our

Table 4.9   The most common swap basis and frequency of payment in major currencies

Currency	Fixed frequency	Floating frequency	Fixed basis
EUR	Annual	Semi-annual (quarterly for 1-year swaps)	30/360
CHF	Annual	Semi-annual (quarterly for 1-year swaps)	30/360
GBP	Semi-annual (annual for 1-year swaps)	Semi-annual	Actual/365
JPY	Semi-annual	Semi-annual	Actual/365
USD	Semi-annual	Quarterly	30/360

yield curve (having swaps which jump from 3 to 5 years, for instance, skipping the 4-year point).

The classic way to fill in missing points is to interpolate. We can interpolate the swap rate itself if we wish, for instance. So, if we have a 3-year swap rate of 3 per cent, and a 5-year rate of 4 per cent, we could infer a 4-year rate of 3.5 per cent.

The recipe would become: create swap rates for every period in the future, and use them one by one to extend the curve. This is certainly easy, undeniably quick, and gives so-so results. Nonetheless, it is often used, and if one is not too fussy about the pattern made by forward rates, it will give a good-enough result. We'll write down the recipe first using this approach, then we'll do some simple analysis and look at alternative approaches.

4.14   Swap basis, frequency for major currencies

We can write down the recipe for swaps using the (imperfect) rule of interpolating missing rates:

1. Find the rates for all the swaps you will need to fill in the ZCR table, using interpolation if needed.
2. In order of maturity, extend the ZCR table by finding the missing, final discount factor using the above equations.

As mentioned, this is imperfect, but let's look at the ZCR table that results (Table 4.10).

The ZCR, as we see, can sometimes track the 'flat' interest rate quite closely.

In addition to measuring zero coupon rate, and discount factors, many practitioners use the yield curve model to estimate the levels of interest rates in the future. Using the single-curve for this purpose is not ideal, but we can do the analysis in any case, to see what forward rates the model implies.

Table 4.10   Extending a curve table with FRAs

Interest rate curve example: today's date being 16 January 2013					
Instrument type	Term or code	Starting date	Ending date	Market rate (%)	ZCR (%)
Swap	2 Years	18 Jan 2013	18 Jan 2015	1.25	1.23
Swap	3 Years	18 Jan 2013	18 Jan 2016	1.3	1.28
Swap	5 Years	18 Jan 2013	18 Jan 2018	1.65	1.63
Swap	7 Years	18 Jan 2013	18 Jan 2020	1.95	1.94
Swap	10 Years	18 Jan 2013	18 Jan 2023	2.3	2.3

To measure a forward rate, we simply need to measure the zero coupon rate to two points in time: the start and end of the desired rate period. The formula, as mentioned before, is:

$$f_{1,2} = \frac{ZCR_2 T_2 - ZCR_1 T_1}{T_2 - T_1}$$

We can convert this to another basis (such as simple interest, with 360 day-count) by a simple formula:

$$f_{360} = \frac{e^{f_{1,2}(T_2 - T_1)} - 1}{n / 360}$$

Here n refers to the number of days in the period. With the example rates above, using the formulas given, the zero coupon rate and one-day forward rates look as shown in Figure 4.1.

A number of features are clear from this. First, we notice that the forward rates jump upwards abruptly at the 3-year point, and exhibit a 'jagged' appearance at other points. This jagged appearance, depending on the level of rates, can be quite pronounced. In general, it is wise to be aware of the shape of the forward curve when using a simple approach such as this. The curve will still function well enough, especially if pricing products that do not depend solely on rates near these inflection points. However one can imagine that in the unlikely case we were valuing a 1-month FRA just before and just after 3 years from spot, we would get wildly inaccurate results.

The source of these jagged lines lies simply in the mathematical necessity of having a yield curve that matches all the inputs we give it. If the forward rates must stay low to match the rate of the 3-year swap, they must also by the same rule, do whatever jumping is needed to match the rate of the 5-year swap. There is no 'smoothing rule' in place.

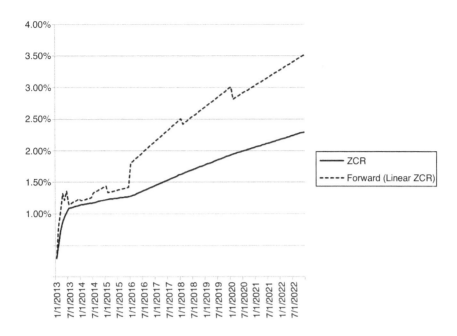

Figure 4.1 An example of the forward rate plotted versus the zero coupon rate

Should we smooth the forward rates? The advantage of smooth forward rates, of course, is that they seem more realistic financially. In addition, if we are able to use the curve to price more complex products that depend on forward rates, we can potentially invite trouble if we don't have smoothness.

4.15 Extending the ZCR table with swaps: Newton–Raphson

We extended the ZCR table in the previous example by interpolating swap points that were missing. If we add a swap to the yield curve and are missing a discount factor for more than one fixed payment date, we needed to create another swap to fill in that date. This meant that, for instance, on a semi-annual swap, we would 'invent' a 2.5-year swap to fill in between the 2- and 3-year points.

Another, better approach is to simply make the assumption that the zero coupon rate between 'known' data points will increase (or decrease) linearly. This means, of course, that we have to find the values for two (or more) discount factors simultaneously. The procedure for this is not difficult, however, and gives better results than simply guessing the rates for missing swaps.

The step-by-step method for estimating ZCRs when more than one point is missing is:

1. Enter a *guessed* value in the ZCR table for the final ZCR: the last needed time-period in the swap. Initially this can be simply a duplicate of the previous ZCR point.
2. Using the swap rate formula, find the swap rate implied by the curve.
3. Add a small increment to the guessed final ZCR in the table, and repeat the process.
4. By geometric extrapolation, estimate the ZCR that would be required for the swap rate to equal the input, market rate. Enter this in the ZCR table (as our new guess), and repeat from step 2.
5. Stop when the swap rate from curve matches the market rate to within a reasonable tolerance (say, 6 decimal points). (Also stop if we've tried more than a given number of times without success.)

This procedure is known as the Newton–Raphson method of root finding, and is widely used in many financial applications, for a large number of different purposes. It is impressively effective, and invaluable in many circumstances.

A good way of imagining the operation of Newton–Raphson is to draw a diagram (Figure 4.2).

To re-iterate the procedure, referencing Figure 4.2, we would start by adding a new swap to the end of our yield curve model. The swap would have a rate (from the market) equal to *Target* (as marked in the diagram). We start by putting ZCR_1 (our arbitrary, guessed ZCR) at the end of our ZCR table. We then extract (using the swap rate formula) the rate R for the swap from the yield curve. This rate, of course, will differ from *Target*, since our curve has an arbitrary ZCR in it. We then add a small amount d

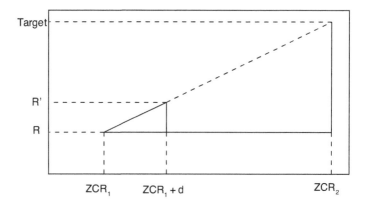

Figure 4.2 Using Newton–Raphson to find a zero coupon rate

to the final ZCR in the curve and repeat the procedure. Again getting the rate for the swap yields a new rate R.

We can see from Figure 4.2 that if we wish to have the yield curve produce *Target* as the rate for the swap, we need to add some larger amount to ZCR_1. Using the rules of proportions, we see that the final ZCR should theoretically be set to be:

$$ZCR_2 = \frac{d \times (\text{Target} - R)}{R' - R}$$

Since the yield curve model is non-linear, this new ZCR will also be an estimate. We'll need to repeat the procedure several times to get an appropriate result. As mentioned in step 5, it's always wise to think carefully about what precision is needed (extreme precision is neither useful nor even always possible) and when to give up (some non-linear problems can be un-solvable, especially if some of the other points in the yield curve are erroneous or otherwise out-of-line.)

It is impossible to overstate the usefulness of the Newton–Raphson process in financial calculations. It allows any number of operations to go forward where the answer is known, but the parameters giving the answer are not. (Examples are many, and include finding the volatility to match an option price seen in the market, or finding the yield of a bond if we know only the price.)

4.16 Methods of interpolation

We've used linear interpolation of the zero coupon rate from the ZCR table to assist us in making our yield curve model work. This is not the only interpolation method used, merely one of the simplest.

Another popular approach is to use linear interpolation of the logarithm of the discount factor. In our yield curve model we can easily implement this. Remembering that the discount factor is equal to e^{-rt}, we see that the log of this is proportional to simply ZCR times time. As such, we can simply do linear interpolation on rt, to get a result as shown in Figure 4.3.

As we can see, using linear interpolation of the log of the discount factor yields flat forward rates between yield curve data points. This results in even greater discontinuities of the forward curve, giving a staircase pattern between swap dates. That is not to say that it is not financially justified (given that we don't in fact know the level of forward rates), simply that using a curve of this shape without awareness may lead to unexpected results.

Another popular method of interpolation is the use of *splines*. Splines are mathematical formulas (simple polynomials) which are constructed so that the curve they represent is continuous between *knot points*. Since

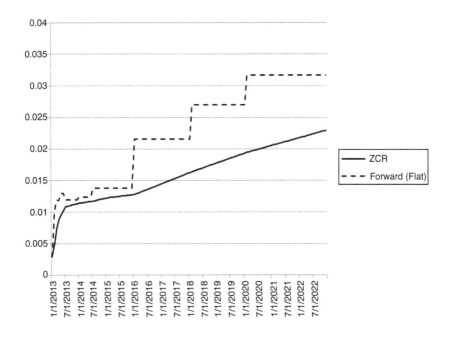

Figure 4.3   Comparing flat forward rates to the zero coupon rate

the curve is constructed in segments (from one known ZCR point to the next), we call the end-points of each segment a *knot*.

We can define a function for the forward rate between knot points which will fit into the spline. A typical spline function (there are several families) might look like:

$$f(t) = c_i t^4 + b_i t + a_i$$

This gives the level of what is known as the *instantaneous forward rate* in the *i*th line segment of the spline.

The instantaneous forward rate is another mathematical construction. We can derive the ZCR from the instantaneous forward rate by recalling that the ZCR is *continuously compounded,* which means that

$$ZCR(t) \times t = \int_0^t f(t)dt$$

Now suppose we want to find the formula for the ZCR at an arbitrary time, given that we've already built a yield curve with known ZCRs in a table. We can use this formula to tell us the ZCR at an intermediate point, let's say sometime after the first known ZCR. Recalling a bit of elementary calculus, and applying it to the spline formula, gives us:

$$ZCR(T) = \frac{ZCR_1 T_1 + \int_{t=T_1}^{T} \left(ct^4 + bt + a \right) dt}{T}$$

or

$$ZCR(T) = \frac{ZCR_1 T_1 + \left(\dfrac{cT^5}{5} + \dfrac{bT^2}{2} + aT \right) - \left(\dfrac{cT_1^5}{5} + \dfrac{bT_1^2}{2} + aT_1 \right)}{T}$$

This is the equation for the ZCR in a single *segment* of the curve, between two points of known zero coupon rate.

That's all very well, but how do we estimate the parameters a, b and c for each segment?

The general approach is to set up a series of constraints on their values, and solve for them. The constraints we set (for each curve segment) are:

- The forward rate at the end of one segment must equal the forward rate at the start of the next.
- The *slope* of the forward rate curve (the first derivative) must also match at the end of one segment and the start of the next.
- The equation for the ZCR must be satisfied at the end of each segment. That is, applying the integral from point ZCR_1 at time T_1 all the way to time T_2 must result in us getting ZCR_2.

These constraints are easy to specify. We notice that there are three constraints, and three variables per line segment, so this should satisfy the requirements perfectly?

Well, almost perfectly. The constraints hold at the *meeting* of two segments – so we in fact have an extra segment left over with no constraints for it.

We must solve this problem by setting three more constraints. Firstly, by the rules of the curve family, we can set the final c parameter to zero. This is a pre-condition, and intuitively we can see that it prevents the curve from exhibiting overly complex behaviour near the last meaningful data point. Secondly we should assume the first ZCR is flat to the first point. We can do this by setting the first a parameter to equal the ZCR itself. Finally, we can assume that the slope of the forward rate curve is zero at the last point (i.e. it flattens out). Since there are no data points beyond, this is a reasonable assumption. We can do this by setting the final b parameter to zero.

Producing the splined forward rate curve then becomes an exercise in finding the solution to a series of linear equations. There are many available tools and libraries for this – we won't go into details on the implementation. Suffice to say, that when implemented on our example, the forward curve looks somewhat similar as shown in Figure 4.4

We can see the vast improvement in the *appearance* of the curve. That said, some practitioners prefer the more ugly, step-wise construction nonetheless. This is because while the splined curve appears more attractive, and perhaps represents something more economically defensible, the forward rates it postulates have no more reality than the step-wise rates of the simple curve methodologies.

Suppose we are measuring the value of a forward rate sensitive instrument. Suppose further that this instrument depends on (among other things) the interest rate between 4 years and 4-years-6-months from now. This rate is probably derived mainly from the surrounding rates of the relevant swaps that we have used to build our curve. Suppose these are the 3- and 5-year IRSs.

On day one, the 3-year swap has a rate of 1.5 per cent, and the 5-year swap has a rate of 2 per cent. We measure our forward rate (between 4 and 4.5 years), and see that it lies comfortably at, suppose, 1.7 per cent.

On day two, the 5-year rate has moved to 2.1 per cent If we are using a linear model, we can assume the forward rate has probably increased

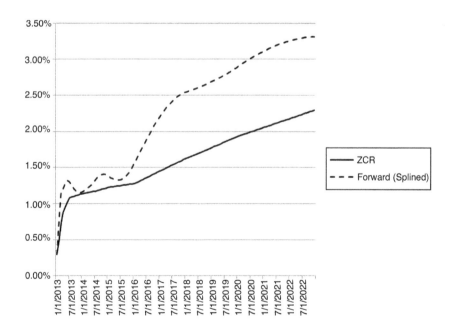

Figure 4.4 Comparing splined forward rates to the zero coupon rate

by a similar, linearly scaled amount (to, say, 1.785%). Furthermore, if the swap rate increases again the next day, we can be quite sure that the forward rate will increase by a completely proportional amount.

However, if we are using splines, we can be sure of no such thing. Because we are imposing a post-process onto the curve, we have in fact also added *noise*. The noise will manifest itself in forward rates that rise and fall in unpredictable ways with the rise and fall of the input swap rates. If we are *hedging* our exposure to a series of trades priced on the curve, we'll need to have accurate assessments of the sensitivity of these trades to movements in the swap rates. If there is no easily predictable pattern, hedging becomes equally less predictable.

We've used a fourth-degree polynomial for our spline function in this example, but there's no reason to stick with that. Some practitioners would suggest doing something even simpler: simply posit a quadratic function of the form $+bt + ct^2$, and derive the solution in the same manner as we've done above. The solution would also exhibit smoothness, perhaps not of the mathematical exactitude of the fourth-order equation, but with the added benefit of simplicity. Alternatively, there is a great deal of literature on the use of much more complex spline forms, which can be manipulated to produce curves which exhibit better hedging characteristics or more realistic-looking forward rates. The fourth-degree polynomial, however, seems to be a simple compromise solution.

4.17 Other second-order corrections: futures convexity, turn-of-year and swap adjustments

We discussed previously the fact that futures prices, while quite liquid and offering a view of interest rates far into the future, exhibit some bizarre characteristics based on the fact that they settle *today* based on the value of rates far in the future. The magnitude of this effect varies depending on the *volatility* of interest rates. If we expect rates to be quite volatile, we'll then have an expectation of the level of futures prices that will differ from their level in less volatile times.

The magnitude of the correction can be estimated based on a number of formulas and approaches. For the case of curve construction, however, we'd rather not be tied up in complex derivatives mathematics, especially formulas which rely on volatilities observed in the options market, which may be something we're not even faintly interested in.

One popular approach is to use an estimate for the level of the correction, based on the heuristic formula:

$$\text{Correction} \approx -\frac{1}{2}\sigma^2 t^2$$

Here σ is the so-called *annualized basis-point volatility* of the forward rate, and *t* is the time until the maturity of the futures contract. Some practitioners will simply input a value for σ which gives a good result (something between 1% and 3%, say) and leave it at that. A more sophisticated approach would be to establish some link between the curve model and an options system which can supply a value for σ.

Another approach, appealing in its simplicity, is to estimate a value for σ based on the market. Since futures contracts extend well past 2 years into the future, we can simply use the 2-year swap point to estimate a value for σ. The procedure would be to build the curve out past 2 years, using futures, then (using Newton–Raphson) find a value for σ whereby the curve model will return a rate for the 2-year swap which matches that seen in the market. (The 3-year swap point can also be used, and a value for σ settled on which gives a best fit for both.)

The turn-of-year effect

During certain times of year the overnight rate will be quite high. This is especially true around the new year, as banks are keen not to fund too much between 1-year and the next. The amount of this increase is unknown, and variable, but can have an effect on the level of rates seen over this period.

As a result, curve constructors often put a 'turn-of-year' adjustment into their models. This takes the form of a parameter (usually a fixed number of basis points) which shows how much we think rates will increase over the few days comprising the new year's holiday.

In our examples, we've been using a ZCR table to represent the curve (at least in the initial building stages). If we were to incorporate the turn-of-year in this model, we'd have to include two new ZCR points (one before, and one after the holiday), to allow us to represent an internal rate during the holiday period which is higher than the surrounding rates. Some simple algebra can arrive at the rates for these points if we assume linear interpolation.

Dealing with complex adjustments like the turn-of-year effect in a splined environment becomes more difficult. One approach would be, once the basic ZCR curve is built, to compute the splined forward curve, and make the turn-of-year effect be an adjustment applied afterwards. The approach makes the curve model more complex, but could be applied as a simple algorithmic adjustment.

Swap point adjustments

The IRS portion of the curve, as we saw, assumes that the floating side of the IRSs we use *does not come into the calculations at all*. This was an interesting, and welcome, addition to our analytic tool-set. Unfortunately, even in the single-curve environment, this is not *quite* correct. The reason for this is that each floating rate period of the swap assumes that the payer of the floating rate will pay (for example) 3-month LIBOR, every 3 months. The swap, however, has payment dates determined by a strict schedule (see the section on IRSs for more information). The swap schedule is determined from the start of the swap, and is focused around the concept of the *roll day* (the day of the month on which the payments are made, one period ends, and the next begins).

The roll day of a swap may not correspond in each instance to the LIBOR rate being quoted, however. For example, consider a swap that starts on the 15th of the month, and the floating side resets every 3 months. If, 3 months from now, the 15th is a Saturday, the end of the period will be moved to the 17th (Monday). Which is correct, and the first LIBOR contract will also extend to the 17th. However, the *second* period will start on the 17th, and extend (3 months further) to (barring weekends) *the 15th*. The LIBOR contract, however, will extend to the 17th (being a 3-month contract starting on the 17th). With weekends and holidays popping up, the difference between the LIBOR contract and the actual period could be 4 days or more in some cases.

This effect is small, but some may wish to account for it (as with the turn-of-year effect) to be extremely accurate. To account for it, however, the method by which swaps are added to the yield curve must be changed.

The basic approach would be to build a small, algorithmic swap pricing routine which adds up both fixed and floating sides, discounts each, and subtracts. The floating side could then be engineered to extract the forward rate from the curve using the LIBOR tenor exactly, but apply the floating rate to the actual swap dates. We'll see this approach is useful in the section on the modern forward curve: accounting for the full swap is also necessary if we break the assumption that discounting and forward rate generation don't occur on the same curve.

4.18 Summary

We've examined the *classic* yield curve in great detail. The classic curve is a useful context in which to understand the tricks and techniques of curve construction. However, the classic curve is not widely used as it used to be. Of more importance now are different *families* of curves, which can be used in different contexts to fulfil the needs of trading desks, risk departments, and other parties who which to analyse the market.

The next step will be to back up to the beginning, and look at how we can more accurately estimate the present value of cash-flows.

Further reading

Deventer, K. J. (1994) 'Fitting Yield Curves and Forward Rate Curves with Maximum Smoothness', *The Journal of Fixed Income*, 52–62.

Patrick S. Hagan, G. W. (2008) *Methods for Constructing a Yield Curve, WILMOTT magazine*.

Ron, U. (2000) 'A Practical Guide to Swap Curve Construction', *Bank of Canada Working Paper 2000–17*.

West, G. (n.d.) 'A brief comparison of interpolation methods for yield curve construction', *www.finmod.co.za*.

5
Discount and Forward Interest Rate Curves

5.1 The overnight index swap and discounting

As we saw in previous chapters, the interest rate curve constructed from LIBOR instruments no longer is very useful for estimating value in modern financial settings. Initially, the events of 2007, when the markets changed their operation, led to much confusion. Many banks were slow to change their systems, but some moved faster. Those that moved faster gained an advantage, and slowly other banks began to see the importance of changing their view of the world of interest rates.

One of the key drivers to the change was the increasing demand that customers provide collateral when trading with banks. It's worthwhile to review briefly the rules around collateral, to see how it affects our view of value.

When a customer deals with a bank, a certain amount of collateral will naturally be required in the event they default while owing money. An initial amount (or initial margin, or IA) will be demanded to cover the riskiness of the trade. A particularly leveraged long-dated derivative will require more IA than, say, a short-dated swap.

In addition to IA, the bank will also demand a variable amount to cover losses in the market. If a customer trades a swap, and rates change to make the swap worth less to the customer, that change-in-value must be reflected in their collateral. This *variation margin* is then added to the initial margin. (In reality, the process is more complex, as the swap will often be *given up* to a clearing house, which holds the collateral, but this chapter will not examine this part of the mechanics.)

What is variation margin? If the present value of the swap is negative (for the customer), this means the cash-flows from the swap add up to some number N today, and we should demand the same amount from the customer as collateral. But what is *present value?* We could imagine it to be the amount the bank could re-invest to get the same amount at the future date: investing N today would give the bank the equivalent of the missing cash-flows in the future.

A better way to imagine collateral is *the amount which, if re-invested today, would cover all expected payments in the future.* Collateral cannot change form. If a customer gives us $1,000 today, we can't go off and purchase a 6-month deposit with the money. The $1,000 is *cash,* and cash is re-invested at the *overnight rate.* (The same holds for the bank: the bank *might* be able to invest in 3- or 6-month deposits, but it doesn't, for obvious reasons of trust, flexibility and counterparty creditworthiness. The bank also invests cash at the overnight rate).

The above argument makes it clear that we should discount our cash-flows at the overnight rate as well. The problem is, of course, that the overnight rate is just that: *overnight.* How can we take a rational view of the level of the rate for months, or years, in the future?

Fortunately there is a very liquid market in *overnight index swaps* (OISs). The overnight index is something like LIBOR, in that it is a rate that is *set,* rather than a rate available for investment. One major difference from LIBOR is that the central-bank often plays a role in the setting of overnight rate targets. Rather than being a passive player, the central-bank may take deposits itself at a pre-defined rate (as with the ECB) or intervene in the markets to assure that inter-bank overnight lending stays within an agreed range (as with the US Federal Reserve). Because of this central-bank intervention, we have some short-term certainty that rates will be stable, and can predict on what dates (after central-bank decision-making meetings) the rates will change.

LIBOR is a poll of banks on a certain day about what they *estimate* unsecured lending rates to be, for a period in the future. The OIS rates, however, are an average of deals that have actually occurred, published either that evening (as in the Euro area) or the next day (as in the United States). (This fact alone makes OIS a superior measure. LIBOR is, especially after 2007, an imaginary rate; the average of where banks *feel* they would lend money for a given term. OIS, however, is based on real transactions.)

The OIS operates as a way to provide a longer term hedge against the overnight rate. As an example, a 1-month OIS would require one party to pay a fixed rate on a notional amount at the end of the month, while the other party would pay the daily-compounded overnight index rate. OIS mechanics are discussed in detail in Chapter 2 on swap transactions – but it is useful to review the mechanics somewhat.

In an OIS, the *floating* leg consists of the compounded overnight rate. If we write this down, for a 1-week swap (consisting of five 'overnight' periods, with 1 weekend in the middle), the floating payment would be:

$$\text{Notional} \times \left(1+\frac{o_1}{360}\right) \times \left(1+\frac{o_2}{360}\right) \times \left(1+\frac{3o_3}{360}\right) \times \left(1+\frac{o_4}{360}\right) \times \left(1+\frac{o_5}{360}\right)$$

or, for an n day swap:

$$\text{Notional} \times \prod_{i=1}^{n}\left(1+\frac{o_i d_i}{360}\right)$$

This looks different from the simple LIBOR swap, but economically it is identical. This is because *compounding* is simply *re-investment*. If the interest accrued over the floating period is re-invested every day, and repaid at the end, the present value will be the same (using no-arbitrage arguments) as if it were paid on a daily basis.

This means, as with LIBOR swap in the pre-2007 single-curve, if we assume that we are using the curve to both estimate the levels of overnight rates and to discount interest payments, then the floating side of an OIS can be ignored in swap curve calculations. Simply put, if we imagine borrowing $1, investing it overnight compounded for 1-month, then receiving the proceeds – the present value of those proceeds should be $1, irrespective of the level of overnight rates. This makes further calculations simple in the basic case. As with the LIBOR curve however, we may wish to re-produce the entire floating side calculation when building curves if we wish to add second- or third-order corrections for increased accuracy.

5.2 Building the basic discounting curve

The basic discounting curve, as mentioned, can be built around the OIS. As with the single-curve, the simplest way to proceed is to create a table of zero coupon rates (or discount factors, as preferred) to keep track of the information we collect as we build the curve. This ZCR table will allow us to either interpolate zero coupon rates, discount factors or even extract estimates of future overnight rates.

The simplest approach (in addition to using the ZCR table, and ignoring the details of the floating side of OISs) includes using log-linear interpolation of discount factors between ZCR points. Which is to say, *assume that forward rates are flat*. Putting this rule in place will give us a good reproduction of flat overnight rates between central-bank meeting dates. The procedure for creating the basic ZCR table is as follows:

1. Add a ZCR for the current overnight rate. This can be simply $\ln\left(1+r_{on} \times d/360\right)/t$ where r_{on} is the overnight rate, d is the number of

days until the next business day and t is the time until the next business day measured in our preferred internal calendar (such as days/365, for instance). In this analysis, we're assuming the *index* requires a day-count of 360 (hence the 360 in the formula above). Of course, for rates such as UK SONIA, 365 would be more appropriate (see Table 5.1).

2. For each quoted OIS of term less than 1 year:
   a. Add the ZCR to the table, using the same formula as for the overnight case.
   b. Determine if there are any central-bank meeting days between this ZCR and the previous one. If there are *more than one*, we should consider adding more, intermediate swap points, since this means an indeterminate rate. If there are none, we do nothing. If there is *exactly one:* then:
      i. Add an intermediate ZCR point on the day the central-bank meeting decision becomes effective (i.e. the day on which the new rate environment will become effective).
      ii. Solve for the level of this intermediate ZCR point. Build the curve model in an intermediate state, and find the level which makes the implied 1-day rate at the intermediate point equal to the 1-day rate just prior to the previous point.

3. For each OIS greater than 1 year but less than 2 years:
   a. Determine the first coupon date. There will be one payment date, which will be 1 year before maturity. (For an 18-month swap, the first payment date will be 6 months from the start.)
   b. Add the final ZCR with value $-\ln\left(\dfrac{1 - RB_1 D_1}{1 + RB_2}\right)/t$, where B_1 and B_2 are the *basis fractions* for each period (the number of days over 360), D_1 is the discount factor to the end of the first period, and as before t is the time to maturity in our preferred measure. Since we're assuming the curve model has already been constructed out to 1 year, the value for D_1 should be available by querying the curve itself.

4. For OISs greater than 2 years, proceed as with normal interest rate swaps. At greater than 2 years, swaps normally have yearly payments. So the procedure is simply to generate the swap schedule (determine the dates), and find the last ZCR.
   a. If there is only one coupon period since the last swap insert the last ZCR using the analytic formula where only the nth period is unknown: $ZCR = -\ln\left(\dfrac{1 - R\sum_{i=1}^{n-1} B_i D_i}{1 + RB_n}\right)/t$.

b. The more general procedure is to insert the final ZCR into the curve model (with a provisional value, equal perhaps to the penultimate ZCR) and solve such that $R\left(\sum_{i=1}^{n} B_i D_i\right) + D_n - 1 = 0$.

The above procedure is the simplest way forward, assuming that the OIS curve represents the best estimate of present value. The procedure is in fact simpler than that for the old-fashioned single-curve, inasmuch as there is only one type of asset (the OIS) involved. However there are some drawbacks.

Firstly, the OIS market does not extend far into the future in every currency. Certainly in US dollars, Euros, Swiss Francs, Yen and UK Sterling, OIS quotes are available out past 10 years. (Indeed, these five currencies have been identified by ISDA as key, liquid OIS currencies, and receive preferential treatment in the new proposed Standardized Credit Support Annex governing bi-lateral collateral agreements).

One question in this case is: how are the central-bank meeting dates determined? Of course, since central banks are public institutions, their meetings are a matter of public record. Furthermore, since they understand the importance of transparency in operation (if not transparency in reasoning) the meetings are often publicly scheduled far in advance.

The European Central Bank's Governing Council meetings are listed on their web-site, as are the US Federal Reserve's Open Market Committee meetings (federalreserver.gov), the Bank of England's Monetary Policy

Table 5.1 Major overnight indices used in OIS trades

Currency	Index	Day-count (360 or 365)	Overnight index source	OIS quote source
USD	Fed Funds	360	US Federal Reserve: Reuters FEDFUNDS1 page, Bloomberg FDFD Index, or http://www.federalreserve. gov/ releases/h15/update/	Bloomberg OIS page (with choice of currency); Reuters USDOIS= (or EUROIS=, etc.). Some Euro historic swap quotes available on euribor- ebf.eu.
EUR	EONIA	360	European Banking Federation: Reuters EONIA page, Bloomberg EONIA index, or http://www.euribor-ebf.eu/	
GBP	SONIA	365	British Bankers' Association: Reuters SONIA1, Bloomberg WMBAGO, or (by paid subscription) http://www. wmba.org.uk	
JPY	TONAR	365	Bank of Japan: Reuters TONAR page; http://www. boj.org.jp	
CHF	TOIS	360	Cosmorex Brokers: Reuters CHFTOIS=, Bloomberg ICAF 6 or http://www. cosmorex.ch	

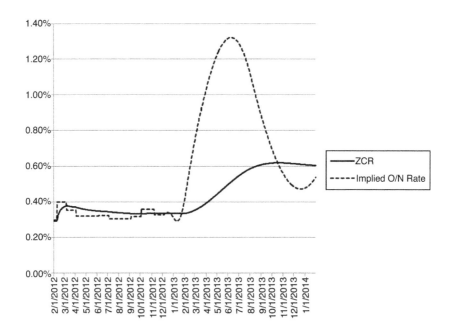

Figure 5.1   Implied forward overnight rates from the OIS curve

Committee (bankofengland.co.uk), the Bank of Japan's Monetary Policy Meetings (boj.or.jp) and the Swiss National Bank (snb.ch) (under Media; Time Schedule).

All of these meetings, however, are typically only projected for the next year or possibly two. Beyond that, the actual meeting dates are less precise. When constructing a curve, when moving beyond the known meeting dates, it may be desirable to consider moving to another form of curve interpolation (rather than flat forward rates), since remaining with flat forward rates would make the curve transitions be at swap maturity dates (hardly realistic).

To make things easier for curve builders, some markets include OISs whose expiry coincides with a central-bank meeting. In the United Kingdom, the Monetary Policy Committee (MPC) sets rates, and the SONIA OIS market has accommodated by providing a widely used (hence fairly liquid) MPC date adjusted swap market.

All of this said – using central bank meetings as artificial jumping-points is not always needed, especially in a smooth curve environment. Jumps of less than 25 basis points are hard to interpret as 'policy related' in any sense; some are due to simple market forces. It may be defensible, depending on how the curve is used, to simply smooth the forward rates with a standard algorithm and continue.

Figure 5.1 is a graph, produced using the above procedure, based on EONIA swap rates. For dates less than 1 year, flat overnight rate levels are assumed between meeting dates. After 1 year, we've reverted to a standard splined forward rate fitting algorithm.

Figure 5.1 shows that in many cases, for small variations in overnight swap rates, the rationale for using meeting dates over swap maturity dates is not water-tight. The variations in rates seen in Figure 5.1 are small enough to reflect not only probabilistic expectations of ECB rate changes, but supply and demand in the swap market as well. For steeper curves, the meeting date methodology makes sense, however. Indeed, the smoothed section of Figure 5.1 could probably be made more rational by using fitted flat forward rates between the second year's meeting dates.

5.3 Which curve to use?

The latest proposed ISDA credit support annex (SCSA) imagines constructing 'silos' for trades, based on collateral currency. So a trade in Euros would have its variation margin needs also in Euros. For example, if a customer trades with a bank, and the trade does not go through a clearing house (which would have its own collateral rules), the bank would first demand some collateral to account for the riskiness of the position (the initial imount or IA). The IA could take the form of either cash or securities. However, if the trade lost value, the bank could demand additional margin to cover the mark-to-market loss. This amount is the *variation margin* and *must be cash.*

The cash, also must be the same currency as the trade. Imagine it was not: imagine a customer posts 1,000 dollars as collateral for a trade whose mark-to-market (MTM) value is 1,300 *Euros* in the bank's favour (and the exchange rate is exactly 1.3). The collateral clearly equals the MTM. So why is it not correct?

It's not correct, simply put, because if USD overnight rates were (suppose) less than EUR rates, all other things being equal, the collateral would not grow enough to cover the potential loss.

Also, more seriously from the bank's perspective: if the bank offers the customer a *choice of collateral currency*, the customer will choose the currency that is cheapest for them to deliver to the bank. Any choice of collateral currency generally is a dangerous thing, and can result in subtle problems. Banks can hedge the exposure to interest rates across currencies, but they have to be aware of it first! We'll have a closer look at this relationship in the section on cross currency trades.

We see that we must use the correct curve to discount trades, and collect collateral for those trades in the correct currency (hopefully the same currency as the discount curve).

5.4   What curves are being used in practice?

Most major dealers are currently discounting their swap market curves based on OIS discounting. That said, for swaps quoted at par (with zero value, that is – where fixed and floating payments exactly offset) many still use the older-style single-curve based on LIBOR, and discounting at LIBOR. The difference between the two is truly *second-order* in nature, in that it does not manifest itself greatly until one is valuing swaps that are off-market.

The consensus approach to building yield curves for use in valuing interest rate instruments based on LIBOR, at this time, seems to be to use the standard boot-strapping procedure as explained in the previous chapter, but discounting all cash-flows based on the overnight swap curve. In addition, as we did in the previous chapter, we must be careful not to mix tenors. That is to say, when building a curve for 3-month LIBOR-based pricing, we must use only 3-month deposits, 3-month FRAs or futures, and swaps where the floating leg is 3-month LIBOR.

As mentioned, the difference in pricing swaps, FRAs, or other instruments initially is exactly zero – by definition. Only when there is a non-zero present value will any instrument show a difference between the OIS-discounted and LIBOR-discounted versions. Even then, the difference is minor in the shorter tenors – because the magnitude of the adjustment is not as great.

5.5   Building a reasonable LIBOR-based curve

The approach, as mentioned, that seems to be the consensus is to build a standard bootstrapped LIBOR curve, but discount based on OIS. This curve-building, however, is not completely straightforward.

When building the LIBOR curve, using deposits and FRAs (or futures) is exactly as before. The zero coupon rates we compute, however, are *no longer representative of anything other than an internal measure of return for that tenor of LIBOR*. We will not use the LIBOR curve any more for discounting cash-flows, rather it will be solely to estimate levels of rates in the future.

Two questions arise. First, since the swaps quoted in the market are largely against one tenor of LIBOR only (3 or 6 months, for US dollars or Euros, for instance), how do we build curves for the other tenors? Second, on a technical level, how do we bootstrap the curve from swaps when the swaps involved depend on both the LIBOR and OIS curves?

The question on tenors (1, 3, 6 or 12 months) is easily addressable. One solution is to simply use swaps where the floating side is of the correct tenor (major brokers will quote many tenors for swaps). Another solution is to 'basis adjust' the swaps, by adding a spread to the floating leg to correct for the basis. This spread is derived from the basis swap rate (where the basis swaps are quoted as a spread in basis points against the shorter floating tenor).

For instance, suppose we are building a Euro curve. The standard convention is to quote swaps as paying a fixed amount annually, and a floating, EURIBOR based amount, every 6 months. Suppose the 5-year swap rate is 2 per cent. Suppose that the 5-year 3-vs-6 EURIBOR basis swap quote is 20 basis points. We would add those 20 basis points to the floating side of a new 5-year swap, to get a swap paying 2 per cent fixed against 3-month EURIBOR plus 0.20 per cent.

This shows how we can use basis swaps to transform inputs, if needed.

5.6   Two curves at once

The next question, on boot-strapping two curves at once, is more difficult, but still quite do-able. The recipe for boot-strapping is still quite simple.

1. Bootstrap the OIS discounting curve as normal. The OIS curve is the basis for all discounting, and does not depend on other inputs.
2. Bootstrap the LIBOR curve as normal, with desired cash rates and FRAs or futures of the appropriate tenor. Note that we assume that FRAs and Futures are naturally discounted by the market at something like OIS rates, so they require no special treatment.
3. Continue boot-strapping the LIBOR curve with swaps. Rather than use the closed-form formulas for the zero coupon rates of the curve, however, we must do a two-phase solving exercise.
   a. First we must create a method to solve for the swap rate of a given swap using both a LIBOR curve and an OIS curve. This is done by solving for the fixed rate of the swap which gives a zero value. Recall the formula for a swap's value is:

$$V = F\left(\sum_{i=1}^{n} B_i D_i\right) - \sum_{j=1}^{m} f_j b_j d_j$$

where B_i is the basis factor for the fixed side, b_j is the basis factor for the floating side, F is the fixed rate, f is the floating rate, and d and

D both the relevant discount factors. When solving for the value of *F* which makes the swap have zero value, we must be sure to get the floating rate from our LIBOR curve, and the discount factors from our OIS curve.

b. When boot-strapping the LIBOR curve, insert a final zero coupon rate which makes the swap we're adding to the curve have a rate equal to the market rate. We'll have to *solve for this rate too.* (This means we are in fact solving for a rate, which depends on a rate we've also had to solve for. Careful construction is called for here.)

4. Finalize the curve-building as before: add splining and/or other corrections as desired.

Notice that the solving in step 3 is quite involved: we're solving for a zero coupon rate when building the curve, and that rate depends on us solving for a swap rate using two curves at once. This is typically not a large problem, as long as we keep our solving approach simple. A typical Newton–Raphson style solution finding algorithm might take less than five or so steps to reach its answer: compounding this leaves us with something that's still extremely fast. Indeed, in tests for short-dated swaps, with a tolerance of 0.01 basis points, the solution was found in two steps.

5.7   What difference does using OIS make?

Does adding complexity to our swap curve make a difference? And if so, where would that difference be noticed?

From an intuitive perspective, we can say that clearly adding OIS discounting to the swap portion of the curve would make no difference at all in a flat yield curve environment. This is because the difference in discounting between the fixed and floating leg of the swap would cancel out exactly. Only when the level of forward rates is rising or falling will there be a difference worth noticing.

In an environment where interest rates are rising, we'd see the fixed side of the swap dominate the value during the early periods, while the floating side would dominate during later periods. If we use OIS discounting when building the curve, we are typically using *lower* rates to discount, this emphasizing the contribution of later periods. This should result in such a curve having *higher* forward rates.

In the rate environment of early 2012, we can see practically no difference under 10 years between the forwards generated with a single-curve and those using OIS discounting. However, if we add a (perfectly realistic) slope to the curve, adding 0.5 per cent to each swap rate per year, we see a dramatic difference between the forwards at 10 years (Figure 5.2).

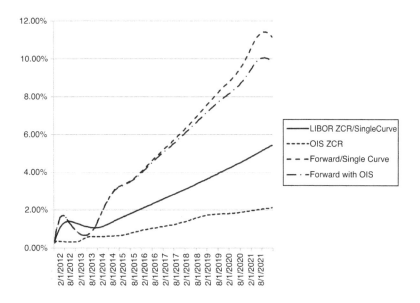

Figure 5.2 OIS discounting effects in an upward-sloping yield curve environment

By 9 years, in fact, the difference between forward rates extracted from a yield curve using OIS discounting and a stand-alone curve has risen to over 1 per cent, an enormous amount if we're calculating the value of rate-dependent trades.

We can see that incorporating OIS is a helpful tool, and will allow our yield curve model to give better performance. With the difference in forward rates, above, noted, we can ask: what difference do we see in swap values? Using the same example rate environment, pricing swaps using single curve and LIBOR/OIS models yields some interesting results (see Table 5.2).

We see, as expected, that there is no difference in the value of par (at-the-money) swaps when using one or two curves. However, as we move away from par, even by as little as half a percentage point, the difference becomes pronounced. The greatest difference seen in Table 5.2 would amount to 50,000 on a 10-million notional swap, an amount which could quite easily remove a trader's profit margin.

5.8 Other considerations: what the curves mean

The addition of the OIS curve to the market has created a great number of changes to the methodologies used to price not only vanilla swaps, but also other more complex instruments. In fact, most of the option pricing models used by banks have needed to be re-written.

Table 5.2 Difference in swap values using LIBOR curve, or LIBOR+OIS combination, in an environment where par swap rates rise by 0.5% per year tenor

Swap tenor	Difference in swap rate from par					
	0	0.10%	0.20%	0.30%	0.40%	0.50%
2Y	0.00%	0.00%	0.00%	0.00%	0.00%	0.01%
3Y	0.00%	0.00%	0.00%	0.01%	0.01%	0.02%
4Y	0.00%	0.00%	0.01%	0.02%	0.03%	0.04%
5Y	0.00%	0.01%	0.02%	0.04%	0.05%	0.07%
6Y	0.00%	0.02%	0.04%	0.06%	0.09%	0.11%
7Y	0.00%	0.03%	0.06%	0.10%	0.13%	0.16%
8Y	0.00%	0.05%	0.10%	0.15%	0.20%	0.24%
9Y	0.00%	0.07%	0.14%	0.20%	0.27%	0.33%
10Y	0.00%	0.09%	0.18%	0.27%	0.36%	0.45%

Fortunately, vanilla instruments can still be valued with approaches very similar to the old model approaches, if appropriate calibrations are undertaken.

More difficult is the situation many find themselves in if they wish to fully understand the risks they are exposed to. Whereas before, the owner of a portfolio of swaps could estimate their value by simply knowing the swap market, today they must also be aware of the OIS market if they truly want to be fully hedged against all possible contingencies.

For instance, if I have a portfolio of interest rate trades (of any sort) with a value of $1,000, that means that I have *expected future cash-flows.* If overnight rates go up, the value of those cash-flows would decrease. To be fully hedged, I should enter into a set of OISs whose value will rise to counter-act the loss.

All of this complexity is daunting. Practitioners have seen the world move from simple models to complex ones in a matter of a few short years. The necessity of OIS discounting is understandable, and the continuing need for LIBOR is correspondingly questionable. Why not dispose of LIBOR altogether, and move to a pure OIS-based model?

It seems likely that this will happen at some point, or something like it at least. However at present we have thousands of institutions world-wide whose entire business process is built around LIBOR. ISDA, for example, has hundreds of legal agreements which enshrine LIBOR as the basis for inter-entity lending. To re-negotiate all of this requires understanding, agreement and a lot of motivation. The people in the position to make these changes are, to put it mildly, distracted by other, more pressing problems. LIBOR is here for a while yet, and we must adapt.

5.9 Using the yield curve to estimate risk

A final subject of great importance is how the yield curve model is used for risk estimation. A yield curve model is a very flexible tool. Not only is it useful in obtaining valuations for a wide variety of financial products – it's also key to estimating risk in a wide range of circumstances.

'Risk' of course means a lot of things. In this context, by 'yield curve risk' our goal is to find out exactly what instruments we should buy and/or sell to make ourselves immune, financially, to shifts in the yield curve.

In practice that means finding a portfolio of simple hedge instruments (swaps, interest rate futures, etc.) that we could buy, which will have the opposite risk to our current portfolio. Adding the two together will protect us from changes in the market.

The simplest way to evaluate the risk on a portfolio of interest rate sensitive trades is to follow a basic procedure:

- Value our portfolio using a set of base interest rate curves made of swaps, futures, and so on.
- For each instrument in each curve:
  - Add a small amount, such as one basis point, to a single input quote
  - Re-build the curve
  - Re-value the portfolio, and take the difference at that point from the base value
  - Return the curve to its original state

In the example below, we're starting with a portfolio consisting of a single 5-year swap. We've valued this swap using two curves, a forward-curve and the discount curve, which we've then 'bumped' as described above. The forward-curve sensitivity is as follows:

Tenor	OND	...	2Y	3Y	4Y	5Y	6Y	7Y	...
Rate (%)	0.38	...	1.116	1.1725	1.3265	1.5255	1.7205	1.8925	...
Sensitivity per basis point	0	...	0	0	0	−489	0	0	...

The discount curve (based on OISs) has a sensitivity of:

Tenor (OIS)	1W	...	2Y	30M	3Y	4Y	5Y	6Y	...
Rate (%)	0.377	...	0.4	0.45	0.5	0.75	0.95	1.2	...
Sensitivity per basis point	0	...	−1	−1	−1	2	2	0	...

This gives us a simple view of rate sensitivity for our portfolio, and allows us to hedge – purchasing a portfolio of swaps whose risk offsets the numbers above would insulate us from valuation changes (to the first order, at least) due to yield curve movements. As expected, the forward curve sensitivities are much greater than those for the discount curve. Any reasonable hedger would probably hedge the forward-curve risk more frequently, leaving interest rate hedging as a second-order occupation.

The example above uses a 5-year swap: in reality, we don't need to restrict ourselves to swaps – this procedure works for arbitrary investments which rely on the yield curve. Swaps can be used to hedge forward-curve risk for a large variety of investments. In reality, one would wish to match the type of hedge instrument to the type of investment one is hedging, to remove the need to periodically re-hedge. For instance, if you're hedging a zero coupon bond, swap dealers will allow you to buy a swap in zero-coupon-like form, where fixed and floating coupons compound to maturity.

One thing to notice is the effect of yield curve smoothing. Many yield curves have some sort for forward rate smoothing procedure applied to them. If we move one point in such a curve up by a basis point, several things could happen. Some curve-smoothing techniques could actually smooth out our point, returning a curve identical to the one we started with. Other techniques, such as forward smoothing with splines, could introduce strange, unpredictable wobbles in the forward-curve.

The most reliable way to build curves when computing risk-reports in this way is by simple boot-strapping using a linear interpolation method between points, such as linear zero coupon rates. By doing this we can, for one thing, guarantee that the effect of moving each point is truly additive. We want to ensure that if (in real life) every rate increases by one basis point, then the net effect on the value of our portfolio will be the same as the sum of increases to each point.

5.10   Delta and gamma in yield curve risk

The risk we computed above is the *interest rate delta* for a given position. The delta shows us the equivalent hedge position we should be holding. To hedge a portfolio given its delta, we simply assemble a portfolio with the opposite delta composed of as few simple hedge instruments as possible.

This way of measuring delta is known as *external perturbation*. We call it external perturbation because the interest rate delta is not supplied by the model which is valuing our instruments, rather we're externally changing the environment in which our instruments are valued. External perturbation is an easy way to get an approximate value for delta, and given the inflexibility of much valuation code, it's often the only way.

Another useful measure, beyond delta, is gamma. Where delta is a numerical approximation of the first derivative of value with respect to an input, gamma is the second derivative. To get gamma we'll need another data point, however. Gamma computation, in the external perturbation method, requires bumping each input point again, in the opposite direction.

For each point, in the report above, we've said that

The ith delta, $\Delta_i \approx \left(V_{+1bp} - V_{base} \right)$

Similarly, we can say for gamma,

The ith gamma, $\tilde{A_i} \approx \left(V_{+1bp} - 2V_{base} + V_{-1bp} \right) \times$ Scale

The scale factor in the above equation is arbitrary, it just is to make the result readable. A typical value may be around 100. Without a scale factor, gamma will measure the change in delta per basis point movement. If we are looking at a portfolio of interest rate options, for instance, gamma will be larger for short-term options near their strike.

5.11 Another approach to interest rate risk – forward rate sensitivity

Two problems with measuring delta in this way are, firstly, that the hedge instruments you may want to use may not include all the instruments used in the yield curve, and secondly, that the forward rates in the curve may cause instabilities in delta reporting. For this reason, many will report sensitivity in terms of *forward rate delta*.

This procedure divides the forward rate curve into a series of buckets, each (perhaps) 3 months long. We add a 'bump', again of perhaps one basis point, to each period in turn, re-value the portfolio, and report the delta for each period as the difference in valuation for each period. Whatever the bump amount, the delta is usually scaled to be shown in terms of change-in-value per basis point.

(One common variation in methodology is to compute so-called *symmetric* delta. (Not that it makes much of a difference.) To do this, we first bump each period by half the delta amount (say, one-half basis point) downward, then again by one-half upwards, and use the difference between each as the delta.)

Fwd Tenor	...	3/2017	6/2017	9/2017	12/2017	3/2018	6/2018	9/2018	...
Rate (%)	...	1.327	1.338	1.342	1.348	1.352	1.359	1.362	...
Sensitivity per basis point	...	25	25	26	25	26	25	25	...

The risk computed in this way is much more stable – since we bump the forward rate curve *after* any smoothing occurs, we guarantee that it will be accurately applied in the pricing model we use.

As Figure 5.3 shows, a 'bumped' forward rate curve results in a small increment being added to a particular part of the curve. The curve above shows the 'instantaneous' forward rate at each point in time – the forward rate as measured at each point in time.

A forward rate incrementing procedure like this is quite straightforward to add to a general yield curve methodology. A yield curve, in fact, can be abstractly represented as simply a method, or function, which returns the zero coupon rate to any point in the future, which can then be used to find discount factors, forward rates, or other useful things. For instance, the discount factor to time T (measured at time t) can be written as:

$$D(t,T) = e^{-r(t,T)(T-t)}$$

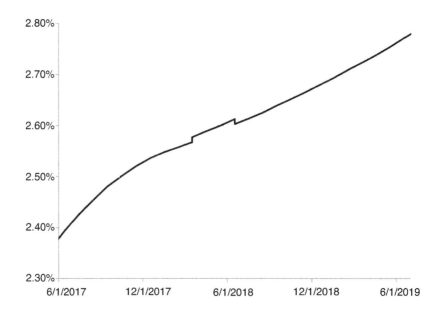

Figure 5.3 Bumping the forward rate to compute forward rate sensitivity

Of course, if we've bumped the forward rate at some time before time T, we'll get the wrong discount factor. Therefore, for any discount factor to a time after the start of the bumped period, we'll need to factor in the bump amount.

$$D(t,T) = e^{-r(t,T_1)(T_1-t)}e^{-(r(T_1,T_2)+b)(T_2-T_1)}e^{-r(T_2,T)(T-T_2)}$$

Here we've added a small bump b to the middle period (measured in continuously compounded terms). Similarly, we can create functions to find forward rates based on ZCR in the same manner. What we should not do is simply add the 'bump' procedure directly to forward rates we calculate, since most forward rate periods will not correspond directly to the bumping period we wish to use.

The main problem with this procedure is that we can't really hedge forward rates directly – especially if we are using swaps. (Well, this is not exactly true. We can hedge using interest rate futures, or FRAs. Interest rate futures actually make a very good hedge instrument, particularly at the shorter ends of curves, and in liquid markets such as USD, EUR, GBP and JPY. For longer term hedging and in other currency markets, swaps are often preferred).

5.12 Converting from forward rate delta to swap delta

As the example Table 5.2 shows, the forward rate sensitivity will be spread out among many buckets. A small bump to the forward rate at the short end of the curve will affect the price of instruments with even the longest maturities. Every bump is changing the price of a great many of the instruments we'd like to hedge with.

To deal with this, we need to also compute the sensitivity of the hedge instruments as well. The procedure is:

- Compute the sensitivity of your portfolio to forward rate buckets
- Compute the sensitivity of each hedge instrument individually to the same forward rate buckets.
- Find the best-fit for the set of linear equations

$$aH_a + bH_b \ldots + zH_z = P$$

Here H represents the vector of sensitivities for each hedge instrument and P is the portfolio sensitivity. We find the least-squares best-fit for the values a, b, and so on. These represent the hedge-equivalent risk representation based on the hedge instruments – selling the same amount of notional of each hedge instrument should provide a hedge for the portfolio delta.

The end result will be similar to the external input rate perturbation result we saw before – by bumping the curve input instruments directly. The advantage, as we mentioned, is that we can choose our own set of hedge instruments, as long as we are careful to choose instruments whose delta profiles are mutually exclusive, more or less.

We can also extend this methodology to include gamma. By computing forward rate gamma for each bucket, we can get another sensitivity vector, to which we can do best-fit analysis for a new set of hedge instruments. Gamma might be best represented, in an options portfolio, by zero-delta swaption straddles. As before, measuring gamma individually for a set of straddles, then finding the best-fit set of weights for each straddle, can give an indication of the gamma hedge.

5.13   Other simple risk measures from the yield curve: carry and theta

'Carry' is a generic word for the value that accrues (or diminishes) over time. A portfolio of vanilla non-option instruments with a net positive present value (PV), for instance, will generally have a positive carry. As values due in the far future come closer to the present, they are discounted less. Even portfolios of negative PV can have positive carry, however, if the positive cash-flows are on steeper sections of the curve.

Related to carry, theta is the term given to gain (or loss) in value in an options portfolio due to time's passage. If we consider an option which is out-of-the-money, and the spot rate does not change from one day to the next, it will have a negative theta value. This is because the option's value will become less over time – the chance of it expiring in-the-money decreases if spot does not move. Essentially, theta is a measure of what happens from one day to the next if realized volatility is zero.

The simplest way to measure theta and carry is to measure them both simultaneously. Generally, this relies on having a pricing infrastructure where one can change the pricing date in a flexible manner. The method becomes:

- Value the portfolio as-of today, using today's yield curves (and volatility surfaces).
- Move the pricing date 1-day forward, to 'today+1'.
- Re-value the portfolio using today's yield curves, re-built as-of today+1, but with all rates unchanged.

- The difference in value will be a combination of the effects of theta and carry.

Being able to easily compute theta and carry relies on having a pricing infrastructure that is not tied down to today's actual, calendar date. A pricing model (for any instrument) should be completely generic. If I want to be able to price anything: a swap, a swaption, an equity option, a commodity swap – I should be required to give the pricing date as a parameter which I can change externally:

$PV = F(t, T, ...)$

The important thing about the hypothetical pricing function above is that we are able to change the first parameter: the time at which we are valuing the instrument. Being able to change this parameter will enables us to easily re-value our portfolio as-of any date we choose.

(The hypothetical second parameter, T, might represent the expiration date of an option trade. Having the ability to modify expiration date for each trade could allow computation of theta as a separable number).

Of course, we will have to re-build the input yield curves as well. This means that the curve-building methods we use must also not depend on today's actual, calendar date. Having a generic curve-building tool-kit is essential.

One (potentially) obvious thing to notice about computing theta is the effect of weekends and holidays. The date to which we increment is generally one *business* day forward – so the theta+carry amount will generally be three times greater over a weekend. When holidays are thrown in, the effect can be amplified as well.

Further reading

Deventer, K. J. (1994) 'Fitting Yield Curves and Forward Rate Curves with Maximum Smoothness', *The Journal of Fixed Income*, 52–62.

Patrick S. Hagan, G. W. (2008) 'Methods for Constructing a Yield Curve', *WILMOTT Magazine*.

Ron, U. (2000) 'A Practical Guide to Swap Curve Construction', *Bank of Canada Working Paper 2000–17*.

West, G. (n.d.) 'A brief comparison of interpolation methods for yield curve construction', *www.finmod.co.za*.

6
Foreign Exchange

6.1 Buying and selling currencies

Perhaps the simplest of all transactions in theory, foreign exchange (FX) is simply the buying and selling of other currencies. One could imagine it to be a risk-free exercise. If I have 1,400 US dollars, and a Euro costs $1.40, I could purchase 1,000 Euros. Where is the risk in that? The Euros won't disappear, and I've spent the dollars. I am, in fact, immune from financial risk.

While this is true, in fact most participants in the markets take positions in a different way. They will (essentially) borrow the $1,400 and purchase 1,000 Euros, without involving any of their cash. So they are exposed to risk, in reality, since they may need to sell the Euros again to repay their loan.

This chapter will examine the risks, pitfalls and intricacies of this and similar manoeuvres. The first step looks at the theory of FX trading, and why it has developed the way it has.

The theory goes like this: I want to purchase, say, Mexican Pesos in exchange for US dollars. I go to my friendly bank, demonstrate that I have enough dollars to do the transaction, and they provide me with some Pesos. The number of Pesos delivered depends on the rate of exchange, which is readily available for me to check my bank's honesty (Google 'USD/MXN' for a look).

But here we hit the first snag. The first thing one requires, if one is to take control of cash in anything but your native currency, is a bank account. Getting accounts set up in different currencies is not always straightforward. So, were I to go to my bank and ask for 1 million Pesos, the first question would be 'for delivery where?'.

The snag in speculating in foreign exchange (or FX, as we'll call it) is the difficulty of taking delivery of currency. This primary quandary has led to the development of several ways to trade currency without taking delivery, such as the non-deliverable forward (or contract for difference), and the currency future. Both of these instruments allow one to speculate in the level of foreign currencies without having to take delivery. (The third way is to roll positions forward with FX swaps, a strategy discussed later).

Whether one takes delivery or not, the basic FX transaction is the *spot trade*. This trade allows you to purchase one currency in exchange for another (at an agreed exchange rate), in an agreed amount of time. The agreed amount of time is usually 2 business days.

The spot trader does not need to have accounts in every currency traded. Most brokers will accept spot trading accounts with only one settlement (cash) currency. We'll discuss how to prevent *settlement* of FX trades when we discuss the rolling of positions.

The spot trader will trade at published FX rates. FX rates are widely quoted, but there is no exchange or global clearing-house for FX. FX rates are mostly an aggregate of rates quoted by major banks, compiled by market data resellers. Major banks will look at each other's rates and try to determine what their own should be (along with looking at order flow, internal positions, strategy and all the rest). A spot trader will have to accept the rate given by whatever bank they choose to deal with.

6.2 Quoting conventions for FX

To buy Japanese Yen for US dollars, I call my bank, who might quote me something like '80.75/85' – meaning they'll sell you 80.75 Yen for $1, and they'll buy 80.85 Yen for $1. Simple enough. (For most of this book, we'll ignore the spread conventions, and simply discuss the *mid* price of assets, the average of the buy and sell price, in this example 80.80).

The Yen/Dollar exchange rate symbol is USD/JPY – each currency as a unique three letter code, of which there are hundreds. An exchange rate has two codes, separated (or not) by a '/', '-' or other symbol. The first code is that of the *base* currency, the second the *term* currency. The quote is always in the form of 'amount of term currency one unit of base currency will purchase', or 'term per base'. (Slightly confused, since the '/' in normal usage implies 'per' as well).

So, theoretically, since USD/JPY might be 80.80, there should also be a JPY/USD rate available on the market, of around 0.012376. There *should be*, but there isn't. (Or at least not readily available). The market will typically quote each currency one way only, and typically each non US dollar currency will be quoted against the US dollar as its second currency. Some currencies are quoted against the Euro, or the Japanese Yen, but the US dollar is by far the global leader in FX *currency pairs*. (Euro-Yen, or EUR/JPY, Euro-Sterling, EUR/GBP, and Aussie-Yen, AUD/JPY are some common non-USD pairs seen on the market).

Table 6.1 Main currency pairs with US dollars as the term currency

EUR/USD	Euro	GBP/USD	UK sterling
AUD/USD	Australian dollar	NZD/USD	New Zealand dollar
XAU/USD	Gold (*see note on precious metals below*)	XPT/USD	Platinum
XAG/USD	Silver	XPD/USD	Palladium

Most currencies are quoted against USD, with USD being first in the pair. USD/JPY, as above, is joined by USD/CAD (Canadian Dollar, or 'Loonie'), USD/MXN (Mexican Peso), USD/RUB (Russian Rouble) and hundreds of others. There are major exceptions. Table 6.1 shows the main currency pairs chiefly quoted with USD as the *second* currency. It's useful to remember, when looking at these rates, that when you *buy* a rate, you are buying the *term currency*.

If I look at USD/JPY at 80, and think it will go up (to 81, say), then I want to effectively *buy* USD and *sell* JPY. I'll tell my broker I want to 'Sell Yen'. If the rate then goes to 81, I've made money. For example:

- Starting Position: 0 USD, 0 JPY
- Trade: Buy 1,000,000 USD, Sell 80,000,000 JPY (Rate 80.00)

My position is now *long* 1 million USD, *short* 80 million JPY.

- *USD/JPY goes to 81.00...I call my broker and close out my position...*
- Trade: Sell 1,000,000 USD, Buy 81,000,000 JPY (Rate 81.00)
- Ending Position: 0 USD, 1,000,000 JPY (*1,000,000 JPY profit*)

One sometimes has to remember that FX is not like stock trading. Everyone watches the USD/JPY rate go up and down – but when the rate goes up, we must remember the Yen is in fact losing value in dollar terms. So 'the Yen is Up' means, in fact, the USD/JPY rate has *fallen*. It's all relative of course: if you work in Japan, then the USD/JPY rate falling means that the US dollar has lost value relative to the currency you care about: the Yen.

Precious metals

One might notice that the last eight entries in Table 6.1 are not currencies per se: they are metals! The fact is, many precious metals trade as currencies. One can think of this as a sensible trade-off. Precious metals are used world-wide as a value store as well as an industrial commodity. Many of them have *lending rates*, which in effect operate like interest rates in a currency.

Commodities in general (such as oil, gas or rubber) are definitely not like currencies. The prime reason they are not is that they have large storage costs. If I want to buy Euros (for dollars) today, because I think the EUR/USD rate will go up within 6 months, I'll have no problem doing that. Someone, at some point, will set up the necessary Euro accounts to hold the Euros, and a single account can hold a limitless supply.

If I want to buy oil today, because I think it will go up in 6 months, I will have to go to the futures market, and decide *when* I want to buy the oil. I'll have trouble purchasing oil and *storing* it for 6 months: storage is hard to arrange. For this reason, oil is traded in contracts for delivery at a specific place and time, whereas currencies can exist anywhere, any time.

Precious metals are between these two extremes. Storage is needed, it's true, but it's cheap relative to the value of the commodity. So the intrinsic value and lending rates of the commodity completely overwhelm the storage costs, and it becomes like a currency.

The difficulty with precious metals, from a bank's perspective, is that the back-office functions needed to trade and settle precious metals are different from that needed for currencies. Precious metals cannot be transferred in the same way currencies can, thus often requiring different computer systems. Nonetheless, from a trading perspective, they are often lumped with currencies.

In US dollar terms, FX trading makes intuitive sense when USD is the second currency in the quoted pair of currencies (as in EUR/USD). So when EUR/USD goes from 1.3 to 1.4, then in fact the Euro has become more valuable *in dollar terms*. Buying Euros will generate a profit (in dollars) if the quoted rate goes up.

6.3 Trading FX and FX positions

We've mentioned the concept of the FX *position* a few times now, and it might be worthwhile to elaborate on this. Suppose we start out with nothing. We decide to borrow $1,400 US dollars, and use that to buy $1,000 Euros. We can build a table of our currency holdings like so:

Currency	Position
USD	−1,400
EUR	1,000

Simple enough. Our *position* is therefore simply our cash holdings in a given currency. (Typically, FX positions are measured including amounts due for payment at any time in the future as well. So a contract for delivery of Euros in 1 month's time is treated the same as one for delivery today.)

We can extend the table, as we trade more currencies. Suppose we now borrow 1,600 USD to buy 1,000 GBP:

Currency	Position
USD	–2,000
EUR	1,000
GBP	1,000

We could also borrow a further 1,000 USD to buy 80,000 Japanese Yen:

Currency	Position
USD	–3,000
EUR	1,000
GBP	1,000
JPY	80,000

This is a table showing our overall FX *position,* on a currency basis. The next thing we'll need to do is keep track of our profit and loss (P&L) as the FX market moves. If we want to liquidate our EUR position, we'd have to sell the Euros at the prevailing rate, and move the proceeds back to USD. Our net position in USD would then reflect any profit or loss from the EUR FX rate movement.

To keep track of this properly, we should first add a column showing the initial rate at which we bought the non-USD currency:

Currency	Position	Initial FX	USD equivalent
USD	–3,000	1.0	–3,000
EUR	1,000	1.4000	1,400
GBP	1,000	1.6000	1,600
JPY	80,000	80.00	1,000
Total USD			0

Naturally, the USD equivalents of our initial positions add up to zero (since we started with nothing). Now, we can add a column showing the *current* FX rate, including any moves it may have made during the day. We can use that to compute the current USD position, and (consequently) any P&L.

Currency	Position	Initial FX	USD equivalent	Current FX	In USD	P&L
USD	–3,000	1.0	–3,000	1.0	–3,000	0
EUR	1,000	1.4000	1,400	1.4100	1,410	+10
GBP	1,000	1.6000	1,600	1.6100	1,610	+10
JPY	80,000	80.00	1,000	82.05	975	–25
Total USD			0			–5

This shows simply enough that, since we started the position, we've lost a total of 5 US dollars. If we were to liquidate our positions (by selling EUR, GBP and JPY at prevailing rates) we would have a small loss which we'd have to make up. The table also breaks down our performance by currency in a nice way.

Using tables like this, one can break down P&L on a daily basis as well, showing the start-of-day positions (using last night's FX rates) and any change during the day. A spreadsheet version of this might have links in the 'current FX' cells to a market data source, allowing real-time P&L estimation.

By using current FX rates, we've *marked our position to market*, and the terms P&L and mark-to-market (or MTM) are often used interchangeably (even though P&L refers to the *change* in value, and MTM to the total value itself).

6.4 Margin

Once we have a table showing positions, we can see how brokers often charge customers *margin*.

In the example above, we were able to trade currencies in an artificially simple manner. We borrowed USD to buy EUR, and there was no real cost to this transaction. In real life, there would be a cost (of sorts), typified by the margin requirement.

Brokers will normally require a small percentage of each position to be deposited on a margin account. For liquid currencies, this could range anywhere from 1 to 5 per cent, depending on what sort of customer you are, and how large the position is. Suppose, as in the example above, we are buying 1,000 USD worth of EUR. The broker might require us to put 2 per cent, or $20, into a margin account.

This amount will serve as a safeguard against movements in the FX rate. Since an individual customer has no great deal of creditworthiness, the broker must protect themselves from default by the customer. If the EUR/USD rate moves against the customer, they might find themselves unable to liquidate the position to pay the broker. The broker will have lent them $1,000 USD – and they will be unable to pay it back. Hence the $20 margin. In the event of customer default, the broker will liquidate the customer's position and keep whatever margin is needed to cover any losses.

Of course, in the event that the customer does not lose money, and closes their position nicely, they can get their margin back with interest (typically paid at the prevailing overnight rate of the currency of their margin account).

We should mention that margin-trading is not something that banks do so much of with each other. Banks that deal in FX will trade currencies inter-bank, and may have credit arrangements that differ considerably from simple margin-rate agreements. Banks, however, often have margin-trading agreements with large hedge-fund or consumer-brokerage customers via a specialized prime brokerage unit, whose purpose is to allow larger customers to trade with their FX desk while mitigating risk.

For a broker, margin rates vary, as mentioned, by customer type (individuals are charged more than, say, corporations) position size (small positions cost more than mid-sized ones, but large ones may cost more again), and riskiness (positions in weird or volatile currencies may cost more).

As mentioned in the previous chapter, we call this margin amount the *initial margin* (IM), or *independent amount* (IA). The IA is supplemented by the *variation margin*. Variation margin is a fancy way of saying P&L. Each day, as the FX rates change, there will be a certain amount of profit or loss which will accrue to our account. This profit or loss can be added to our margin account.

Typically, if the margin account drops below a certain point we will get a margin call from the broker. This will be a requirement from them that we 'top-up' our margin account to reflect the loss in value of our position. If the P&L keeps moving against us, we'll get repeated margin calls.

If, on the other hand, the P&L goes in our favour, we should be able to demand a return of margin from the broker. This will be a request to them to return to us some of our margin account, due to the fact that we are *over-collateralized*.

A brief example may help. The below table shows our initial position with example margin rates, and initial margin:

Currency	Position	Initial FX	USD equivalent	Margin-rate	IA required
USD	–3,000	1.0	–3,000	N/A	
EUR	1,000	1.4000	1,400	2%	28
GBP	1,000	1.6000	1,600	2%	32
JPY	80,000	80.00	1,000	2%	25
Total USD					85

In this example, we see the total IA is $85, based on the total from three positions.

One question arises from this, however. What happens when the positions are negative? Suppose, changing this example, we have *sold* EUR. Would we be charged margin?

Of course we would. The approach taken by most banks or brokers is to only charge based on one side of the position. This could be the positive or negative side (depending on the broker). Suppose our broker only charges based on positive positions, and we had sold EUR rather than bought it; the table above would change as follows:

Currency	Position	Initial FX	USD equivalent	Margin-rate	IA required
USD	−1,400	1.0	−1,400	N/A	
EUR	−1,000	1.4000	−1,400	N/A	
GBP	1,000	1.6000	1,600	2%	32
JPY	80,000	80.00	1,000	2%	25
Total USD					57

We've reduced our margin requirement by offsetting some of the EUR position against the other currencies. This approach (counting positive or negative positions towards IA) is known as *net open position* margin calculation (or NOP margining). NOP margining is probably the most popular form of margin or collateral computation for FX; other approaches include VaR margining (value-at-risk), but this is typically much more complex and useful only when including more complex transactions. FX cash trading largely uses NOP.

6.5 Cross rates

Typically, if US dollars are *not* mentioned in a currency pair, it is referred to as a 'cross rate'. So, theoretically, EUR/JPY is the 'Euro-Yen Cross Rate', whereas USD/JPY is simply the 'Yen Rate'.

Simply enough, one can figure out how to derive cross rates from US dollar rates with a little algebra.

Suppose USD/JPY = 80 and EUR/USD = 1.5, what is EUR/JPY? Well, 1 dollar buys 80 Yen, and 1 Euro buys 1.5 dollars... so 1 Euro should buy 120 Yen, obviously.

EUR/JPY= EUR/USD × USD/JPY

As with ordinary algebra, the currencies can cancel out in the currency pairs, leaving the desired pair.

One should keep in mind the bid/ask spread when looking at crosses. If I want to *buy Yen for Euros* (in effect, selling EUR/JPY) then I'll want to sell Euros to buy dollars, then sell dollars to buy Yen.

Suppose I want to trade EUR/JPY this way.

- EUR/USD = 1.3000/1.3010
- USD/JPY = 80.00/80.10
- So EUR/JPY = 104.00/104.93

The bid/ask spread becomes magnified by this process, since we're in effect doing two transactions. Not surprising, but worth keeping track of.

6.6 Spot days

The most basic FX trade, as mentioned, is the spot trade. This means that we agree to exchange notional amounts of each currency in (typically) *two days' time*. Typically, the date on which the currencies actually change hands is called the settlement or *value date*. But what does this mean?

The actual rules for calculating the value date are usually simple, but there are a few caveats that creep in from time to time.

Settlement day rules

- Typically settlement is after *2 business days*, skipping weekends. So a trade done on Thursday will typically be for value Monday.
- If the value date turns out to be a bank holiday *in either currency's country or US dollars*, then the value date will move to the next day that is not an official bank holiday. Notice that US dollars have a special meaning in the FX market: US holidays are relevant even in crosses such as AUD/JPY.
- If the intermediate date (between trading and settlement) is a holiday in the non-USD currency, then it will be counted like a weekend, and settlement will also move forward a day.
- If the intermediate date is a US holiday only, then no special notice it taken, unless the second currency is ARS (Argentina), CLP (Chile) or MXN (Mexico).
- If the currency pair is USD/CAD (Canadian), USD/TRY (Turkish), USD/PHP (Philippines) or USD/RUB (Russian), then there is typically only *one day* of settlement lag. USD/UAH (Ukraine) has same-day settlement.
- Arab currencies treat Friday and Saturday as weekend days, and Sunday as a working day. Most such currencies then will take the settlement day as Monday for trades done the previous Wednesday or Thursday (thus being fair to both USD and the local currency). The exceptions are SAR (Saudi) and JOD (Jordan), where Thursday trades settle Tuesday.
- Trades after 5 p.m. New York time are typically counted as having been traded the next day. (Except NZD/USD, which moves over at 7 a.m. Auckland time).

Most practitioners naively implement 2 spot days for most currency pairs, which works fine in most circumstances. The special rules above are needed for settlement systems, or short-term traders who wish total accuracy.

Table 6.2 Common tenors and their meaning

T/N or TN	Tomorrow-Next, that is, the business day after the next business day. Usually the same as the *spot* value date, and quoted for FX swaps.
S/N or SN	Spot-next, that is, the day *after* the default spot value date.
O/N or ON	Overnight, from today until the next business day.
1W, 2W	One or 2 weeks. Here, '1-week' means 1-week forward from the standard *spot* value date, adjusted for holidays. So if today is Tuesday, and spot value date is Thursday, the 1-week tenor would refer to the Thursday in the following week.
1M, 2M, 3M, 6M, 9M, 1Y	One to 12 months. This also takes the spot date, and moves it forward by the given number of months. So if the spot value date is the 12th of June, the 1-month forward date would be the 12th of July, subject to the modified following convention (see Chapter 2 on).

6.7   Forward trades

It is possible to trade FX in terms other than 2-day spot. In fact there's a moderate sized market around forward FX. Later chapters look at this in more detail; here we'll look at forward FX from the perspective of the cash FX trader.

Any trade to a date that's not the spot date is generally called either an *outright* (or *forward outright,* or *outright forward*) or a *broken date* trade.

Outright trades are those trades which settle on a pre-defined *tenor.* These are dates in the future which are commonly traded, and include fixed terms like 1-week, 2-weeks, 1-month, and so on (Table 6.2).

An outright trade is just like a spot trade: it's an agreement to trade an amount of one currency for another, at an agreed rate, on a given date. The rate for a forward trade will be different from that of a spot trade, given all the various factors, such as interest rates and different supply and demand conditions which may pertain to future dates.

6.8   FX swaps and managing positions

As we mentioned, it is unusual for those who trade FX to settle all their positions. Typically, someone might trade, say, USD/MXN (Mexican Peso) during the day using spot trades. At the end of the day, they can prevent this from settling by *moving the position to the future,* or *rolling* their exposure.

Rolling of positions is not something banks do – rather it is something that non-bank FX traders may engage in. Rolling of positions is necessary because its often undesirable, or even impossible, for many traders to settle payments in currencies in which they are only speculating.

The simplest way to roll positions forward is with an FX swap. FX swaps are simply two FX trades, offsetting each other, which settle at different times.

For example, a 1-month EUR/USD FX swap would have a *near leg* (typically settling in 2 days, at the spot date) and a *far leg* (settling in 1-month).

Example: EUR/USD swap; today's date 21 February		
Currency	Settle date	Amount
EUR	23 Feb	−750,000
USD	23 Feb	1,000,000
EUR	23 March	750,750
USD	23 March	−1,000,000

In the example above, the first two rows represent the near leg (the spot transaction, in other words) and the last rows are the far leg.

Notice that the far leg in this example has amounts that do not match the near leg. Normally, a dealer will charge nothing for an FX swap transaction – the transaction is free, all the customer has to do is provide the cash for any settlement. However, as always, nothing is free: the dealer will take a margin on the transaction. In addition, future amounts will generally be larger than spot amounts because of interest rates. So assuming the spot FX rate is 1.3333, and the forward (1-month) rate is 1.333111, and EUR and USD interest rates are 1 per cent and 0.8 per cent respectively, the *present value* of the transaction is actually about −500 dollars: it has cost the customer 500 dollars to do this trade.

Suppose we did this trade to roll forward the spot trade in the first example. If we add up all our trades, we can look at our actual *FX position*. The term 'position' here simply means the sum of all amounts in each currency.

Trade	Settle date	EUR	USD
Spot trade	23 Feb	750,000	−1,000,000
FX swap near leg	23 Feb	−750,000	1,000,000
FX swap far leg	23 March	750,750	−1,000,000
Total position		750,750	−1,000,000

The position we have then is 750,750 Euros, settling in 1-month.

The forward FX rates quoted in the market are *outright* rates. The *swap* is the opposite of an outright trade. The FX swap exposes the holder to no risk due to changing FX rates (at first), and has little or no value on its own. Most people do transactions in the spot market to speculate, or transfer funds and risk, then move the settlement dates forward to ensure that they keep the risk in place without settling into currencies for which they have no account.

One typical strategy is to always roll positions forward by a set amount. A trader could trade every day for a week, for instance, using spot trades. At the start of the day, the previous day's trades would now be only 1 day from settlement. To prevent settlement, those positions would be rolled forward to the spot date using a *tomorrow-next swap* ('Tom/Next'), and today's trades would be added to them.

Once per week, the net daily position can be rolled forward to the next week, using a 1-week swap. If desired, that can be further rolled forward on a monthly basis. The typical goal is to minimize the number of trades needed to manage positions, and ensure that the Tom/Next swaps don't become unwieldy and over-large.

6.9 Forward points

Forward *points* are the way FX forward rates are quoted in the market. Forward points are usually quoted to two further decimal places than the spot rate. So, for instance, if EUR/USD is quoted at 1.3333 (four decimals), the 1-month forward outright might be quoted as 1.333111 (six decimals). The quotes are usually given as *additive adjustments* to the spot rate (to

EUR/USD example forward points	
Spot	1.3333
1-week	−0.52
2-weeks	−0.98
1-month	−1.89
2-months	−3.52

prevent them changing as rapidly as the spot, which might change several times per second).

In the example above, the forward points are quoted in 'magnified form' as well. To get the additive adjustment to the spot rate, we must divide by 10,000. So, to get the 2-month forward outright, we would take 1.3333 and add (−3.52/10,000) to get 1.332948.

Note that these examples are using *mid* rates. Typically the market will quote bid and ask: if you are a customer of the bank or broker, you will buy the *term* (second) currency at the ask rate, and sell at the bid rate. To make matters more confusing, the *sign* is often not quoted. One must determine whether the forward points quoted are positive or negative by seeing if the bid is *below* (positive) or *above* (negative) the ask.

For example, using EUR/USD as above, the 2-month point might be quoted as 4.54 (bid) 2.50 (offer), implying that the numbers are negative.

The FX swap market has several forms of trade, which dealers are happy to quote. The most common form is (as in our example) to keep the notional amount of the swap in the *base* (first) currency constant, and to vary the amount in the term currency. As in our example, this means that we exactly match our position in US dollars (with no interest accrual), but have some difference in EUR (to reflect interest accrual in both EUR and USD).

Customers may wish, however, to keep the term currency flat, and dealers will quote this option as well.

Note that because of the habit of distributing the interest accrual from **both** currencies into the term currency (if the base amount is kept constant), the FX exposure is slowly shifted as well. An FX swap is not totally risk-neutral: if, for instance, you have a JPY exposure, and you swap the position forward, your exposure will slowly grow at a slightly greater rate than would be expected from interest alone. (This effect is called *tail risk*, and simply becomes another risk-management artefact).

Pips and big figures

FX rates are often quoted with only the last two numbers of the relevant rate. For instance, if EUR/USD is 1.3340 (bid) versus 1.3345 (ask), the quote might be given as '40/45'. These numbers are the 'price points', or pips, in which the rate moves.

Often, if you've been away for a while, seeing just the pips will tell you nothing about the rate: you'll need the rest of the quote as well. The part of the quote before the pips (1.33 in this example) is the 'Big Figure', or 'handle'. Asking a broker 'what's the handle' is always a good idea if you're unsure.

6.10   Deliverable or not?

Whether or not one wants to take delivery of currency, there are some currencies that can't be settled, even if one had all the machinery in place. For example, Brazil imposes a number of controls on its currencies to prevent 'speculation'. This makes it hard for banks to offer customers a meaningful way to trade Brazilian *reals*, at least directly.

The answer is the *non-deliverable forward*, or NDF. NDFs are like normal FX spot or forward transactions in their economic effect. The difference lies in the fact that they are really a *derivative*, that is, when one trades an NDF one is not actually buying FX, one is entering into a contract *based on FX rates*.

A 1-week USD/BRL (Dollar/Brazilian) NDF might look like this:

- For reference: today's date: March 20
- Expiration of NDF: March 27 (1-week)

Table 6.3 Common non-deliverable currencies

Currency code	Name	Typical fixing source (Reuters)
ARS	Argentinian peso	BNAR
BDT	Bangladesh taka	
BRL	Brazilian real	BRFR or BRLPTAX=
CLP	Chilean peso	CLPOB=
CNY	Chinese yuan/renminbi	SAEC
COP	Columbian peso	CO/COL03
EGP	Egyptian pound	
GTQ	Guatemalan quetzal	
IDR	Indonesian rupiah	ABSIRFIX01
INR	Indian rupee	RBIB
KRW	Korean won	KFTC18
MYR	Malaysian Ringgit	ABSIRFIX01
PHP	Philippine peso	PDSPESO
PEN	Peruvian neuvo sol	PDSB or PDSC
RUB	Russian rouble	RUB/1
TWD	Taiwan dollar	TFEMA
UAH	Ukrainian hryvnia	GFIU
VEF	Venezuelan bolivar	BCV28
VND	Vietnamese dong	

- Sell BRL/buy USD
- BRL amount: 1,750,000
- USD amount: 1,000,000
- NDF rate: 1.75
- NDF fixing source: Brazilian PTAX rate as quoted on reuters (BRLPTAX=)
- Delivery date: 2 business days from expiration.

This looks like a normal forward outright, really. The difference is, on March 27, rather than transferring the USD and BRL amounts to and from various accounts, the NDF is settled by taking the difference between the *NDF rate* (1.75 in this example) and the actual rate (as observed via the *fixing*, typically seen on a Reuters or Bloomberg page). The difference is then multiplied by the term amount (the USD Amount in this example) to get the final payment, which is converted to USD at the fixing rate.

The economic effect of an NDF is exactly the same as an ordinary FX forward which is converted to US dollars when the value date becomes the spot date.

Let's look at what happens when the NDF fixes, and in the example above, suppose the rate fixes at 1.77:

$$BRL\ payment = (1.77 - 1.75) * (USD\ amount)$$

Since this is equal to 20,000 Brazilian reals, we can compute the final payment amount:

$$\text{Settlement amount} = \frac{20{,}000}{1.77} = 11{,}299 \text{ US dollars}$$

A few things to note:

- Naturally, if selling dollars, we would pay rather than receive the settlement amount.
- Settlement is always in the *deliverable* currency of the pair. So EUR/KRW will settle in Euros, and GBP/RUB will settle in Sterling.
- Fixing happens, typically, 2 days before delivery. The fixing date's relationship to the delivery date is the same (economically) as the relationship in a normal cash trade between the trade date and the value date. The number of *spot days* determines the lag between fixing and delivery (Table 6.3).

6.11   A note on the carry trade

While we're not typically concerned with trading strategies in this book, it is useful to look at the 'FX Carry Trade' strategy as an illustration of how spot and forward FX work together.

The first thing to notice is that forward FX rates are in no way a 'prediction' of the future. They are simply a point in the future where supply and demand (and interest rates) have put the forward point. For instance, consider the USD/TRY market (US dollars against Turkey). If Turkish rates are, suppose, 10 per cent, and US rates are 1 per cent, people will prefer to invest cash in Turkey, and borrow cash in the US. So the simplest version of a trade to take advantage of this would be: Sell USD/Buy TRY spot, Buy USD/Sell TRY forward.

Unfortunately, the simple trade won't work. The forward market is almost always built to eliminate any such arbitrage: the forward rate realized in the above trade will be at such a level as to remove any possible profit.

What traders *will* do however, is to sell USD/buy TRY spot, and invest the TRY in an account paying Turkish interest rates (either cash rates, or bonds and securities). Ideally the USD loan can be secured with the Turkish securities. As the Turkish investment will grow at a rate much greater than the interest due on the US loan, an almost cost-free profit ensues.

Cost-free, but not risk-free. The strategy is based on a perception that spot FX rates are in fact unrelated to forward rates. Indeed, if one looks at history, one sees that the evolution of the spot rate is almost always completely disconnected from the direction implied by the forward points. It's true, if everyone pursued the carry trade (buying Turkish in this example), the currency would appreciate slowly but surely; it does not. The holder of the USD/TRY position will earn excess returns if spot continues a steady path, and not too many others try this same trading strategy.

The FX spot rate does move a lot, of course, and carry traders are frequently surprised by moves that go against them. In our example, a 9 per cent rise in the spot rate could wipe out a year's profit. Carry traders are in fact hoping that FX spot rate volatility will be low for the duration of their investment (i.e. they are *short volatility*).

6.12 Bid/ask spreads, and skew

FX brokers compete fiercely, and one of their selling points is often the narrowness of the spread they offer on spot rates. It should be noted that there are more components to market-making in FX than spread.

In addition to spread, there is *skew*. FX brokers (and banks) naturally must closely monitor the flow they see from their customer. If a broker of EUR/SEK (Euro-Swedish) sees most customers on a certain day *buying* Swedish, they may choose to raise the price of SEK against the Euro. The spread would remain (suspiciously) narrow, but the mid (average of bid and ask) would move down to reflect the flows for the day. In fact, many banks and brokers will move slightly further than what they see in the inter-bank market, thus allowing themselves to make some excess profit from the flow.

Another component of FX strategy is to customize quotes above a threshold. Many FX spot rates are streamed over market data providers, or made available over automated trading systems. However, these automated quotes are typically available only for a limited size. Above a threshold, customers are forced to ask individual banks or brokers for customized quotes, which may be based further on order flow and customer history. Generally speaking, for customers, it is always wise to shop around and request multiple quotes, especially for larger orders.

6.13 Measuring risk in FX trading

Risk, in FX trading, is necessarily a relative term. A gain in one currency is a loss in another, after all. However, for purposes of margin calculation, for instance, the currency of one's collateral (and the currency of one's bank account) make a huge difference. If you are posting margin in USD, you'll want to know the USD equivalent value of your positions in other currencies, and monitor your risk against USD.

Currency	Net position in USD	Rate	Net position
USD	1,250,000		1,250,000
EUR	150,000	1.3	115,385
JPY	600,000	80.0	48,000,000
PLN	–2,000,000	3.0	–6,000,000

The simplest starting point is a simple table of position (in each currency, and also converted in to US dollars).

Each of these currencies will be for delivery on a certain day in the future. A spot FX trade, for instance, will generally settle in 2 business days. Settlement is a tricky thing, however. If a trader is merely speculating (or hedging other trades) and they trade, say, USD/PLN (US dollars versus Polish Zloty) in the spot market, they may never actually wish to take delivery of any Zlotys. Taking delivery means having an actual bank account in Poland, after all, which is a complex thing to arrange. Most traders will rather *roll* their FX positions, by arranging an FX swap transaction to take the Zlotys in 2 days time, and return them in (say) 1-month. Doing this on a daily basis will keep any foreign currency from ever settling.

To manage the challenge of keeping all the balls in the air, FX traders need not only a position report, but also a report showing all the cash amounts along with the dates on which they are being paid:

Currency	Net position in USD	Rate	Net position	1 March	2 March	5 March	6 March	7 March
USD	1,250,000		1,250,000	200,000	–600,000	2,000,000		–350,000
EUR	150,000	1.3	115,385	–153,486				269,231
JPY	600,000	80.0	48,000,000		48,000,000			
PLN	–2,000,000	3.0	–6,000,000			–6,000,000		

In this report the values for net position are shown in terms of US dollars, for ease of comparison. The other amounts are all in the individual currency.

(Note that we're not limited to FX cash payments in this reporting structure. Any arbitrary investment can have an FX position assigned to it, which can show up in the net position for subsequent hedging. See Chapter XX on FX forwards for an example of how to compute the FX components of an arbitrary investment.)

As well as showing the FX delta, another risk this report helps manage is *settlement* or *delivery* risk. This is a form of *operational risk*, which basically covers anything under the rubric of 'general screw up'. This sort of thing, not surprisingly, is very common. Managing a large number of positions and keeping them from settling is quite important.

Another common risk measure in FX is something called *net open position*, or NOP, which we mentioned briefly in section on Margin. NOP is simply a measure of your overall exposure to the FX market within a portfolio. To measure NOP, we would take the net position in USD column of the settlement report above, and add up (typically) either the *positive* entries, or the absolute value of the *negative* entries. This gives an indication of how much we have outstanding in risky FX trades.

In the example above, the NOP (by either measure) is 2,000,000 USD. If we were trading with a broker, they might have a margin requirement based on NOP of a few per cent. If we were charged margin of, say, 3 per cent on the above positions, that would mean we'd be required to deposit 60,000 USD with them.

Notice that since we're measuring everything in USD, if the exchange rate moves, positions will move as well. Suppose, in the example above, the PLN exchange rate moves to 3.1. The position in PLN will not change (the cash amounts in the future are fixed, because we've already traded at the previous exchange rate of 3.0). The USD amount of the PLN position will change – to –1,935,484. This means that our NOP (if we measure as the sum of the short positions) may fall as well.

NOP is not always measured for all currencies together. A broker may decide to measure NOP for major currencies separately from minor, risky currencies. This is the decision of the broker or bank. However, NOP is still one of the most popular risk measures for FX. (The other popular measure is value-at-risk. This is more of a black-box measure, and varies in its implementation from broker to broker.)

7
Cross-Currency Trades in the Future: Forward FX and Cross-Currency Basis Swaps

We've looked at the meaning of forward foreign exchange (FX) trades and swaps in a previous chapter. Here, our aim is to do a little more analysis around both how forward FX rates are computed and how a trader can value their FX position once it's been traded. The first thing we'll look at is how FX rates in the future are derived.

7.1 Computation of forward FX in the collateralized world

The classic method of explaining the computation of forward outright points involves interest rates and a simple no-arbitrage argument. Let's continue with our example from the world of EUR/USD.

The classic no-arbitrage argument goes like this. If I want to pay someone 100 Euros in 1 year, I should not care whether I invest the money in the United States for 1 year, and enter into an agreement to convert at the forward rate, or convert now at the spot rate and invest in Euros for 1 year. Why should it matter? If there was any difference, all the banks and investors would have exploited the difference and ironed it out long ago. We must assume, in general, that if there are two ways to do something (in finance, at least) and they are both valid, then they *must be equivalent.*

Similarly, the present value of 100 Euros received in 1 year can be estimated by converting the 100 Euros to dollars today (at the spot rate) or in 1 year (at the forward rate). It should not matter which one we choose.

So:

$$\frac{100 \text{ EUR}}{\text{Spot FX}} \times D_{\text{EUR}} \quad \text{should equal} \quad D_{\text{USD}} \times \frac{100 \text{ EUR}}{\text{Forward FX}}$$

(Here D_{EUR} is the discount factor for Euro interest rates, and D_{USD} is the discount factor for USD interest rates.) We usually know the Spot FX rate. By the rules of no-arbitrage, the market participants should make the forward FX (Fwd FX) rate such that we don't care which of the conversion routes we choose.

Sensibly enough, the formula for the forward FX rate becomes

$$\text{Forward FX} = \frac{\text{Spot FX} \times D_{base}}{D_{term}}$$

Here D_{base} is the generic discount factor in base-currency interest rates (EUR, for instance, in an EUR/USD Quote) and D_{term} is the generic discount factor in term currency. We can see that dealers could then, in fact, base their bid/ask spreads on the bid/ask spreads of the underlying interest rates. A simple spreadsheet could make a useful dealing platform.

There are problems with this formulation, however.

First, *what interest rates should we use to compute discount factors?* The obvious answer would be to use the rates at which the currency amounts are expected to grow, typically the compounded overnight rate. This tells us that we should rely on overnight index swap (OIS) as a basis for forward FX. Indeed, the OIS interest rate curve makes a good basis to build upon.

Traditionally, practitioners used (and some still do use) the LIBOR-based deposit curve to build their FX calculations. The problem, as we have seen, is that LIBOR does not any longer represent, realistically, any return that can be achieved in the real world for collateralized trades. FX, by and large, is collateralized, and so should depend on OIS.

Another problem with this formulation is that, no matter what interest rate curves you use, whether LIBOR or OIS, using the equation above will generally not return a realistic representation of the forward point market.

7.2 Why are forward points not exactly right?

The forward FX market is based, like all markets, on supply and demand. So if (as is often the case) European banks want to get access to US dollars, they might buy dollars now (spot) with the promise of giving them back later (in, say, 3 months).

A large number of banks doing the same thing (all for 3 months) would push the price of dollars *up* today, and *down* in 3 months' time, simply by the law of supply and demand. This means that the 3-month forward point would be skewed.

Any supply and demand relationship in the forward points, however, *has little or no effect on interest rates.* The supply and demand of US dollars or Euros for overnight deposit is so large with respect to the foreign exchange market that the interest rates will not move.

This means, with the large inter-bank flows moving the forward market, the classic forward rate equation no longer holds.

To illustrate, let's look at an actual snapshot from the market.

On this example day (actually, a day in February 2012), we saw the following rates quoted:

EUR/USD spot FX rate	1.3245
EUR/USD 3-month forward	1.324980 (spot + 0.00048)
3-month EUR OIS rate	0.35%
3-month USD OIS rate	0.11%
3-month EUR deposit	0.94%
3-month USD deposit	0.48%
Number of days in 3-months	90 exactly

We can use the interest rates and the spot rate to determine the *theoretical* forward, using our choice of the (logical) OIS rates, or the (often used) LIBOR-based deposits.

First, using OIS we get,

$$\text{Forward rate} = \frac{D_{EUR} \times \text{Spot FX}}{D_{USD}} = \frac{\left(\dfrac{1}{1+\dfrac{0.35\%}{4}}\right) \times 1.3245}{\dfrac{1}{1+\dfrac{0.11\%}{4}}} = 1.323706$$

Market quoted forward rate = 1.324980

As we see, not only is this different from the result we get from forward points, it is *in the other direction entirely.* Using interest rates implies that the EUR/USD rate will *decrease* at longer tenors; looking at the market shows us the opposite: it *increases.* (At the time of this writing, EUR/USD is an extreme case, but the differences seen are obvious in all currency pairs.)

The forward points implied by OIS for 3-month EUR/USD are –12.7, and by 3-month LIBOR, –20.0. The market quote of +4.8 differs from these considerably, and the differences grow larger as one looks at longer tenors.

Examination of GBP/USD yields similar results: a difference of 3.5 points when using OIS, and 11.3 points when using LIBOR.

These skews make sense if one looks at the market dynamics. When this snapshot was taken, banks were buying dollars now (pushing the Euro down in the spot market) and re-selling them later (pushing the Euro up in the forward market). This leads to forward FX rates being *higher* than would be normally implied by interest rates.

The lesson from this is simple: *obey the market*. When looking at forward FX rates, one must look at the forward FX rate market, and not speculate about the operation of interest rates. The FX market has its own dynamics, and forward FX should be treated almost as a special asset-class of its own.

This is an important result. The implications have far-reaching consequences, not only for the understanding of the forward FX market, but for the valuation of any currency position. The implications are not simple to see, but they're very important to fully grasp.

7.3 The question of present value

When looking at an FX position, what is its value? This is an interesting question, of course, and depends on your point of view.

The classic approach says that one can use interest rates, and one should not care too much whether one chooses to discount payments in one currency or another. As we've seen above, however, *the foreign exchange market does not get along well with the interest rate market*.

But why? Surely, from an economic perspective, if I am due to receive 1 million Euros in 3 months, the value today *is* the present value in Euros (using the Euro discounting curve), and the value in US dollars *is* that value converted at the spot rate? Alternatively, I should be able to convert at the forward rate, and discount in US dollars?

This is a tempting argument, but we need to look at what can actually be realized.

If I am transacting foreign exchange with a broker, bank or other FX provider, they will ask me to post *margin* to cover any losses in my position.

There will be an *initial margin* amount (to cover any risk) and a *variation margin* (which rises and falls with the market). As we saw with interest rates, it is important that the margin we post accumulates interest. Typically, it will accumulate interest at the rate given by the overnight index in its own currency. This may be Fed Funds for US dollar collateral, EONIA for Euros, and so on.

This margin (or *funding*) currency should determine the value of the trade. If I deposit enough *today* to pay any demand in the *future* based on the margin funding interest rates, then I've succeeded in determining the present value of the trade. Any other currency may give the wrong result.

Let's look at EUR/USD again. Suppose we have a 3-month forward trade, executed at a point that's slightly off market. What's its value today?

EUR/USD forward trade example	
EUR/USD 3-month forward	1.324980
EUR notional	1,000,000
USD notional	−1,300,000
EUR value (at forward rate)	18,853
USD value (at forward rate)	24,980
EUR OIS rate	0.35%
USD OIS rate	0.11%
EUR value 'today'	18,837
USD value 'today'	**24,973**
Spot FX rate	1.3245
EUR value in USD	**24,949**
EUR interest rate which makes both sides match	−0.04%

Astounding as it may seem, the market actually provides a small *negative interest rate* to Euro notionals in this example. This is totally fictional, of course, since the adjustment to interest rates is purely relative, and simply relates to the rates which make the forward properly match.

It may be clearer in this case to draw a picture (see Figure 7.1). This rather tortuous drawing illustrates the two ways to value a forward FX trade: convert to the base-currency, then discount, or convert to the term currency, then discount. As we see, the results are slightly different.

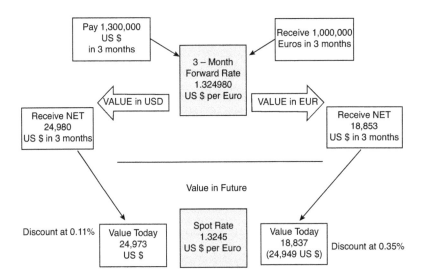

Figure 7.1   Two possible ways to value a forward FX transaction

Complete correctness demands that we take care and only use appropriate discounting. This means, typically, doing any discounting in margin currency.

Quite often, however, due to the restrictions of our systems, or the desires of traders, we can't choose our discounting currency. Other adjustments must be made.

Ideally, we'd like a way to discount any amount in any currency, without having to convert all amounts to the funding currency at forward FX rates. We'll see how to do this when we look at basis swaps.

7.4 Choice of collateral

Things are simple if we know, in the example above, which currency our collateral is in. If the customer or the bank has a *choice* of collateral, however, we're in a more difficult situation. If the trade is un-collateralized, it becomes even more complex.

The basic rule should be: *value FX trades in the collateral currency.* As we saw before, this is justified by the fact that if the customer deposits collateral, we want to ensure that the collateral grows to match the value owed in the future. The only way to do that, of course, is to use the same interest rates for valuation and collateral growth.

If there is a choice of collateral on the customer's part, the customer should choose the collateral that is *cheapest to deliver.* That is to say, the customer with obligations in two currencies (currency A and currency B) should (if they are really paying attention):

- Value their obligations, converting to currency A at forward rates, and discounting in currency A.
- Repeat the process for currency B.
- Choose as collateral currency whichever makes the amount owed the *least.*

In the example above, if we owed the amounts shown, it makes sense that US dollars would be the cheapest to deliver currency. So even if we had no dollars, and needed to convert Euros into dollars at the spot rate, it would still be cheaper to deliver dollars.

Of course, in many collateral agreements there is no choice of currency in which to deliver. In these cases, we must stick with the agreed funding currency.

If there is no collateral agreement in place, such as when a bank owes you money but you have no collateral agreement on the bank's side, the correct valuation of the obligation becomes more complex. Effectively, the proper procedure is to include the credit spread in the discounting (a number of basis points to add to the LIBOR curve, effectively), and in addition take into account the volatility of that spread.[1]

7.5   How did the market get skewed away from interest rates?

Banks often want to engage in FX swaps. The reason is simple: to get access to currency needed for current obligations. Many banks need US dollars on a regular basis for funding purposes, but European banks will have more Euros on hand than dollars. Swapping these Euros for US dollars is a popular pastime.

The typical EUR/USD swap will consist of:

1. Payment of notional amount of Euros now for X units of US dollars (spot).
2. Receive regular interest on the Euro amount (at EURIBOR, typically, plus or minus a spread).
3. Pay regular interest on the US $ amount borrowed (at USD LIBOR, with no spread).
4. Receive the notional amount of Euros back, return the US dollars.

This simple arrangement is known as a *constant-notional basis swap*. Basis swaps form a large part of inter-bank international funding. Until around 2007, the spread paid on top of LIBOR was small, and represented nominal shifts in supply and demand.

After 2007, US dollar funding became heavily in demand, and the basis swap curve started to really shift. Supply and demand in the international lending market was moving the basis swap curve away from LIBOR, and in fact, LIBOR itself was losing its connection to the FX markets. This explains the shift we saw in the forward points for EUR/USD.

Another way of looking at the constant-notional basis swap is as a way to borrow one currency, using another currency as collateral. In Figure 7.2, the customer is borrowing US dollars, using Euros as collateral. The bank is not paying a very good rate of return on the Euros it's holding, presumably because it is not happy at having to give up dollars.

How does this relate to the FX market? Figure 7.3 shows that the basis swap and the FX forward are two different views of the same thing. The two columns on the left show a hypothetical 3-month basis swap. The payments at the start and end exactly match the forward FX market.

The difference between a constant-notional basis swap and an FX swap is the *coupon schedule*. The basis swap pays interest every 3 months (on both sides), whereas the FX swap only pays at the end.

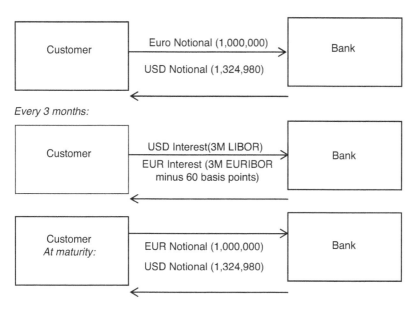

Figure 7.2 Payments in a constant-notional basis swap

The advantage, then, of the basis swap is that the notional amounts are fixed, and the interest rate component is separated.

The basis swap market offers banks (and others) an easy way to borrow other currencies on a long-term basis. For instance, suppose I am a French corporation that wishes to issue debt in the UK market. I will issue a bond, paying a fixed rate of interest, for say 10 years, in Sterling (GBP). I'll sell that bond to UK buyers, who will pay me Sterling, and I will then pay them (in Sterling) the fixed coupon rate on the bond (5%, for instance) every year, with the final repayment in 10 years.

The French corporation, however, may prefer to pay interest in Euros, at the prevailing Euro interest rate (3-month EURIBOR plus a spread, for instance). The easy way to do that would be to first purchase a standard UK interest rate swap to convert the GBP fixed payments into GBP LIBOR (plus a spread) payments. We can then combine this with a EUR/GBP basis swap, to convert the GBP LIBOR into EURIBOR. *Et voila.*

In this example, the corporation has hedged its exposure perfectly: the fixed payment in GBP in 10 years has become a fixed payment in Euros in 10 years. The corporation can also choose whether to pay a EURIBOR-based interest rate, or (via another EUR swap) convert this to a fixed rate.

Banks may, because of their more complex outlook, prefer a different view. A bank that uses a 10-year basis swap to secure access to US dollars may accept that it must return those dollars in 10 years. But the bank's view of the position is that it is exposed to the EUR/USD exchange rate.

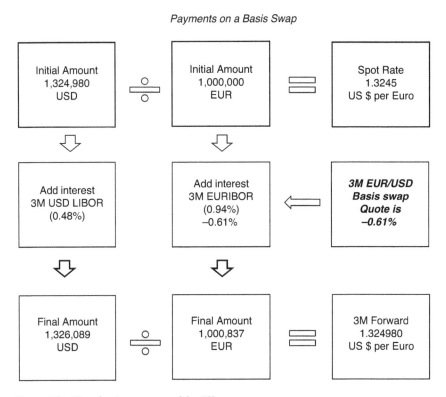

Figure 7.3   How basis swaps are like FX swaps

If, in 10 years, the dollar has fallen in value, exchanging those Euros and returning the dollars looks like a bad deal.

Constant-notional basis swaps create *FX risk* in the future. The bank that holds one has a large FX position at the maturity of the deal. As the FX rate changes over time, that FX position could accumulate a large net positive or negative value. As we've seen, because of credit concerns, the one counterparty would probably require more collateral to balance this risk.

Rather than deal with this constant shifting of risk over time, which possibly could tie up considerable collateral, another form of basis swap has become popular: the *mark-to-market basis swap*. In a mark-to-market basis swap, the notional amounts are *reset* every 3-months to reflect the prevailing spot FX rate. This amounts to, in effect, the swap turning into a series of small, 3-month long, constant-notional swaps all strung together.

Tables 7.1 and 7.2 show the payoff details of each type of basis swap. Contrast this with the mark-to-market version.

Another advantage of the mark-to-market version is the riskiness, of course. The major counterparty risk is limited to a 3-month horizon.

Table 7.1 Terms of a constant-notional basis swap

Start date	2-days from Trade date
Initial notional payment	N amount of currency 1.
Initial notional receipt	N × (Initial FX rate) amount of currency 2.
Payment frequency	Variable, but typically every 3-months.
Payment index	LIBOR (USD, GBP, EURIBOR, etc.).
Spread to add to payment	Typically quoted spread is applied to non-US side of swap. For example, GBP/USD swap quoted at −20 basis points would pay USD Libor versus (GBP LIBOR minus 0.20%).
Final notional payment	N × (Initial FX rate) amount of currency.
Final notional receipt	N amount of currency USD.

Table 7.2 Terms of a mark-to-market basis swap

Start date	2-days from Trade date
Initial notional payment	N amount of USD.
Initial notional receipt	N × (Initial FX rate) amount of currency.
Payment frequency	Variable, but typically every 3-months.
Payment Index	LIBOR (USD, GBP, EURIBOR, etc.).
Spread to add to payment	As with constant-notional swap.
Notional adjustment	At every payment date, reset the non-USD notional to N × (Current FX rate). Pay or receive the difference between this amount and the previous notional.
Final notional payment	N × (Last FX rate) amount of currency.
Final notional receipt	N amount of currency USD.

There is, of course, some risk embedded in the basis swap spread (which may change), but the majority of the credit risk is in the FX rate.

7.6 Help, I'm trading basis swaps!

Perhaps the most surprising intrusion of basis swaps into the trader's portfolio is via collateral. If, say, a bank's customer is trading a large number of US dollar transactions over the counter, and the bank lets that customer collateralize the trades with Euros, then the bank is running (like it or not) a basis swap position with that customer.

This makes sense. The collateral account accumulates Euro floating rate interest; the US dollar portfolio is exposed to US interest rates. To properly be aware of the exposure, the bank needs to value the portfolio in Euros. Only when the value of the portfolio is known in Euros will the bank be able to know how much collateral to demand.

As we saw before, the proper way to value a set of payments in another currency is to use the forward FX rate. Sometimes, however, that's either not convenient, or not possible. Many OTC trading systems do not make forward FX rates available in a nice way, and, in any case, doing such conversions can be quite messy.

A far more standard way to deal with cross-currency pricing issues is to use what is called *basis adjustment.*

We are familiar with standard discounting curves. As we saw, they can form a model which allows us to estimate the present value of future cashflows. However, as we also know, they do not agree with forward FX rates.

The standard way to deal with this problem is to shift one of the discount curves, so that the forward FX rates match. This can be done within the yield curve model itself, by super-imposing a spread on the zero coupon rates.

The table below illustrates the approach, using two example currencies with a spot FX rate of 10.0:

Term (years)	Currency 1 ZC interest rate (%)	Actual currency 1 discount	Forward FX	Implied currency 2 discount	Actual currency 2 discount	Currency 2 ZC interest rate (%)	Implied rate spread (%)
10	5	0.6065	8.950325	0.6777	0.6703	4	–0.11
5	4	0.8187	9.685012	0.8454	0.8395	3.5	–0.14
3	3	0.9139	9.97132	0.9166	0.9139	3	–0.10
1	2	0.9802	10.0392	0.9768	0.9753	2.5	–0.11
Spot	1.5	1.0000	10.0	1.0000	1.0000	2	n/a

In this example, we've laid out the zero coupon rates for each currency and, using these rates, the actual discount factors. The *implied discount factor* is the discount factor in currency 2 that would give us the forward FX rate shown.

So, if:

Spot currency 2 amount = Spot FX rate × Currency 1 amount

The classic formula for forward FX rates, using discount factors is:

$$\text{Forward FX rate} = \text{Spot FX rate} \times \frac{\text{Currency 1 discount}}{\text{Currency 2 discount}}$$

And so, solving for the *unknown* currency 2 discount factor:

$$\text{Implied currency 2 discount} = \text{Spot FX rate} \times \frac{\text{Currency 1 discount}}{\text{Forward FX rate}}$$

We construct an *Implied Zero Coupon Rate* by simply saying:

$$\text{Implied ZCR} = -\frac{\ln(\text{Implied discount})}{T}$$

The *spread* is simply the difference between the implied and the actual zero coupon rate in currency 2. Using this spread will allow us (if we wish) to get so-called *basis-adjusted* discount factors.

Once we have built a table of spreads, we can super-impose these spreads on our currency 2 yield curve model. The goal would be, with the currency 2 yield curve, to adjust (if desired) *discount factors* to use the ZCR-plus-spread amount. Typically the spread will be linearly interpolated, and added to the ZCR retrieved from the curve model.

Care should be taken, of course, to remember that this procedure applies to the discount curve, not to the forward curve. In a typical rate environment, interest rates would be implied from the LIBOR curve, and discount factors from (for instance) the OIS curve: it would be the OIS curve which would be basis-adjusted, and the basis adjustment would happen only after the curve is constructed.

7.7 Basis adjustment using basis swap spreads

While it is easy enough to basis-adjust using forward FX points, most people prefer to use basis swap market to make the basis adjustment. There are several reasons for this, but most notably the fact that the liquid market for currencies beyond 1 year *is* the basis swap market; the forward FX points mentioned above are often quoted based on basis swaps.

The procedure for building the basis adjustments using basis swap quotes is a little trickier than for forward FX points, since we must basically arrive at a present value estimate for both legs of the swap. Briefly, the procedure is as follows:

1. Construct LIBOR and discount curves for each currency as normal. Build the basis spread-adjustment mechanism so that any discount factor can be basis-adjusted based on linearly interpolating spreads between dates.
2. Choose which side of the curve you wish to basis-adjust. Remember, when pricing a basis swap, one currency is discounted normally and the other has the basis spread added or subtracted.
3. Basis-adjust the short end of the curve based on the forward FX points (out to 1 year) if possible, using the method described above. While not necessary, this does give more detail in the short end of the curve.
4. From the shortest to the longest basis swap quote:
   a. Compute notional amounts for each leg, based on the spot FX rate.
   b. Price the non-adjusted leg, by computing the LIBOR estimates from the LIBOR curve, adding a spread if required, multiplying by the notional and discounting on the discount curve.

   c. Price the adjusted leg in the same way, using basis-adjusted discount
      factors. Insert a new entry in the basis spread table for the curve,
      corresponding to maturity of this basis swap quote.
   d. Solve for the new basis spread such that the values of each leg are
      equal.

Ideally, we should provisionally basis-adjust *both* currencies. This is
because we'd like flexibility. If we have, for instance, curves in EUR and
USD, we should be prepared to price trades for customers who want to
collateralize in USD (thus using the basis-adjusted EUR curve), or customers who prefer collateral in EUR (thus using the basis-adjusted USD
curve).

   To re-iterate: *all payments not in the collateral currency should be discounted
on basis-adjusted curves.*

7.8   Getting the present value of a basis swap

Now that we understand the process of basis adjustment, we have all
the tools we need to get the value of a basis swap after the trade has
occurred.

   There are two questions to answer before valuing a basis swap. First,
what currency is the swap to be valued in? Second, what currency is
the collateral in? Once we have determined these things, the procedure
becomes:

1. Determine the cash-flows in each currency.
   a. Using the LIBOR curves for each currency, determine the forward
      3-month LIBOR rates for each period. If a period has already started,
      this requires using the historical LIBOR fixing.
   b. Using the day-counts, schedule and notional amounts, determine
      the cash amounts to be paid at each date in the future.
2. Discount these payments to the present.
   a. If a payment is in the currency of the collateral, use the normal dis-
      counting curve (such as OIS) for that currency.
   b. If the payment is *not* in the collateral currency, use the basis-ad-
      justed discount curve.
   c. Don't neglect the notional exchange at maturity.
3. Combine the payments at the spot FX rate, in the currency of the trade.

Many trading systems are quite fussy about the *trade currency*, even for
cross-currency deals. This has led to some confusion over this process,
with sometimes bad results.

Basis swaps can be quite confusing as well. The basic procedures for valuation, quotation and trading are simple enough, but the details are not obvious. It's important to keep track of the different parameters of the swap:

- What is the trade currency of the deal? This is often the currency in which the present value will be reported in, but has no bearing on how the trade is quoted or valued.
- What is the currency to which the quoted spread is applied? This is usually the non-USD leg.
- When valuing a basis swap post-trade, which side should be basis-adjusted? This is usually the side in which the collateral is *not:* the cash-flows in the collateral currency should be discounted without adjustment.
- Is the notional amount adjusted with each LIBOR payment? It's important to distinguish mark-to-market basis swaps and constant-notional basis swaps.

7.9 The FX components of an arbitrary investment

One interesting question, which comes up surprisingly often, is simply: what is my FX position on a given trade? Typically, this comes up in the context of a portfolio of diverse trades, but it can also apply to single trades which are of a complex nature.

Suppose I am presented with a spreadsheet, giving the value of a series of contracts with a counterparty. The spreadsheet creator has helpfully given several inputs: *Euro interest rate, GBP interest rate, EUR/GBP FX rate*. One cell on the left is helpfully labelled 'Present Value (EUR)'.

We can see from this that our spreadsheet creator has helpfully done all the work of adding up all the cash-flows from the trade or trades, summing them in their respective currencies, done (we hope) the appropriate basis adjustments and arrived at the present value in Euros.

However, we know also that we have an implied FX position. If the EUR/GBP rate changes, the value of the trade in EUR will change as well. What is our FX position?

The answer is surprisingly easy to arrive at. Let us suppose that, with a given (fixed) set of interest rates, our investment is equivalent in value to some (hypothetical) EUR cash amount and some GBP cash amount. So:

Total value (EUR) = Value (EUR) + Value (GBP) * FX

This is interesting. Now, for argument's sake, let's (using very basic calculus) take the first derivative of the Total Value with respect to the FX rate:

$$\frac{d(\text{Total value})}{d(\text{FX})} = \text{Value}(\text{GBP})$$

That was easy! Now we can simply get the EUR value by saying:

$$\text{Value}(\text{EUR}) = \text{Total value}(\text{EUR}) - \text{Value}(\text{GBP}) * \text{FX}$$

We can now say that our FX position is Value (EUR) (Euros) and Value (GBP) (Pounds Sterling). Therefore, to *hedge* our exposure to FX, we would simply put in place an FX position in the FX market of the opposite sign.

But how, in practice, do we take the first derivative of the value of an arbitrary trade or portfolio? The typical approach is to simply use numerical methods. For instance, we can manipulate the FX rate a small amount up and down.

Let's create two FX scenarios. Imagine going back to the hypothetical spreadsheet, and putting new FX rates into the 'FX Rate' cell. One rate will be slightly smaller than the market rate, one rate will be slightly larger. So, again by basic calculus:

$$\frac{d(\text{Total value})}{d(\text{FX})} \cong \frac{(\text{Total value: Rate 1}) - (\text{Total value: Rate 2})}{\text{Rate 1} - \text{Rate 2}}$$

This is straightforward, and requires only choosing an appropriate amount for the shift to use between Rate 1 and Rate 2. The shift amount should not be so small that the total value does not change, nor should it be so large that non-linear effects dominate the result. Typically, somewhere around 1 per cent is used.

It should be noted that if the FX rate is used to *divide* rather than *multiply*, the result is different. Suppose the total value in the example was in GBP rather than EUR. The resulting equation of value becomes:

$$\frac{d(\text{Total value}(\text{GBP}))}{d(\text{FX})} = \frac{-\text{Value}(\text{EUR})}{\text{FX}^2}$$

Not quite as friendly an equation, but still fairly straightforward. The key thing is, if implementing this approach, to ensure that one keeps track of the nature of the rates, and the currencies of the results.

Further reading

Masaaki Fujii, Y. S. (2010) 'A Note on Construction of Multiple Swap Curves with and without Collateral', *Financial Services Agency, Government of Japan*.

Masaaki Fujii, Y. S. (2010) 'On the Term Structure of Interest Rates with Basis Spreads, Collateral and Multiple Currencies', *Bank of Japan*.

8
Basic Equity Trades

Stocks are the most basic and popular investment. A share in a company is one of the most widely understood securities. That said, how many people understand what a stock is?

Stocks are (often) shared ownership in a company. So, with proper notice, anyone who owns more than 50 per cent of the stock in a company effectively controls it. But is that their claim to value? A large number of stocks have a 'free float' (i.e. the proportion of stock which may be held by the public) of under 50 per cent. These stocks are still quite popular.

Stocks may have value by virtue of their claim to future dividends. Many stocks pay regular dividends just like bonds pay coupons. However, many technology companies pay no dividends, and keep huge cash hoards which may never go to shareholders. These stocks are also quite popular.

In short, we may just say that stocks have 'value' – for some reason. Banks deal in stocks either as primary market makers (who maintain orderly markets in stocks they have launched), or as market access providers (giving investors access to stocks and stock markets they might not otherwise reach via derivatives), or as proper derivatives dealers (offering simple or complex options on stocks). Once these trades are in place, a host of tools are needed to put value on the stocks and the trades that depend on them.

8.1 Stock prices

Stocks go up and down in price, and the most basic hardware in many banks is aimed at getting these prices delivered accurately. The mechanics of stock price recording are well known: at any moment during the day (when the exchange is open) there are bid and ask prices on any given stock. The exchange aggregates orders and produces a ladder of prices at which customers wish to buy or sell. If a customer wishes to buy a stock at a price which is equal to or above the lowest price at which someone wishes to sell, the order is executed and a sale is made.

The exchange publishes details of all of this activity, which is available on many market data networks. The most basic details are the bid and ask prices, and the last price at which a trade was done (typically referred to as bid, ask and last). Also important are the day's highest trade price, and lowest price (high and low). Beyond this, the order book shows the ladder of prices at which people are prepared to buy or sell, below the current bid or above the current ask.

Stock prices are streamed, and often used for later analysis. In financial institutions, the most common way to store prices is in a *tick database*, the most common of which is a system called kdb (by a company called Kx systems). Such a system can do analysis on large amounts of data, and present the results to other end-user systems.

8.2 Lending

The most basic problem institutions have with owning stocks is just that – they are stocks, have variable value and offer no guarantee of any predictable return. Banks which hold stocks generally do so in a completely hedged manner. So any stocks they hold will be either as a side-effect of their obligation to make a market in certain securities (if they have one) or on behalf of customers, or to hedge other complex positions (such as an equity swap).

In all of these cases, the bank has a reason for holding the stock that has nothing to do with its value. The bank doesn't care whether the value goes up or down (except inasmuch as failing stocks hurt customers, who might then move away from being customers).

Banks can, however, make excess return by lending the stocks to customers. A customer will borrow stocks from the bank, after posting appropriate collateral. The customer then typically sells or transfers the stocks. At the end of the loan period (which may be open-ended) the customer will re-purchase the shares on the market and return them to the bank in exchange for the collateral being returned to the customer.

For the bank, this is in effect exactly the same as selling the shares to a customer, with an agreement to buy them back in the future at a pre-arranged price. In fact, this is another way of formulating the stock loan agreement: since the ownership of the stock has changed hands, it is in fact a form of sale, with an agreement to re-purchase later.

In an ideal world, stocks would spend as little time as possible on a bank's balance sheet[1]. Stocks would be replaced by cash collateral, which would be adjusted by the variation margin as the value of the stocks rose and fell. And of course, each time the stock is lent, the bank receives a fee. (Unlike bond repo, rather than charging a rate of interest, stock lending records the charge as a 'monthly fee'.)

Settlement for lending agreements is governed by market practice, but in the United States and the United Kingdom it is 3 days.

The basic outlines of a securities lending transaction are shown in Table 8.1.

The process of stock loan is triggered, typically, by a *locate* request from the borrower. A prospective borrower (such as a hedge fund) will query an institution for a list of securities they wish to borrow, along with the sizes they wish to borrow in. The lending institution will respond with a list of available securities that match – typically a small subset of the requested securities. When a locate request is served, however, the lending institution may put a hold on the securities (like a library would on a book) for a certain time, to reserve them for the borrower.

The key thing about lending stocks is that it is pretty much valuation-neutral. If you own a stock and lend it out, you still own the stock (effectively). Since financial institutions rarely hold stocks on their own balance sheets, unhedged, in any great quantity, the process of stock borrowing and lending is a way to use equities to make a bit of excess return for the institution, while keeping the stock on the books.

Table 8.1 Basic outline of a securities lending transaction

	Customer	Bank
At start of trade	Customer delivers initial collateral amount equal to the market value of the securities, plus initial margin (measured as percentage of market value).	Lender delivers securities.
Settlement	Generally $T+3$ for both cash collateral and securities. In certain markets where DvP[2] is not available, collateral may be required to be posted $T+2$, against securities delivered $T+3$.	
Payment	Borrower pays monthly fee, plus any payments (such as dividends) which the stock would pay. Monthly fee is measured as basis points of market value, multiplied by day-count (typically Act/365).	Lender pays interest on collateral account, accrued daily.
Collateral adjustment	Variation margin payable if market value of the stock exceeds purchase price, as measured daily.	Margin can be repaid if stock value falls below purchase price[3]
Termination	Borrower can terminate at any time for delivery $T+3$.	Lender can demand securities back at any time, for receipt $T+3$.
Legal arrangements	Useful starting points for documentation on stock borrowing include the Global Master Securities Lending Agreement[4].	

Stock loan operations within banks are usually run from a *prime broker-age*. Prime brokerage operations typically will arrange for their customers the ability to purchase stock on margin (much like a conventional broker) and to borrow stock from others. (In addition, one key feature of prime brokers is that they allow customers to put all their collateral in one place. A prime broker should be able to take stock purchased on any exchange and hold it as collateral.)

Outside of prime brokerage, banks will hold stocks generally as a hedge against liabilities they may have elsewhere. One example of this is over-the-counter trades such as *equity swaps*.

8.3 Equity swaps

An equity swap is a simple swap transaction where one party pays a floating rate of interest, and the other pays the return of a stock (or basket of stocks, or stock index).

A simple outline is given in Table 8.2.

In this example, party B is paying the 'total return'. But what is total return? Total return is simply:

- The amount of any dividends paid during a given payment period.
- The amount by which the stock basket appreciates during a given period.

So if we invest $1,000,000 at the beginning of the period in a given stock, and it pays $10,000 in dividends, but the price falls such that the stock holding is only worth $995,000 – then we pay the net income: $5,000.

If the stock *loses* value we may well *receive* money instead of paying. In this case we might make money both by receiving interest and by profiting from the loss in value of the stock. (As such, an equity swap is a convenient way to short-sell a stock. If you want to profit when stock

Table 8.2 Basic outline of an equity swap

Reference equity	A single stock, or collection of stocks.
Notional amount	$1,000,000 for instance.
Trade date	The date on which the trade is agreed.
Start date	Trade date plus three business days (typically).
Payment schedule	Every 3 months, adjusted for holidays as per a normal swap agreement.
Party A pays	3M LIBOR + x%
Party B pays	The return generated by investing the Notional Amount in the Reference Entity at the closing price quoted on the trade date.

prices fall, then simply enter into an equity swap where you are paying the equity side.)

Customers who cannot legally invest in stocks (because, for instance, the stock is traded in a country that doesn't let foreigners invest directly) can use equity swaps to get the return of a stock investment. Customers who cannot *divest* from stocks (because, for instance, they want to keep their voting rights) can use equity swaps to hedge themselves against losses the stocks may make.

8.4   Notional amounts

The notional amount of the equity swap is an amount of currency (on the interest rate side), and a number of shares on the other. The computation of returns on the interest rate side is straightforward: interest is paid as usual in an interest rate swap with a floating rate.

The equity side is more interesting. For the first period (which we'll say is 3-months, as it often is) the return is simply the amount by which the shares gained (or lost) in value. In addition, any dividend payments are made (usually) when they occur. (Dividend payment is an optional feature: in a *price return* equity swap, the settlement is based solely on price with no dividend adjustment.)

In the second period of the swap, however, if the number of shares does not change, the swap will become unbalanced. This is because we've paid the return already: in the real world (if we had purchased shares to hedge our position) we would have had to sell a number of shares to make the swap payment. If we don't adjust the number of shares, we'll end up paying returns on an equity portfolio we never could have realized. For instance, if our $100 of shares appreciates to $105, we would pay $5 on the equity side of the swap. In the next period, however, would we want to pay the return on $105 worth of stocks, or $100? Given that we've already had to pay away the profit, $100 is more suitable.

Typically, swap documentation will take this into account. The number of shares will be re-adjusted in each period to reflect any gains or losses which have occurred. In effect, this means the swap behaves like a series of 3-month 'swaplets', each with the same cash notional amount.

8.5   Forward prices

Once the equity swap has started, we are left with the issue of valuation.

Valuation of the interest rate side of the swap is straightforward, inasmuch as we have the interest rate tool-kit at our disposal to find the present value of a series of cash-flows.

The equity side is more interesting.

The first thing to recall is that, at least in terms of agreed procedure, we must stick to a no-arbitrage theory of pricing. This means that we must assume (due to the lack of any other information) that the future value of a stock will simply be the same as its present value times the risk-free rate of return. This is not the whole story, however.

If we are holding a stock for a given amount of time (say, 3 months) – why not lend it out? In fact, we must assume the rational investor *would* lend it out, for a certain *borrowing fee*. The fees charged to lend stocks vary widely. Highly liquid stocks generate small fees, but smaller, less easy-to-locate stocks can be more lucrative. The general formula used would be a certain number of basis points on the notional amount (measured in currency) per day.

So, given that we can count on receiving a borrowing fee for our stock, we could assume that the forward price is given by:

$$\text{Forward stock price} = (\text{Spot price}) \times \left(1 + \left[\frac{r \times d}{365}\right]\right) - \text{Lending fee} - \text{Dividends}$$

This representation of the forward stock price is simply another way of saying that (aside from the fact that stock prices go up and down) we should be indifferent between investing money at rate r for d days, and holding a stock and receiving fees and dividends.

(We could simplify this further, by rolling the lending fee into the interest rate r, making r represent the net rate less lending fees.) In this formulation, however, r must be a realistic representation of the rate at which we can borrow money.

Alternatively, we could borrow money to hold a stock. In this case, we might not be able to lend the stock out, because we'd be using it as collateral for the loan. We'd have to provide a certain initial margin on the transaction, and then pay interest on the loan amount.

In this way of looking at the world, the expected price of a stock in the future might be given by:

$$\text{Forward stock price} = (\text{Spot price}) \times \left(1 + \left[\frac{r' \times d}{365}\right]\right) - \text{Dividends}$$

Here, the interest rate (r') is the *stock-collateralized* rate, which is somewhat lower than the risk-free rate in the first case. The lower rate should make the forward price computed more or less equivalent.

In both these formulations, the interest rate used is very important.

Table 8.3   Cash-flows in an equity swap

	Bank pays	**Bank receives**
Bank selling 1-period 3-month equity swap		
At end of 3-month period	Price appreciation on stock position + Dividends	Floating rate
Hedge position for bank selling equity swap		
Equity hedge purchase at start of transaction	Price of stock	Stock position to use as a hedge
Lending transaction – to maximize profit	Stock position	Price of stock as collateral for lending
During transaction	Interest accrued on collateral	Lending fee + Price appreciation on stock (as variation margin) + Dividends
End of lending at end of swap	Price of stock + Appreciation	Stock position
Sale of hedge	Stock position	Price of stock + Appreciation

The key point, really, is that the interest rate used in computing an equity forward must match the funding costs. If you are selling an equity swap, and the interest rate you use in computing forward stock prices is not the same as the rate you pay when *hedging* the swap, then there will be a huge potential for mistakes.

This might make more sense if we draw out the cash-flows of the transaction. In Table 8.3, a bank is entering into an equity swap, paying the equity returns to a client and receiving a floating rate for 3 months.

This is fairly convoluted, but the end result is that the bank:

– Receives from the customer a floating rate.
– Pays a floating rate as interest on collateral.

In addition, the bank:

– Receives the price appreciation on the stock, as well as any dividends.
– Pays the price appreciation on the stock to the swap customer, as well as any dividends.

As an extra bonus, the bank receives a lending fee.

The thing to ask here, of course, is whether the floating rate from the customer is enough to cover the interest on collateral? If collateral interest is calculated daily (using an overnight rate) and customer interest is LIBOR based, it might be safe to say that the customer's floating rate is more than enough. However, as we've seen, LIBOR and OIS are not necessarily linked in their dynamics!

8.6 Valuation

Swap valuation is typically done in two parts: the floating (interest rate) leg and the equity leg. The floating leg of the swap can be valued using traditional interest rate swap methods: using a LIBOR forward curve and OIS discounting, for instance.

As we see from Table 8.3, the bank can perfectly hedge in the stock position it is holding. As such, the valuation of the equity leg matches the valuation of the lending transaction, it makes no difference.

However, often the lending transaction and the stock position are on different systems, or will be reported separately.

We can write out the valuation formula for 1-period of the equity leg of the swap as follows:

$$\text{Present value} = \text{Equity notional} \times \left(\text{Forward price}(t) - \text{Starting price}\right) \times D$$

(Here, D is the discount factor from the end of the period.)

8.7 Equity dividends

One of the most important parts of computing the expected forward price of a stock is the level of dividends.

A few market data providers (such as MarkIt) will provide expected dividend levels on individual stocks. Many companies have dividend schedules that are published in advance, making forecasting easier. Even with published schedules, however, there is no requirement for a company to pay dividends.

The market (usually the market for options) can provide some feedback for the expected level of dividends. If the forward price seen in the market is higher than expected (due to interest rates alone), one could speculate that others anticipate a lower level of dividends. By and large, however, the published dividends are an accurate reflection of expected levels.

Dividends behave like coupons on a bond. A stock's value just before a dividend is paid will be higher (of course) than after it is paid. If a stock is worth $100 today, but will pay a $5 dividend at the close of the business day, I would expect (other things being equal) that the stock would be worth $95 tomorrow.

We might imagine we could see the effect of this by looking at dividends over time. If we track stock prices over time, we'd see regular dips on post-dividend days – perhaps (as in the chart below) a saw-tooth pattern over the course of a year. Of course – go to any stock price web site, and you will see no such thing. This is because equity prices are regularly re-based in historical charting systems. Each time there is a dividend, past prices are artificially *reduced* to make the chart smooth. (This can be disconcerting if you've followed a stock over time, and suddenly see its price in the past a bit lower than you remember. However, it's just an artefact of the market data supplier's graphing software.)

More interesting than dividends in the past, however, are the future dividend levels.

Published dividends come in two forms: *discrete* and *continuous yield*. Discrete dividends represent an amount-per-share, paid on a certain date in the future. Dividend yields are more of an approximation, and represent an adjustment to the risk-free rate used in computing the forward. The classic formation, in fact, of an equity forward is:

$$F = Se^{(r-q)t}$$

Here, S is the current stock price, r would be the risk-free rate (either collateralized, or less lending fees) and q would be the continuous dividend yield.

Usually market data providers will give discrete dividends up until a certain point in time (up to which there is confidence in the company's schedule).

To make a basic forecast of the forward price of a stock, therefore, one must:

– Know the dividend schedule for discrete dividends as far as it is applicable.
– Subtract discrete dividends on each of the *ex-dividend* dates which are available from the dividend forecast.
– After the last discrete dividend date, subtract any continuous dividend yield from the interest rate used to grow the stock price.

One question that sometimes arises is: how do we compute the continuous dividend yield on a stock, given a set of discrete dividends?

The first thing to do in computing the dividend yield is to decide on a time horizon in which to do it.

Figure 8.1 shows the assumed price appreciation of a stock (assuming no price volatility) over a 2-year period. If we wanted to compute the dividend yield to a point at the end of 1 year, one can see that we'd get greatly different answers if we set the time horizon to November 30 (when the price is above 101.5) or if we set it to December 1 (when the price is <101). Carefully choosing the horizon is a useful first step.

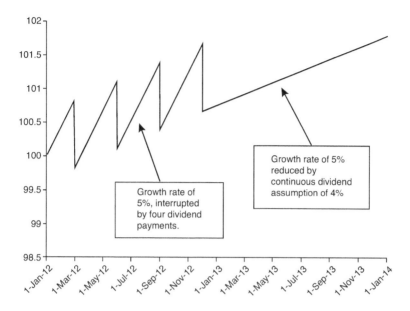

Figure 8.1   Equity dividends

Note: Figure showing the computed forward values for a stock with value 100 on 1 January 2012. The stock pays discrete dividends quarterly for the first year, and after that is assumed to have a dividend yield of 4 per cent. We assume that, apart from dividends, the stock will grow at 5 per cent annually.

After that, recalling the classic equity forward equation on the previous pages, we can make the assumption that

$$F = Se^{(r-q)t} \quad \text{so} \quad \ldots \quad q = \frac{-\ln\left(\dfrac{F}{S}\right)}{t} - r$$

Here *F* is the forward which we compute as in Figure 8.1: by growing the spot price at our chosen interest rate, subtracting dividends as they are paid.

Typically, computing the dividend yield on a stock is done to provide the number for some other, inflexible system or equation. Far more useful than dividend yield calculations done in this way, however, is simply having a function or procedure which can give the expected forward level at any point in time, by using either discrete or continuous dividends as applicable. Such a function can be used to give valuations for equity swaps, forwards and can even be used in pricing plain vanilla equity options.

Further reading

Bank of England (2010) 'Securities Lending: An Introductory Guide', *http://www. bankofengland.co.uk/markets/Documents/gilts/sl_intro_green_9_10.pdf*.

European Central Bank (2011) 'Settlement Fails – Report on Securities Settlement Systems (SSS) Measures to Ensure Timely Settlement', *http://www.ecb.int/pub/pdf/ other/settlementfails042011en.pdf*.

Faulkner, M. C. (2007) 'An Introduction to Securities Lending', *http://www. bankofengland.co.uk/markets/Documents/gilts/securitieslending.pdf*.

International Securities Lending Association (2010) *Global Master Securities Lending Agreement*.

9
Government Bonds

9.1 Basic features of bonds

To many, government bonds and securities are examples of the simplest *fixed-income* investments. We've introduced them after our discussion of LIBOR and the interest rate curve because it's really useful to understand how they operate in relation to standard interest rate markets. Indeed, it's typical for the term 'yield curve' to refer not to an interest rate model, but to a simple chart of government bond yields.

Before going too much into the details, we should examine what we mean by 'government bond' in this context.

A bond is a security – a legally defined contract that can be bought and sold. Most government bonds are sold by dealers, and have a pre-defined 'face value' of 100 dollars, pounds, Euros or whatever. Some bonds are traded on exchanges (typically, the bonds of a sovereign country will be traded on its stock exchange), but most of the volume in dealing is done directly between counterparties. Banks trade with other banks, and with hedge funds or large investors, or even individuals.

Bonds have a *maturity date:* the date on which they expire. On expiration, they return the face value to the holder of the bond. Most bonds pay *interest*: most bonds will pay, on a regular basis, some rate of interest on the face value. The rate of interest is called the *coupon*. A semi-annual bond with a 2 per cent coupon will pay the holder 1 per cent of the face value every 6 months, and 101 per cent at maturity (since there is a coupon at maturity, which gets added to the face value).

Bonds have an *issue date:* the date on which they are issued into the market. There is also, technically, a thing called the *dated date*, which is the date on which interest begins to be counted – this is usually the same as the issue date. Bonds have a *coupon frequency*, which is typically either annual or semi-annual (sometimes quarterly). Finally, bonds have a convention by which interest is accrued, known as the day-count basis, or simply *basis*.

Some bonds, it should be noted, are very short-term and pay no coupon and are simply an agreement to pay the face value at maturity. These bonds (or *bills*, as they are often called) are typically less than 1 year in duration, and are used for short-term borrowing by governments.

Some bonds go quite far beyond these simple confines and pay interest in complex ways (such as including the rate of inflation) or on strange dates, or with interesting special rules. However, the vast majority of simple government bonds adhere to these parameters: they can be thoroughly defined by a couple of dates and a coupon rate (see Table 9.1).

Most bonds issued by governments will have common attributes: the same coupon frequency, for instance, the same basis, even the same coupon days.

The payments on a bond can be visualized as a series of cash-flows over time. Imagine, as we did before, a bond with a 2 per cent semi-annual

Table 9.1   Parameters defining most simple government bonds

Type of Bond	Interest paying or not?
Face Value	Often 100 (dollars, euros, etc.)
Maturity Date	The date on which the face value is paid to the holder, and the bond expires.
Coupon Rate	The rate of interest paid by the bond.
Coupon Frequency	Annual, semi-annual or quarterly: the frequency on which interest is paid on the face value
Basis	The basis on which interest is accrued. Typically ACT/ACT, ACT/365 or ACT/360 (see below for details).
Issue Date	The date on which the bond is issued into the market.
Settlement Days	The number of days between purchase (or sale) and delivery of the security.

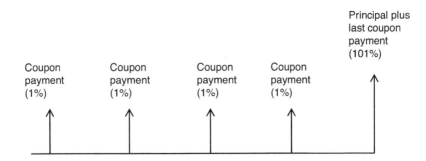

Figure 9.1   An example of a bond payment schedule over time

coupon, with 2 years (plus a few days) until maturity. The payments would be spread out over time like so (Figure 9.1).

Bond payment schedules, by and large, are based on regularly spaced coupons. It is generally easiest to extrapolate the coupon schedule by looking at the maturity date. A semi-annual bond, maturing on the 15th of January, will usually pay coupons on the 15th of July and the 15th of January of each year. (Generally, very rarely, some bonds will have long final coupon periods, meaning that there may be an irregular schedule at the last period.) Unlike in the swap world, these coupon dates are allowed to fall on non-business days. The actual payments, of course, would be made one or more business days after the coupon date.

9.2 Accrued interest

Looking at Figure 9.1, one can imagine that the *value* of a bond would be simply the present value of all the future payments. In fact, it is. The interesting thing about bonds is that since they have coupons, payments will periodically drop off. So, there are two competing forces that act on the price of a bond:

- As time goes by, the payments in the future become closer, and their present value rises.
- As time goes by, coupon payments disappear (since they are paid). This causes the total value of the bond to decrease.

If the coupon level exactly matches the market, these two effects should cancel, thus resulting in a bond whose present value over time rises and falls slightly, but remains hovering around the same level.

In fact, central banks (and other bond issuers) will calibrate the coupon rate such that the bond is initially priced at or around 100 (dollars, Euros, etc.). This value (called 'par') is the simplest to trade, and results in bonds whose value can be easily compared.

Given this, we can imagine (if the interest rates we use to value the bond remain stable) that the present value of the bond would evolve over time as in (Figure 9.2).

In fact, this is exactly what happens to the price paid for bonds in the market. As the coupon draws nearer, the price raises a small amount every day (supposing discounting rates are stable, that is). When the coupon is paid, the price falls.

This price we've graphed is the so-called *dirty price* of the bond. This price represents the full invoice amount that a buyer would pay. What actually happens in practice is that this price is broken down into two parts: the *clean price* and the *accrued interest.*

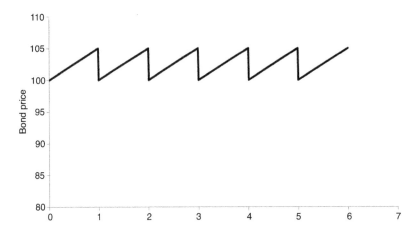

Figure 9.2 The effect of bond coupon payments on bond price over time – assuming no price volatility

Naturally, if one is selling a bond in between coupon payments, one would want compensation for the amount of interest already accrued within that coupon period. If bonds traded solely on *dirty price* (as in the picture above), then this would not be a problem. The seller would always get a higher price before a coupon date and a lower price after a coupon date.

However, the convention has arisen of quoting the price with the effect of the current coupon stripped-out, so to speak. This means that we sub-tract the pro-rata accumulation of interest on the current coupon, to get the so-called *clean price*. The *clean price* is much more stable over time – it has fewer wobbles, and no jagged pattern caused by coupon payments. The pro-rata coupon amount (the *accrued interest*) is simply added to the invoice price when a sale is made.

The simplest way to compute accrued interest is using the so-called Actual/Actual convention (or ACT/ACT as it is sometimes abbreviated). This means that the amount of accrued interest is equal to the number of days since the last coupon, divided by the total number of calendar days in the coupon period, multiplied by the coupon amount.

So if 30 days have elapsed since the last coupon payment date, and there are 182 days between the last and next coupon payments, and the coupon payment is (suppose) $2.00, then the accrued interest will be

$$AI = \frac{30}{182} \times \$2 = \$0.32967$$

Simple enough. The accrued interest payment and calculation is a simple heuristic method to keep the allocation of interest fair and equitable.

It should be noted that, if one is doing complex analysis of bond prices, based on a complete interest rate model, one is going to be most concerned with the *dirty price*. The calculation of accrued interest is chiefly useful if one needs to calculate the *dirty price* from a quoted *clean price*.

Most government bonds compute accrued interest in the same way: by taking the ratio of the number of days elapsed in the coupon period, divided by the total number of days in the period. (Corporate bonds use a different accrual method, analogous to the 30/360 day-count method used in the swap market.) Exceptions include Canada (which always assumes 182.5 days in each coupon period) and Japan (which ignores leap days).

Table 9.2 shows some of the key characteristics of major government bond types.

To restate things, then, for example, if I were to buy a 10-year German Bund today, for settlement in 3 days, for a price of 100.48 Euros. The quoted price, of course, is the *clean price*, to get the *dirty price*, we have to compute accrued interest. Table 9.3 shows the calculation.

The accrued interest is of course rounded where it becomes irrelevant, in this case at the 0.01 Euro level. More typically, the notional amount is larger, and there would be less rounding. The exceptions to this rule (and there always are some) include France (where accrued interest is rounded to 7 decimal places) and Italy (where it is rounded to 5).

Table 9.2   Characteristics of major government bonds

Country	Security name	Typical initial maturity (years)	Accrual basis	Settlement	Coupon frequency
USA	Treasury note	2, 5	ACT/ACT	T+1	Semi-annual
	Treasury bond	10, 30	ACT/ACT	T+1	Semi-annual
UK	Gilt	1–50	ACT/ACT[1]	T+1	Semi-annual
France	OAT	7–50	ACT/ACT	T+3	Annual
	BTAN	2–5	ACT/ACT	T+1	Annual
Germany	Bund	10–30	ACT/ACT	T+3	Annual
	BOBL	5	ACT/ACT	T+3	Annual
	Schatze	2	ACT/ACT	T+3	Annual
Italy	BTP	3–30	ACT/ACT	T+3	Semi-annual
Japan	JGB	2–40	ACT/365[2]	T+3	Semi-annual
Canada	GOC	2–30	ACT/365[3]	T+3/T+2[4]	Semi-annual

Table 9.3 Example of computing dirty bond price

Bund maturity	4 January 2022
Clean price	100.48
Purchase date	26 March 2012
Settlement date (three business days after purchase)	29 March 2012
Previous coupon date (or issue date)	4 January 2012
Next coupon date	4 January 2013
Coupon amount	2.00%
Face value purchased	100
Days from last coupon to settlement date	85
Days in coupon period (4 January 2012 to 4 January 2013)	366
Accrued interest	$\dfrac{85}{366} \times 2.00 = 0.46448$
Dirty price	100.48 + 0.46 = 100.94

9.3 Holidays

Getting the settlement date from the trade date necessitates taking proper account of national holidays. Most European bonds, for instance, will not settle on TARGET[5] holidays, and so the settlement date will move to the next full business day. In addition to TARGET, the national holidays of each state's bond settlement system may also need to be taken into account. For instance, Bund settlement is not possible on the 24th and 31st of December, due to holidays at the Frankfurt clearing system. France and Italy follow pure TARGET holidays, while the US,[6] UK[7] and Japan[8] have their own holiday calendars.

9.4 Yield

The most common measure of the rate of return on a bond is *yield*. In simple terms, the yield is the single, simple interest rate which would apply to a bond given its price in the market. The interest would be compounded at the coupon frequency – for an annual bond, the interest would compound annually; for a semi-annual bond it would compound every 6 months. By far the most common formula quoted in books is the following:

$$\text{Dirty price} = \frac{C_1}{(1+y/f)} + \frac{C_2}{(1+y/f)^2} + \frac{C_3}{(1+y/f)^3} + \cdots + \frac{C_n + P}{(1+y/f)^n}$$

Here, C_1 is the first coupon amount after settlement, C_2 the second and so on. We assume there are n coupon periods until maturity. The variable f refers to the frequency: semi-annual bonds have frequency 2, annual bonds 1 and so on. P is the face value, which is almost universally taken to be 100 for purposes of quotation. Of course y is the yield, in this case – the formula allows you to extract a *dirty price* given a quoted yield.

The formula is close, but as we can easily see there is not much allowance for where we are (at purchase) within a coupon period. This approximation balances out, but is not very useful, and often not used in financial systems. (That said, in some cases, such as Canadian bonds, it is sometimes an officially sanctioned formula for yield quotation.)

A more commonly implemented approach is represented by the slightly more complex formula:

$$\text{Dirty price} = \left(\sum_{i=1}^{n} \frac{C_i}{\left(1+\frac{y}{f}\right)^{(i-w)}} \right) + \frac{P}{\left(1+\frac{y}{f}\right)^{(n-w)}}$$

where

$$w = \frac{\text{Days from last coupon date to settlement}}{\text{Days in coupon period}}$$

This is the formula used in, among other systems, Microsoft Excel. It makes a good approximate formula for representing the rate of return of a bond, in that it takes into account the closeness of the settlement date to the next coupon.

But why measure yield in this way at all? After studying the interest rate market, this formulation seems quite primitive, especially inasmuch as it ignores any sense of term structure for bonds. If a government entity is issuing bonds of many different maturities, and they have different prices, surely we can build an appropriate zero coupon yield curve representing their funding costs as a function of time, without resorting to single-number yield formulations.

This is in fact, correct, and as we will see this is a valid way to analyse the fixed-income market. However, yield has become a widespread, almost universal method of quotation and comparison among bonds. Indeed, in some markets (such as Japan) bonds are often traded on a yield basis – so it is essential to understand how yield is calculated in order to be able to quickly work out the invoice price.

To make things more complex, the yield computations (and accrued interest calculations) almost always have exceptions for each national market. Bloomberg has a document, 85 pages long[9], listing all the different accrued interest and yield calculation types for bonds around the world:

there are literally hundreds of variations. As a general rule, it is unwise to convert yield to price unless one is absolutely certain of the methodology used to estimate yield itself, or one is able to accept small errors in price.

As an example, one of the more common alternate formulations is the so-called *ISMA formula* for calculating price from yield. This is commonly used in the United Kingdom, Japan and other jurisdictions.[10] The ISMA formula includes no summation, so is somewhat easier to implement in a spreadsheet, for instance, but is also somewhat more approximate. (In the United Kingdom, the formula is used to calculate what is called the *gross redemption yield*. It is also commonly used with Bunds, Japanese bonds and others.)

9.5 Yield from price

Given a bond price, how do we compute the yield? The formulas above enable us to generate the price given a yield, but what about the reverse operation?

In general, there is no closed form solution for computing the yield of a bond from the price. The best approach is usually to solve for the yield *iteratively*. We covered the Newton–Raphson technique of solving for unknown variables in the section on interest rate yield curves; the same approach should be used here.

In Excel, of course, there is a formula (YIELD) for this. If we wished to solve for the yield ourselves, we would follow something like the procedure outlined before (Figure 9.3).

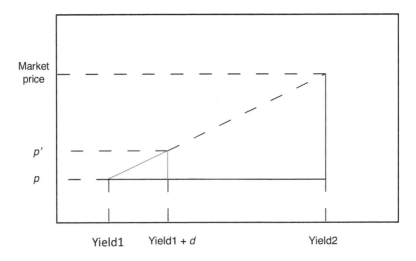

Figure 9.3 Using Newton–Raphson to find yield given price

The general approach is:

- Start with a level of yield (*Yield1*) which is a good estimate, perhaps set to the coupon rate of the bond. From this, use the yield to price formula to get the price (*P*) which this corresponds to.
- Add a small amount to Yield1 (*d*) (perhaps 0.0001 per cent) and re-compute the price (*P'*) from this.
- Extrapolate from these two points the level of yield which should return the market price for the bond (*Yield2* in Figure 9.3). Here, this would be $d \times (\text{Market price} - P) / (P' - P)$.
- Continue (with Yield2 as our new estimate) repeating the process until our estimated yield gives us a price which matches to within our desired tolerance.

As with yield curves, this approach usually converges on an appropriate result very quickly. There are some non-linear aspects (yield being inversely proportional to price), but these do not add much to the computation time.

9.6   Short-term debt instruments

In addition to coupon-bearing bonds, most governments also issue short-term debt instruments, with maturity of less than 1 year. These are issued on what is known as a *discount basis:* they pay the full face value at maturity, and trade at a discount to that value. So, for instance, a US Treasury *Bill* (the US discount instrument) might have a face value of 100, and mature in 6 months. Its price today, therefore, might be 99.5, representing the present value of the 100 dollars it will return in 6 months.

Unlike bonds, of course, discount instruments don't have accrued interest. Their price simply reflects their status as a zero coupon instrument.

Some markets, like the United States, do not routinely quote *price* on bill instruments, rather price must be inferred from so-called *discount yield.* In the United States, the formula to convert discount yield to price is:

$$\text{Price} = 100 \times (1 - \text{Discount yield} \times \frac{d}{360})$$

Here *d* represents the number of days from settlement to maturity. This is a weird inversion of the usual simple interest formula. Discount yield, as we see, is simply a quick rule-of-thumb approximation of a real interest

Table 9.4 Common discount instruments

Country	Instrument name	Day-count basis	Settlement
US	Treasury bill	360	T+0
UK	Treasury bill	365	T+1
France	BTF	360	T+1
Germany	Bubill	360	T+2
Italy	BOT	360	T+2
Japan	Discount bill	365	T+3
Canada	Treasury bill	365	T+2

rate. If we were to write a more normal equation, we would express something closer to what is known as the *bond-equivalent yield:*

$$Price = \frac{100}{1 + \text{Bond equivalent yield} \times \dfrac{d}{365}}$$

(The lesson here is obvious: we should always make sure that we know what kind of 'yield' we are dealing with when we look at any debt instrument.)

In the United Kingdom, yield is quoted as it is in most jurisdictions, on a simple money-market basis, which has the same formula as the US bond-equivalent yield. In most European jurisdictions, the formula is similar, except with 360 days instead of 365 (Table 9.4).

9.7 Funding and government securities: repo

The most common way to trade any government securities is not to buy or sell them directly, but rather to buy or sell them via *repo*. Short for 'repurchase agreement', repo is the tool most banks use for securities trading.

Repo is basically another means to collateralize trading. If a bank is holding bonds, and wishes to borrow money, it can lend the bonds as collateral for cash. Alternatively, a bank that has cash to lend can lend it in the repo market, taking securities as collateral.

Because of this duality, repo is sometimes more confusing than it needs to be. Repo is both a means to borrow cash (with securities) and a means to borrow securities (with cash). In fact, there are two sorts of markets that develop from time to time: those where parties are mostly interested in borrowing cash in exchange for any security (cash-driven) and those where parties are looking for specific bonds to borrow (securities-driven).

Before delving too far into complexities, however, it is useful to review what exactly a repo transaction is. Basically, someone who sells a bond in the repo market also agrees to buy it back *at a fixed price* later. The repo seller (the one selling the bond) will get cash in exchange for the bond, and pay interest on that cash (at the *repo rate*). In addition, the repo seller retains any coupons paid by the bond.[11]

The easiest way to view repo is as a way to borrow cash, using bonds as collateral. Since the bonds are *not* cash, and must be sold on the market if the borrower defaults, there's a risk involved in lending against them. If the price falls, for instance, and the borrower of cash defaults, then the lender is in trouble. To guard against this, a *haircut* is applied to the bond price.

For example, suppose we have a bond (price today, 95, plus 5 accrued interest) and we wish to sell it on the repo market *overnight*. We agree with the buyer to pay us the *dirty price* (100) less 3 per cent haircut, for a total of 97.

At start of repo:
Seller: Sells bond X for 95 + 5, less 3% = 97 in cash.
Buyer: Buys bond X for 97, holds in *margin account* on behalf of seller.

The next day, the agreement can be extended (if it is an *open* repo agreement) or terminated. If we terminate it, we return the cash we borrowed (97) plus interest accrued on the cash at the repo rate. The buyer of the repo returns whatever is in our margin account: in this case, it is the bond itself, which has accrued one more day of interest.

At termination of repo:
Seller: returns 97 in cash, plus 1 day of interest on the cash; receives bond X.
Buyer: returns bond X, receives cash plus interest.

It should be noted that the two interest payments should balance. The rate paid on the borrowed cash (the repo rate) is balanced by the interest which accrues on the bond.

What happens if a coupon is paid on the bond during the repo term? Many repo agreements (such as the standard UK Gilt repo agreement[8]) state that the buyer should apply any coupon payments to the sellers' margin account. If a coupon is paid, the value of the bond will decrease by the coupon amount, but the amount of collateral will be stable, since the coupon will go into a cash account. This is typical: any return from the collateral account must stay in the collateral account.

What this means, effectively, is that the repo buyer must hold records of not only security collateral, but cash collateral as well. In addition to possible coupon payments, the seller of the repo may also give other cash collateral under certain circumstances.

The standard Global Master Repurchase Agreement (GMRA; to which the Gilt agreement mentioned above is an annex) simply says that coupon payments must be either sent to the seller or put on their account. The Gilt annex, however, makes a bit more sense in the case of a bond (the GMRA can apply to any security). If a bond coupon were delivered immediately to the seller, the value of the bond collateral would drop by the coupon amount, potentially resulting in under-collateralization.

Figure 9.4 clarifies this a bit. We can imagine that at the start of the repo, the seller sends a bond to the buyer, in exchange for cash.

What happens if the market value of the bond changes? The GMRA talks about Transaction Exposure – which is the difference between the agreed *repurchase amount* and the value of the bonds held (less haircut).

For example, suppose we have sold a bond on repo, for 95, with 3 per cent haircut. This means that we will get 92.15 in cash at the beginning of the transaction. The repurchase amount will be the price we've agreed for at the end of the transaction (usually the same as at the start). So if

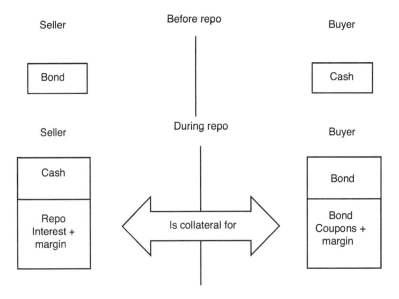

Figure 9.4   Conceptualizing repo transactions

the repo term is 1 week, the initial amount borrowed is 92.15, then the repurchase amount will also be 92.15. If the value of the bond falls to 90 (a steep fall, admittedly), then the Transaction Exposure will be 92.15 minus (90 less 3% (87.3)), or 4.85.[9]

The repo buyer can demand additional margin (more bonds, or cash) to cover the transaction exposure. If the bond had gone *up* in value, the repo *seller* could demand some margin back. (Another simple approach (which can be agreed) is to break the repo, and re-start the agreement with a new repo under new collateral terms.)

9.8   The repo and the reverse

The repo agreement is of use to both parties. The seller can use bond holdings as a means of raising cash. The buyer can use cash to obtain bonds with a guaranteed resale price at the end of the repo term. This means, in most cases, that the buyer will re-sell the bond (or bonds) they have received as collateral, and only repurchase them at the end of the repo term.

In other words, the repo buyer is betting that the bond will lose value – they are going short. If the bond *does* lose value, they will be able to purchase it at a reduced price at the end of the repo term, deliver it at the agreed repurchase amount and make a profit.

A little terminology (which may be familiar to many): the seller of a repo is sending their bond out to the buyer, so they are *repoing out* the bond. The buyer is doing the reverse of what the seller is doing, so they are doing a so-called *reverse repo*. They *reverse in* the bond.

9.9   General and special

Most repo is not actually done on specific bonds, rather it is done on collateral of a certain 'general nature'. A bank, for instance, may wish to raise cash from its bond holdings, but repoing out hundreds of specific issues would be laborious and unnecessary.

What happens, in reality, is that the bank will repo out the holdings as 'General Collateral' or GC repo. The agreement with the repo buyer will be for collateral of a certain nature (US Treasury Securities, for instance), and those securities will get a certain haircut, and receive an overall repo rate.

In the US Treasury market, for instance, a popular form of repo is the so-called General Collateral Finance (GCF) repo – a form of repo typically done via brokers. This form of GC repo allows buyers and sellers to deliver baskets of securities (whose composition may be unknown until late in the day) for repo to a central counterparty. The central, clearing counterparty will match all trades from different dealers, and hold collateral on behalf of buyers and sellers.

GCF repo is marked to market daily – so the margin accounts are topped up based on not only changes in the value of collateral but changes in repo rates. Parties must settle mark-to-market differences each day, and then any excess margin is returned when the repo trade is terminated.

Special repo is the opposite of general – it is repo on specific bonds, often bonds which are in high demand. In the United States, there will always be a number of treasury bonds which are in constant demand, because of their ability to be delivered to satisfy maturing option contracts. These bonds are *on special*, and the repo rate will be often significantly lower than the GC rate. This means that, to buy such a bond on repo, someone will have to accept much less return on the money they lend out.

This is an important point. Managing 'specialness' is critical in the repo market. Since bonds that are on special are in high demand, sellers can negotiate better terms from buyers. This means they can use their bonds to borrow money from buyers for much less – by paying lower repo rates. When US Treasuries are on special, the repo rate has been known to even dip below zero – meaning that the repo buyer is essentially paying for the privilege of borrowing the bond.

9.10   Using the repo rate to get future prices

To recap, then, the seller of a bond on repo will receive, at the end of the repo:

$$P_2 - P_1$$

where P_2 is the (dirty) price of the bond at the end, and P_1 is the *dirty price* at the start. (Which is a fancy way of saying: they get the return on the bond, both relating to price changes and accrued coupon.) Note that this is the *net financial effect* of the repo agreement – not what's said in the agreement (as explained in the sections earlier).

The seller of the repo will *pay*

$$P_1(1-H)r\frac{d}{365}$$

where r is the repo rate, H is the haircut and d is the number of days elapsed (365 may be 360, depending on market convention). This is just simple interest at rate r on the amount borrowed.

Since repo is a big market, and buyers and sellers can easily change places, the two amounts should be the same, largely, if everything is liquid. So we should be able to say:

$$P_2 - P_1 = P_1(1-H)r\frac{d}{365}$$

or

$$P_2 = P_1\left(1 + r(1-H)\frac{d}{365}\right)$$

which, if we ignore the haircut term, becomes

$$P_2 = P_1\left(1 + r\frac{d}{365}\right)$$

The repo rate, in other words, *should* simply be the return on the bond (with a second-order correction coming via the haircut). Therefore, if we want to find the expected price[10.] of a bond at some future time, we could use the repo rate as a way to infer the future price from the present price.

In fact, this is what is often done in practice. For instance, when analysing a bond option, we'll often want to know the expected future price of a bond. One input into the bond option formula will be the repo rate, which allows this amount to be easily computed.

Care should be taken, of course, when computing the forward price of a bond to adjust for two things: *specialness* and *coupons*. Adjusting for coupons is straightforward: simply subtract the coupon amount from the bond price on coupon payment days. Specialness is more complex and warrants further discussion.

9.11 Bonds and yield curves

The formula for getting the forward price of a bond (given its current price and a repo rate) gives us a straightforward relationship between prices and repo rates. In fact, the repo rate is simply another way of viewing the return on a bond over a short period.

We can also infer the return on a government bond by looking at the government bond yield curve. If we assume that all non-special bonds issued by a national government are pretty much interchangeable (except for maturity and coupon), then we can assume that that government has a *rate environment* that applies to it. At any point in the future, there will be a zero coupon rate at which government debt can be discounted to get its present value.

We should be able to graph these zero coupon rates to get a yield curve, in much the same way we do for interest rates.

To build the yield curve, we could simply follow a procedure very similar to that used for interest rates:

1. Starting with bills or discount instruments, build a table of zero coupon interest rates out to 1 year or so.
2. For each bond after 1 year, estimate a new zero coupon rate to maturity which would make all the bond's cash-flows equal its current (dirty) price.

This approach, while attractive, is not much used. One problem is that bonds all have subtly different factors affecting their price, which results in the yield curve resulting from this process being somewhat inaccurate.

In fact, if we look at this problem, we see there are two reasons why we might want to get a yield curve for a bond market, and each has a different, best solution.

First, we might wish to determine the expected future price of a bond. We might need this to compute the payment on a swap, to determine if the bond is useful for delivering into a futures or option contract or to determine the expected future price for use in options calculations. In all of these cases, we really want an estimate of the effective repo rate that will apply to the bond.

A second reason we might wish to have a yield curve is to analyse whether certain bond prices are as expected: do they lie above or below the yield curve? Alternatively, we may wish to determine the price for an illiquid bond-based on bonds whose price we know: for this we'd need some general way to discount cash-flows. In these cases, we need some estimate of the expected discount factors for each point in time: we need a proper yield curve model.

In the first case, where we need the repo rate, we may be able to use the yield curve model instead, since effectively the two are interchangeable. In fact, we might be able to use the repo market to build the short end of our yield curve. Here, however, the paths diverge. Typically, term repo rates are not available for long periods. When building long-term yield curves, practitioners often will use a smooth function which fits (as well as possible) the bonds in the set they wish to analyse.

This means that some bonds (like those on special, or those that are illiquid or those that have non-standard terms) are left out. Which bonds to include and which to leave out are a matter of debate. Sometimes (in the United States, especially) the most liquid bonds are almost always on special. Are these bonds best left out, or perhaps are they best included?

9.12 More on repo: RONIA, Eurepo and other indices

One development that is especially significant is the introduction (in the United Kingdom at least) of an analogue to the quoted overnight lending rate, but for repo markets. In the world of unsecured lending in the United Kingdom, SONIA is a weighted average rate at which lending occurred in the overnight markets. In a similar vein, a new index, RONIA, has been introduced to cover lending in the repo markets. RONIA (Repurchase Over-Night Index Average) is the weighted average repo rate in the inter-bank overnight market, for UK Gilt collateral.

Since its introduction around 2007, RONIA has risen in popularity as a benchmark. The market it measures, repo lending, has remained steady, while unsecured lending has fallen in popularity: lending under SONIA and RONIA was, by the end of 2011, roughly similar in volumes.

By 2012, however, RONIA was just starting to develop a swap market. By April, several brokers were quoting trades out to 12 months. As such, RONIA promises to be a good benchmark on which to base analysis of the UK government market.

Other markets, however, are more complex. There's no equivalent of RONIA in either the US or Europe. Europe, admittedly, has something called 'Eurepo' (with term rates out to 12 months). This is similar, outwardly, to RONIA; however, it allows collateral of the 'most actively traded European repo market', and of the 'best quality' only. Since European government debt is of a widely different quality, and repo market activity can vary, the result is that one cannot be sure what government the Eurepo rate will refer to at any given time. In addition, if one wants to analyse the Belgian government market, for instance, Eurepo is no help.

9.13 Finding the price of illiquid bonds

One of the most common tasks practitioners face is to find accurate price estimates for bonds which may not be widely quoted in the market. For instance, a government may have hundreds of outstanding bonds, only a few of which are widely traded. How can we get price estimates for the others?

Well, based on the analysis above, one way to proceed would be to build a bond-based yield curve along which we can price (accurately) the

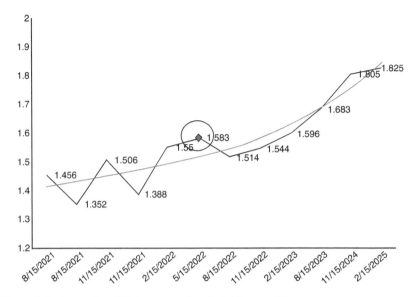

Figure 9.5   Example of US Treasury Bond yields near 10 years

liquid bonds we see in the market. Then, we can price other bonds simply by discounting their cash-flows on the curve. This is a simple, robust approach, but requires some work to develop properly.

One issue is that liquid bonds may have different prices from illiquid bonds, based on their liquidity, their specialness (see the section earlier) or other considerations. A good, general way to see this price differential is to look at the closing, end-of-day price quotations from a major source (such as, for instance, TradeWeb or a major broker such as ICAP).

Figure 9.5 shows the quoted yields of a number of US Treasury bonds, centred near the active (liquid, or on-the-run) 10-year note. As we can see, the yields differ quite a bit. There are a few reasons for this:

- Some bonds have higher coupons. The bond just after the 10-year bond (with a yield of 1.514%) has a coupon of over 7 per cent – the 10-year has a coupon of just 1.75 per cent. This means that actually, if we were pricing this bond by discounting its cash-flows, we would be using far more of the early parts of the curve than we would for a lower coupon bond.
- Some bonds are less in demand. The on-the-run bond (as discussed earlier) is almost always on special, and may be priced accordingly.
- Supply and demand work differently for every bond – there may be idiosyncratic considerations for each. For instance, some bonds may be

eligible for delivery into bond futures contracts, which may also put them more in demand.

One simple approach to finding the price for less-liquid bonds, then, could be:

- Find a benchmark (end-of-day) quoted price for all bonds for this issuer which is trustworthy.
- For bonds near a benchmark, liquid, bond, find the difference in yield between this bond and the benchmark. Call this the *yield spread* for the bond.
- During the day, as the benchmark bond's price moves up and down:
  - Re-compute the benchmark bond's yield (by using the price-to-yield solving method).
  - Add the yield spread
  - From the resulting implied yield for our illiquid bond, compute the illiquid bond's price.

This method (yield-spreading) is quite simple and often used over more complex methods (such as yield curve building). A more complex version might involve using multiple benchmark bonds, and shifting the yield based on an average of the yield shifts of surrounding benchmarks, for instance.

One more concept is important, however, in the world of heuristic tools used to aid price generation: *duration.*

Duration is a way to measure the average maturity of a bond's cash-flows. For instance, if a bond has no coupons, and matures in 10 years, we know that it's duration will be 10 years (exactly). However, if it pays coupons, the duration will be less, because we receive some payments before maturity.

If we add up the cash-flows of a bond, multiply each by its time until payment and then divide by the total value of the bond, we should get some idea of the 'average' time on which a payment will be made:

$$\text{Duration} = \frac{\sum_{i=1}^{n} c_i\, D_i\, t_i + FDT}{\text{Price}}$$

Here, c is the coupon amount, D is the discount factor for each payment, F is the face value of the bond and t is the time until each payment is made (with T being the time until maturity).

If you don't have a yield curve, however, how do you compute the discount factor? One simple replacement (based on the simplest yield formula, given earlier) is to replace D with

$$D_i = \frac{1}{(1+y/f)^i}$$

Here, as before, y is the yield and f is the frequency on which coupons are paid.

Once we can compute duration (even in-exactly) we can use duration instead of maturity to estimate where on the curve our bond should sit. If we don't have a full yield curve model, we can build a fairly good estimation tool by simply ordering bonds by duration, and then yield-spreading them against the nearest liquid benchmarks.

All of this is mostly of interest in major government bond markets.

9.14 Futures markets

In addition to the cash market, there is a large and lively market in bond futures. These, as one might expect, are contracts to *deliver* (or receive) government bonds at some time in the future.

In order to de-couple the futures market (to some degree) from the cash market for bonds, the seller of a futures contract may deliver any of a range of bonds to satisfy the contract.

Typically, the contract will state explicitly which bonds are eligible for delivery.

As an example, let's look at the Long Gilt Future (traded on the LIFFE/Euronext Exchange). Suppose I sell a contract for £100,000, expiring in December 2012 (a date in the past, but one for which, at the time of writing, specific examples are available).

If, after selling the December 2012 Futures contract, I hold it until maturity (in December) I will be in the peculiar position of having to *deliver*. This means that I must send bonds to the clearing firm (or Clearing Service Provider, as LIFFE calls it) which satisfies the terms of the contract. In this case, it means providing £100,000 face value of Gilts.

As the seller, I get to choose which bond to deliver: the exchange makes available a list of deliverable bonds (see below).

How much do I get paid for these bonds, after delivering them? Table 9.5 allows the clearing firm to calculate the contractual settlement amount. In this case, the settlement amount is

$$\text{Settlement} = 100,000 \times \text{Futures price} \times \text{Price factor} + [\text{IA} + \text{DA} \times T]$$

Table 9.5 Deliverable bonds for the December 2012 long gilt future

Potential bond (ISIN Code)	Coupon	Maturity date	Price factor	Initial accrued	Daily accrued	Delivery days
GB00B4RMG977	3.75	7 Sep 2021	0.9816226	870.165746	10.359116	3, 4, 5, 6, 7,
GB00B3KJDQ49	4.00	7 Mar 2022	0.9999507	928.176796	11.049724	10, 11, 12,
GB0030880693	5.00	7 Mar 2025	1.0961319	1160.22099	13.812155	13, 14, 17,
						18, 19, 20,
						21, 24, 27,
						28, 31

Table 9.6 Major government bond futures contracts

Exchange	Bond futures contract on
Chicago Board of Trade (CBOT)	30-year US Treasury bond
CBOT	10-year US Treasury note
CBOT	5-year US Treasury note
CBOT	2-year US Treasury note
Tokyo Stock Exchange (TSE)	10-year JGB
TSE	5-year JGB
LIFFE (NYSE/Euronext)	Long gilt (10 Years ±)
LIFFE	Medium gilt (5 Years ±)
LIFFE	Short gilt (2–3 Years)
Eurex	Buxl (German 30Y)
Eurex	Bund (German 10Y)
Eurex	Bobl (German 5Y)
Eurex	Schatz (German 2Y)

The *Futures Price* above is the agreed settlement price for the day on which *notice of delivery* is given. In this example (for London Gilt Futures), the futures price is called the *Exchange Delivery Settlement Price*, and is the volume-weighted futures contract price for the day on which notice is given. The last term in the equation is simply a contractual method of computed accrued interest: IA is the initial accrued interest for the delivery month, after which one adds the daily accrued interest (DA) times the number of days since the start of the month (T).

What does this mean? Briefly, it says that the exchange is trying to make bonds of different coupon values roughly equivalent. In this example, the 5 per cent bond will have a higher market value (because of its higher total cash-flow value). So, to make it reasonable to deliver this bond, the Price Factor must be increased to make it sometimes worthwhile. Similarly the 3.75 per cent bond will have a lower price factor. If interest rates hover around 4 per cent, then all the bonds in the table *should* be largely equivalent in terms of deliverability. In reality, this usually does not happen.

On a given day, one of the three bonds will be the *cheapest to deliver* (or CTD). We can determine which one it is by computing the settlement amount in the equation above for each bond, and comparing it with the amount it would cost to buy each bond (£100,000 face value) in the market.

Even before the futures contract expires, we can determine the cheapest to deliver bond. This is simply done by finding the future price of the bond using the repo rate. For each deliverable bond, use the future price (via repo) and compare that with the settlement amount (using the current futures contract price). The bond which yields the highest profit is the cheapest to deliver.

The cheapest to deliver bond, not surprisingly, is somewhat in demand for futures traders. If the cheapest to deliver really is cheap, then there's an incentive to buy and hold it until delivery. As more and more traders do this, the bond becomes quite sought after. Not surprisingly, it often ends up on special repo.

There are a wide variety of futures contracts on government bonds. A few of the most popular ones are listed in Table 9.6.

9.15   Gross basis, net basis and implied repo

For bonds which can be delivered to satisfy a futures contract, the difference between the bond price and the futures price (times the price factor) is known as the *basis* (or *gross basis*). On the delivery date, the bond with the gross basis closest to zero will be the CTD. In fact, in a perfect world, the CTD bond will have zero basis on delivery.

Gross basis = (Bond price) – (Futures price) × (Price factor)

As we can see, bonds that cost more will have higher gross basis – cheaper bonds will have lower gross basis.

The trouble with gross basis is that it compares apples and oranges, to an extent. It is looking at the difference between a bond price (today) and a futures price – which is based on the expected price of a bond at some time in the future.

Prior to the delivery date, the more useful number to monitor is the *net basis*: this is the difference between the *forward* bond price and the futures price (times price factor). In the case

Net basis = (Forward bond price) – (Futures price) × (Price factor)

From the section above, we can see that we can get an approximation of the forward bond price by using the repo rate as a simple interest rate:

$$P_{\text{forward}} = P_{\text{today}} \left(1 + r \frac{d}{365} \right)$$

If we know the repo rate of each of the potential bonds we can deliver into the contract, we can put together a spreadsheet to determine which bond has the lowest net basis.

Conversely, if we look at simply the bond prices and futures prices, we can *solve* for the repo rate on each of the CTD candidate bonds. This rate (called the *implied repo rate*) will be highest for the CTD bond – since a relatively cheap asset will need to grow at a high rate to meet a given delivery price.

$$\text{Implied repo} = \left(\frac{P_{\text{forward}}}{P_{\text{today}}} - 1 \right) \frac{365}{d}$$

What is the forward price in this equation? We set the forward price to the futures price (times price factor and accrued interest) for the bond – then use it in this equation to find out what the repo *would be* if the bond's basis goes to zero on delivery.

Sticking with our example from the UK Gilt market, we can show what simple implied repo analysis might look like as shown in Figure 9.6.

This example is taken from a spreadsheet showing how implied repo rates can be obtained using market data. One thing to notice – we put in an explicit *delivery date* for the futures contract.

Each futures contract actually specifies a range of possible delivery dates. In this example, any business day in June would suffice for delivery. We chose the last business day, because this turned out to be the most profitable – as the example shows, for one bond in particular (the 4% of March 2025) we can make a positive return, in theory. (Whether this means any actual profit, given that the yield on the bond is around 1.5 per cent, is another question.)

Long Gilt Futures – Implied Repo Analysis			
Futures Contract Expiration Month: June 2013			
Today's Date	20-Apr		
Futures Price	119.85		
Last Delivery Day	28-Jun-13		
Days until Delivery Day	38		
Possible CTD Bond	1.75% Gilt Maturing September 2022	4% Gilt Maturing March 2025	5% Gilt Maturing March 2025
Bond Price Today	100.55	120.46	132.24
Price + Accrued Interest	100.7877718	121.0034783	132.9193479
Price Factor (Conversion Factor)	0.8271861	0.9999507	1.0930627
Futures Price x Price Factor + AI	99.68389008	121.0823518	132.5498213
Implied Repo	−10.5%	0.6%	−2.7%

Figure 9.6 Example of implied repo analysis

The choice of delivery day is important however. Even though the party that delivers the bonds will make very little guaranteed profit – they do have the option to deliver on any day of the month. This option is worth something. Once the futures price is locked in, the party that's delivering the bonds can watch the market for buying opportunities all month long, and (hopefully) find an opportune moment to deliver. For this reason (as well as the fact the party delivering bonds has the choice of multiple bonds to deliver), implied repo rates are often lower than actual repo rates over a given period.

9.16   Trading against benchmarks and futures

Many traders will hedge their positions with futures – even if the bonds they're trading are not the actual CTD bonds associated with the futures contract.

For government bonds, this makes sense. A single government entity will have the same credit worthiness to any maturity date – whether you buy a 9- or 11-year bond will make little difference if you hedge with a 10-year future. The futures contract will protect against 99 per cent of the price changes you'll see in the market.

Doing such a trade (buying bonds and selling futures, for instance) is known as *basis trading*. By entering into this position, the only risk you are exposed to is that the basis will change: so-called *basis risk*. Basis trading is common, not only with government bonds, but with any sort of bond of a similar credit rating in the same currency. Most of the price movements in the bond market are related, and hedging with futures will capture the large majority of risk – even for corporate bonds.

Related to basis trading is *switch trading* – buying one bond while selling another (benchmark) bond. In the case of governments, a trader may sell benchmark bonds (often the CTD for a futures contract) while buying other bonds of similar maturity. The 'basis risk' here is not with the futures market, but in the yield spread between the benchmark bond and the other, perhaps riskier bond.

9.17   Fixed-income portfolios and bond risk

The primary risk number for a bond position is much like the delta measure we see in yield curve related risk. This simple measure is, in fact, often called 'dpdy', 'DV01' or 'PV01' – for first derivative of price with respect to yield, 'dollar value of one basis point' and 'price value of one basis point'.

If we are hedging bond yield (as is generally the case) we want to find out the sensitivity of the bond to movements in yield. Computing PV01 for a bond is generally straightforward (and can be done numerically, as with delta, by simply bumping the yield slightly and re-pricing). PV01 can also be computed numerically for most bonds by using the formula for *modified duration*:

$$\text{Modified duration} = \frac{\sum_{i=1}^{n} PV(CF_i)T_i}{P(1+\frac{y}{f})}$$

In this formula we add up the present value of each cash-flow in the bond (*PV(CF)* in the top summation) – including any principal return at the end – multiplied by the time until payment of each cash-flow. Present value is usually calculated by discounting at the current yield, *y*. The *f* in the equation above represents the payment frequency of the bond.

To get an estimate of PV01, we use the equation

$$\frac{dp}{dy} = -(\text{Modified duration}) \times \text{Price}$$

Simple enough. The price value of a basis point can be computed by multiplying this result by 0.01 per cent.

In addition, as with gamma, we can measure the second derivative as well: the convexity of a bond. Convexity is simply a term to describe d^2p/dy^2 and can be measured numerically as well as by a number of formulas. As with interest rate products, convexity is greater if a bond includes an option. Callable bonds have greater convexity than vanilla bonds. Also, bond futures exhibit a certain amount of convexity not found in their cash equivalents.

This is all very well – if we wish to hedge bonds with themselves. In reality, fixed-income portfolios consist of a large number of unrelated bonds hedged with a small number of liquid hedge instruments. In many cases, the hedges will be bond futures.

If we take the European market as an example (the United States is very similar), there are three major bond future contracts which act as hedge instruments of the first-order: Bund futures (based on bonds of maturity around 10 years), Bobl futures (5 years or so) and Schatz futures (2 years). Each of these futures trades at a price given by the price of the CTD bond (or bonds). If we are trying to hedge a portfolio of Euro-denominated bonds quickly, we may wish to use futures to hedge against first-order changes in the yield curve.

One common way to determine which future to hedge with is to measure the duration of the bond you wish to hedge, and the duration of the hedge instruments. (For futures, this would be the duration of the CTD bond for the contracts.) Using a weighted average can then help determine the proportion for each hedge.

What this does is provide a proxy for the market as a whole. Bund futures, for instance, are so widely traded that they will rise and fall with overall market sentiment – as will the bonds we're hedging. This hedges only the overall sentiment – unless one is hedging German government bonds, there will be some divergence over time. It's rather like hedging stocks with stock index futures – a good approximation for stocks with beta close to one, but never perfect. (However, overall, if one is hedging a lot of bonds, the effect should even out to some extent.)

The risk, then, can (in broad terms) be represented as pseudo-positions in each of the related bond futures. In Euro-land, Bund, Bobl, Schatz and to an extent Buxl (25+ years), futures would each have a notional amount against which they might be required to hedge. In the United States, this would correspond to the Treasury Bond futures (25+ years), 10-year note futures, 5-year note futures and 2-year note futures.

Another way to hedge, of course, is via interest rates. Many bonds, especially non-sovereign debt, are best valued as a spread from LIBOR or OIS. Discounting the cash-flows on the appropriate curve will allow one to create an interest rate risk profile for the bond portfolio as described in the previous sections.

Further reading

Choudhry, M. (2002) *The Repo Handbook*, Butterworth-Heinemann.
Duffie, D. (1996) 'Special Repo Rates', *Journal of Finance*, 493–525.
Place, J. (2000) *Basic Bond Analysis (Handbooks in Central Banking no. 20)*, London: Bank of England.

10
Corporate Bonds, Credit Spreads and Credit Default Swaps

Like governments, corporate entities like to borrow money. One of the easiest way to do this is by issuing bonds, which many corporations do on a global basis, borrowing from wherever the demand is greatest, and the rates lowest. The corporate bond market is large, and also very diverse.

Like government bonds, there is no real exchange on which corporate bonds are sold. Most bonds are sold by dealers (such as banks) to investors (such as pension funds, investment funds, hedge funds or individuals). The process of issuing new bonds is interesting, involving banks working with borrowers to *underwrite*, or insure, the issue of bonds. The borrower is thus guaranteed to sell the bonds at an agreed price, and the banks effectively lend the money. The underwriting bank (called the *book runner*) then tries to sell the bonds to investors. (In fact, the bank has probably reached an agreement with major investors before the process begins.)

Because the bank has an inventory of bonds on its books (which it sells to investors), it also has the capacity to buy back bonds from investors who change their minds. Typically a bank will agree to maintain a 'secondary market' in a bond for some time after issuance. Maintaining a market typically means agreeing to *buy* bonds at a published price, and sell them (if any are sold – there's no obligation to sell bonds you don't have) at a small spread above the purchase price. Often bonds are listed on an exchange for regulatory purposes, and the exchange enforces such orderly market procedures.

10.1 Modelling corporate bonds

Like government bonds, corporate bonds have certain conventions they adhere to, around computing accrued interest and around settlement. These can differ from the government bond market. The most important details to know are around the day-count conventions and settlement.

Corporate bonds in the United States almost all use the 30/360 day-count convention to calculate accrued interest. In Europe, many use the European variant (30E/360) while others stick to ACT/ACT. (See the section on swaps for more details on the calculation of these conventions.) Most corporate bonds also settle a bit later than their government counterparts, often taking three business days (*T*+3).

The main difference between corporate bonds and government bonds, however, is their price. Since many corporations are seen as less credit-worthy than governments (not always, but sometimes), the rates they must pay in interest are higher. As such, the yield on a corporate bond will often be higher than the corresponding government bond. This difference in yield is sometimes (but not always) called the 'credit spread'.

10.2   The credit spread

What is the credit spread? The simplest definition, as mentioned, is simply the difference in yield between the corporate bond and a government 'benchmark' of similar maturity.

Credit spreads are useful in pricing corporate bonds. Since corporate bonds are very illiquid, trading very rarely compared with their government counterparts, it is often difficult to get a useful price for them from the market. What many practitioners do is assign the corporate entity a 'spread', and then use that spread to infer a price for the bond. So, for instance, if a bank is holding $100,000 face value of 10-year bonds in Alpha Corporation, and wishes to assign a price to its holdings, it might (in a simple scenario) do something like:

- Decide on an agreed credit spread against a benchmark government bond for Alpha Corporation. This may be based on the general price of more liquid bonds they've issued, or the price achieved at their last bond offering, as well as other factors such as their CDS spread (see the section on Credit Default Swaps).
- Add the spread to the yield of the government benchmark, then, given this new yield, determine the price of the Alpha Corporation bond.

This procedure has some drawbacks: first, it ignores the fact that the government bond market has its own dynamics. The government benchmark yield can change dramatically for no particular reason, and this should not affect the value of the corporate bond. Second, the benchmark spread is inexact in that as time goes by, the corporate bond will have a shorter and shorter maturity, making the spread to a generic 10-year government bond less and less appropriate.

One common approach has been to use 'spread-to-LIBOR' as an alternate pricing technique. As we've seen, LIBOR has developed its own problems lately, but the technique is quite good nonetheless.

10.3 Spread-to-yield-curve

Rather than sticking to LIBOR per se, we'll discuss in general how a corporate issue can be priced using a spread to any yield curve (including LIBOR).

As we've seen, the yield curve model gives us a powerful tool to analyse cash-flows. We can use the yield curve model to give us the present value of a cash-flow from any time in the future. Given that, we should be able to 'plug in' the cash-flows from a corporate bond, add up their present values and get a total 'value' representing the bond's worth.

Of course, the present value of a bond's cash-flows, for a corporation with a large credit spread, will be much larger than the bond is actually worth. This is because, as we discount the cash-flows in our yield curve, the lower rates that make up the curve result in larger present values.

So, what good is it to get the present value of a bond's payments? Simply put, if we can do that for a bond whose price we know (such as a liquid, benchmark bond), we can use that information to infer a credit spread over the yield curve.

This is done in a simple manner, albeit one that requires solving for an unknown quantity:

1. Guess at a credit spread (S) for the corporation. Add this spread to every zero coupon rate in the yield curve model.
2. Add up the cash-flows of the bond, using the present value of the (now-adjusted) yield curve.
3. Re-adjust S so that the sum of the cash-flows is equal to the *dirty price* of the bond. (See section on Newton–Raphson for a description of an approach to adjusting for an unknown quantity.)

This simple approach is a quick and easy way to get the spread-to-LIBOR or spread-to-OIS for any reasonably liquid bond for which we know the price. Once we have the spread, we can use it to price other bonds (Figure 10.1).

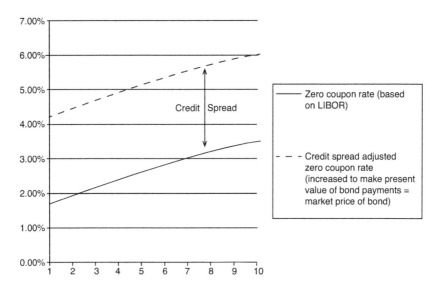

Figure 10.1 Computing a credit spread with a yield curve

Example: 7Y Bond, Market Price $92.
Present value of payments using unadjusted LIBOR curve: $105.
Present value of payments after adding 2.5 per cent to zero coupon rates of
LIBOR curve: $92.
Therefore The credit spread of the bond is 250 basis-points over LIBOR.

The example above shows graphically what happens when we adjust
the credit spread, and how the now-adjusted curve will give higher rates
(and lower prices) for any bond we price on it.

The spread we calculate is a *continuously compounded* spread, of course,
since we have directly adjusted the zero coupon rates in our yield curve
model (which are continuously compounded).

Spreads may have a term structure as well. If we have a corporation
(or state, or agency or any entity that issues bonds) with several *liquid*
bonds in the market, we may be able to calculate several different credit
spreads.

Figure 10.2 shows what would happen in the case of a credit curve
being adjusted around two liquid bond issues. We would first compute
the credit spread for the bond with the shortest maturity.

Then, we would use this credit spread adjusted yield curve to price the
next bond (with longer maturity). In the example, the first bond has

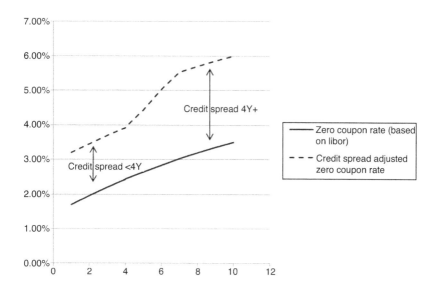

Figure 10.2   Computing a term structure for credit spreads

a maturity of 4 years, and the second bond a longer (7 years, perhaps) maturity.

In finding the credit spread for the second bond, we would use the first bond's credit spread up until 4 years, and only adjust the credit spreads after 4 years for the second bond. Naturally, some form of curve smoothing is needed after the 4-year point (to avoid jumps in valuation). The example above shows a linear spread between points, which is probably sufficient for most estimation.

This process gives us a *term structure of credit spreads*. This term structure can be used to price other bonds from this corporation or entity, or even bonds from other, similar entities with similar credit-worthiness.

It's worth mentioning (after the discussion around LIBOR in the previous chapter) that LIBOR remains an important benchmark, even if it is no longer seen as a truly risk-free rate. What LIBOR provides is a *benchmark*. It's a commonly agreed framework (for yield curves) that allows us to compare entities of different credit-worthiness. Also, it's agreed that LIBOR will not fluctuate unduly because of non-related economic events. For instance, if LIBOR changed suddenly because of economic events unrelated to the borrowing costs of companies, it might cause reported credit spreads to gyrate wildly. Fortunately, LIBOR remains (fairly) closely linked to the borrowing costs of most companies and other entities, making it a decent (if not perfect) benchmark.

10.4   More complex corporate bonds: embedded options

Corporate bonds are famous for their embedded options. They are, in this regard, much more complex than their government counterparts.

Many bonds are *callable*. A callable bond is one that may (on a coupon date) be bought back by the issuer for a pre-set price.

A bond callable at 100, then, can be re-purchased from the buyer at any coupon date for $100. If the bond was bought at $90, this is of little immediate concern, since having someone pay $100 for it would be a nice surprise. However, having such a call provision limits the upside of the investment.

It also makes it difficult to compute the credit spread if using this bond as a benchmark. The reason for this is, simply, that to price these bonds you also have to price the option. Pricing an option like this (which depends on interest rate levels *and* credit spreads) is complex. It means modelling interest rates and credit spreads (probably as two separate, correlated processes) and seeing what happens in a variety of scenarios. There are many models which can do this, of course, but implementing them, calibrating them and using them properly take a small department.

The term used for credit spreads in an embedded-option bond is *option-adjusted spread* (or OAS). The OAS is the spread that, when used inside the model, will give the correct price for the bond. In this way, it's probably going to be very close to the ordinary credit spread we calculated for the plain (no-option) bond.

Common options in bonds include:

- **Callable bonds:** *the issuer can buy back the bond (on a coupon date, or on certain pre-determined dates) for a pre-determined price. A schedule of prices (for different times) may apply (a so-called call schedule).*
- **Puttable bonds:** *the buyer can resell the bond to the issuer (again, at certain pre-determined dates) for a pre-determined price (or set of agreed prices).*
- **Convertible bonds:** *the buyer can exchange the bond for a pre-determined number of shares of stock in the company.*

The first two (callable and puttable) are bonds with embedded interest rate and credit options. The third has an aspect of stock-option about it, and dealing in convertible is often closely linked to the equity departments of many banks or institutions.

10.5   Asset swaps

One of the most common ways to evaluate credit, used more often perhaps than spread-to-LIBOR, is the so-called *asset swap spread*. To understand what this is all about, it's necessary to understand the basic asset
swap trade itself.

An asset swap is simply an exchange of a bond (from the seller) for a
swap. The seller of the bond keeps the coupons from the bond via the
swap. The buyer of the asset swap pays face value (100, or *par*, usually) for
the bond, and receives a floating payment (LIBOR plus a spread) from the
seller for the life of the agreement (see Figure 10.3).

The asset swap seller is paid 100 for the bond at the start of the trade.
But what if the bond is worth less? What if the bond is worth more?

There are two reasons a bond may be worth more or less than par.

- The bond may be credit-risky, making its price lower – people are afraid
  the bond issuer will default, lowering its market value.
- The coupons on the bond could be above or below the current corresponding par swap rate. High coupons make the bond more valuable,
  of course.

In both cases, the difference will be made up in the spread paid by the
seller. If a bond sells for less than par, the seller will get a bonus at the
start of the swap when they receive full par value. They'll have to make
up for that by paying a larger spread on the swap.

So what does this mean? The value of the bond to the buyer must equal
what they're giving up: par value *plus* the value of the swap. For example,
suppose a bond's price is $90, and it's coupon is 5 per cent – which, we'll
say, is 2 per cent above the par swap rate. The seller of the swap will see:

- Payment at the start of the swap: $100
- Value of the bond given to the buyer: –$90

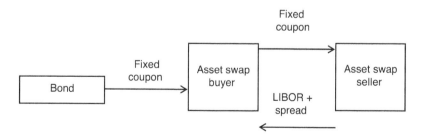

Figure 10.3   An asset swap

From this, we see that:

- Value of the swap to the seller: –$10

The asset swap spread, added to LIBOR, will be such that the value of the transaction will be zero, or near to it.

The asset swap spread is, more or less, related to the LIBOR spread:

$$\text{Asset swap spread} \approx (\text{Coupon} - \text{Par swap rate}) + \text{LIBOR spread}$$

Since the asset swap spread is directly proportional to the LIBOR spread – the riskier the bond, the higher its spread will be.

10.6   Other ways of looking at credit: credit default swaps

The trouble with corporate bonds is that they are so varied. One can talk, and in fact hypothesize, to a great degree about the credit-worthiness of a company without having much evidence. There is the *credit rating* of a company (the estimate put on the credit-worthiness of a company by a third-party agency whose job it is to estimate credit-worthiness). But the credit rating is also subjective and, most importantly, not the product of the market.

Finance loves markets. In the corporate arena, there is a market for bonds, true enough, but this market is not exactly uniform. The market for credit default swaps on individual companies, however, gives a uniform, easily comparable way to compare credit-worthiness.

What is a credit default swap? In its simplest form, it is insurance against the bankruptcy of a corporation. If I own a bond issued by XYZ corporation, which pays 5 per cent per annum, I can purchase a CDS contract on XYZ (for a fee) which will compensate me if XYZ ever decides to stop paying interest (or redeeming) the bond.

The form of the CDS contract has changed a great deal over the years, but the basic swap characteristics are given in Table 10.1, between a buyer of protection (the party paying regular fees) and the seller of protection (the party paying a lump sum if the company goes bankrupt).

The key terms here are:

- The *reference entity*: in other words, the company on which protection is being sold.
- The *reference obligation*: the bond which we are using as a yardstick. All single name CDS contracts like this (single name, in that they are on a single company) will use a reference obligation. This is used to determine

Table 10.1 Standard CDS contract: European version

Protection buyer	**Reference entity: XYZ Corporation**
Fee	X% (typically 1% or 5%, sometimes 0.25% or 10%) of notional amount per annum, paid on 20 March, 20 June, 20 September and 20 December, or the following business day should these dates fall on a weekend or holiday. The final date is not adjusted for purposes of computing interest
	The fee will be paid on each period end date, unless there is a credit event, in which case the fee will be paid *pro-rata* up until the credit event date (Sometimes, such as for CDS on sovereign entities, this is not the case, and no fee is payable on default.)
	Each accrual period starts on the period start date (e.g. March 20) and proceeds up to but not including the next period start date. The last period, however, *does* include the maturity date
Day-count basis	Actual/360
Notional amount	$1,000,000 (e.g.)
Reference obligation	XYZ 4.5% unsecured debt maturing 12 June 2022 (e.g.)
Currency	USD (e.g.)
Holidays	For USD: London + New York
	For EUR: London + TARGET
	For GBP: London
Protection seller	
Payment on credit event	Notional amount multiplied by (1.0 minus the determined recovery value of the reference entity as a percentage)
Credit Event determination	By the Determination Committee. The DC will 'look back' 60 days to determine if Credit Events have occurred

the payout from the contract should there be a 'credit event'. The reference obligation is usually a well-known bond issued by the company, which can be readily sold in the market.
- *Credit Event*: bankruptcy, restructuring of certain kinds and other delays in payment on obligations of the company.
- *Recovery value*: should a credit event occur, the recovery value is the amount that a determination committee (DC) says the bond is worth *after* a credit event. This will typically be much less than 100 – but greater than zero.

In this form, the CDS are quite straightforward. I pay a regular premium (as with an insurance contract) and receive a payment if something bad happens. Unlike insurance, the contract isn't typically cancelled directly – typically traders will enter into a reverse contract to close-out a position they don't want to have any more. (So a buyer of protection can become a seller of the same protection – resulting in a simple cash profit or loss.)

The payments on CDS contracts happen four times a year (in most cases, this is a typical CDS contract as per standard terms in the United States and most of Europe). The dates in the example above are not made up: they are called (confusingly) *IMM* dates, and are the four days on which CDS are typically paid. (These IMM dates have little to do with the IMM dates we encounter in the interest rate market – although the interest rate IMM dates for futures are also in March, June, September and December.)

There are a couple of features (new to the CDS market) that make the CDS different from ordinary swaps.

Full coupon payment. Payment on each IMM date is the full amount of ¼ the annual payment – *even if the contract is entered into just before the IMM date*. This means that you may pay a large amount for just a few days protection. To offset this effect, there is an *up-front fee*, made up partly of the accrued premium payment. So if the premium payment in March is $500, but I have purchased the contract 90 per cent of the way through the coupon period, part of the up front payment (to me) will be compensation for overpayment – in this case, $450 of accrued premium.

The up-front fee also compensates for another strange feature of the standard CDS: **fixed coupon amounts**. Most CDS will have standard fees of either 1 per cent per annum, or 5 per cent per annum.

How can this be? Companies have a wide variety of credit ratings. Insurance against default should cost anything from 50 basis-points to 50 per cent per year. How can there be just two standard fees?

Again, this is where the up-front payment comes in. Purchasing insurance against default on an entity for which it might cost 7 per cent per year, the standard contract would probably stipulate merely 5 per cent. The difference is made up by the up-front fee. The fee should be sufficient to cover the difference between the standard coupon (5%) and the coupon that actually would pay for credit protection (7%). *The fee should include the present value of the difference of the two cash-flow streams: in this case, 2% per annum for the life of the contract.*

10.7   Pro-rata fee on credit events

The standard CDS contract stipulates that, if a credit event occurs, the fee is still payable in that period *up until the credit event.* So, for instance, if a CDS contract would require payment of $1,000 each period, and half-way through the third period there is a default, then the fee payable would be only $500.

This may not apply in all circumstances, however. As mentioned in Table 10.1, CDS on sovereign entities (like countries) typically will have no accrued payment.

10.8 Credit events and restructurings

What determines a credit event? Briefly put, credit events are unsurprising things such as declarations of bankruptcy, or failure to pay obligations of similar subordination to the reference instrument.

In the documentation, in fact, there is a reference to *which* obligations (bonds) may be defaulted on to trigger a credit event. Confusingly, these are often also called 'reference obligations'. Generally, the rule is that a credit event can be triggered by a default on an obligation in certain currencies (similar to the reference entity, to exclude 'exotic' currencies) and on obligations of similar seniority, and not on 'contingent liabilities' (i.e. convertible bonds, or bonds with embedded options).

There are other things, however, which are not typical credit events, but which have often been deemed to be credit events by various forms of documentation. These are *restructurings* – events where creditors and the debtor agree to an amended form for various debts. This can include later payments, reduced principal or such things as longer maturities for certain instruments.

The market is moving away from recognizing restructuring as a credit event, largely, because it makes trading much simpler if it is not. However, there are a great many rules around about restructuring, and what sorts of events it applied to. These rules largely governed the practice of physical settlement – which applied to the types of bonds that could be supplied as settlement when a restructuring occurred. The restructuring rules go by names such as 'Old R' (the old restructuring approach), 'Mod R' (modified), 'Mod-Mod R' and, of course, 'No-R'.

Today, most North American CDS trade with No-R. European corporate CDS trade with Mod-Mod-R.

10.9 Auctions and settlements

The restructuring rules tie in with the settlement process in a rather strange way. The main process for settlement of CDS is the *auction*. This is a process, run by committee, whereby there is a determination of the cash settlement price for the CDS. Auction participants can choose physical settlement when they hold the reference obligation – they can sell it via auction to buyers, and are compensated via the buyer and the CDS protection seller to get par value for each bond. Many CDS buyers, however, will choose cash settlement, and get paid the difference between par and the auction-determined price.

The bonds delivered into an auction don't have to be reference bonds, however. The committee overseeing the auction will publish a list of bonds which are deliverable – usually more than just the single reference obligation. This means that CDS protection buyers can have a choice as to which bond they deliver – and of course will deliver whichever one is cheapest to get hold of.

For example, suppose I purchase CDS protection on XYZ Corporation, which defaults. I own one of their bonds (the 7.9% Bond maturing January 2035).

- The auction system allows me to sell my bond directly.
- If the auction gives a price of $35 for the bond, I'll be paid $35 *plus* $65 (from my CDS protection) to give me $100 for each bond. (Here 35 is the *recovery rate* – more on this later.)
- Alternatively, I can just accept $65 and keep the bond.

In an auction after a major credit event (i.e. bankruptcy) there will be one auction, and one price *for all CDS*. So if the result of the auction is a price of $25, that applies to all contracts at all maturities.

In an action after a restructuring, there may be multiple prices, banded by maturity. So there will be a price for 2.5 year, 5 year and 7.5 year 'buckets' of CDS maturity. Of course, if we are in a No-R regime, this won't happen. But in Europe (using Mod-Mod R) there may well be different maturity buckets, and thus different pay-outs under certain circumstances.

Unless of course, you're a sovereign entity (i.e. a state or country). In which case you use Old-R, which has just a single maturity bucket in restructuring events.[1]

10.10 Succession events

It's worth mentioning briefly one other aspect of CDS which plays a critical part in their definition: succession events. These are not credit events, but rather events where the reference entity is bought by another company, or buys another company and transfers assets or liabilities, or splits itself into parts. The DC in this case must first determine that an event has occurred, and then allocate the CDS contracts to a different entity than the one they started with – essentially rewriting the contract.

Succession events don't play a role in the valuation or analysis of CDS, but they're important to know about in any case.

10.11   Probability of default: another way of looking at the credit spread

All of this discussion brings us back to the credit spread.

Suppose a bond has a 5-year maturity, a 5 per cent coupon and is valued at $101. Suppose again, that this represents a credit spread of around 2.5 per cent above the risk-free rate.[2]

If we valued the bond using the risk-free yield curve (LIBOR, or whatever we choose to represent risk-free-ness), we would get a price of around $113.

What does that extra $12 represent? We could argue that it's the *risk premium* – the amount that we would pay to forgo the risk of default, or the amount we receive to experience the risk of default! We pay less for our bond, in exchange for shouldering the risk of losing money.

If we pay $101 for our bond, we are in fact saying that we are willing to save $12 over a risk-free investment to get extra return.

Returning to our graph of credit spreads, we can label it like so (see Figure 10.4).

The area between the two curves can literally be thought of as representing the risk of default.

To go into more detail – let's look at the premium repayment on the bond.

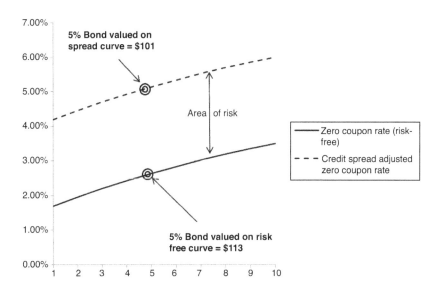

Figure 10.4   How credit spread affects value

- Discounted on the credit curve – $100 in 5 years is worth $89.77 today.
- Discounted on the risk-free curve – $100 in 5 years is worth $79.55 today.

Breaking it down further we can say, by looking at our yield curve:

- The continuously compounded 5-year risk-free rate is 2.16 per cent.
- The credit spread adjusted 5-year rate is 4.58 per cent.
- The difference, therefore, is 2.42 per cent: this is the precise continuously compounded credit spread at 5 years.

So the price of the principal repayment, in mathematical terms, is:

$$e^{-\left(r_{\text{risk-free}} + r_{\text{credit}}\right)t} \times P = e^{-r_{\text{risk-free}}t} \times e^{-r_{\text{credit}}t} \times P$$

Here, r_{credit} is the credit spread (as explained above) at the maturity of the bond, and P is the principal amount.

Basically, we see that we've broken it down into *two separate yield curves*. The credit spread is not just spread above LIBOR (or whatever), it is a yield curve in its own right. The first term in the equation above ($e^{-r_{\text{risk-free}}t}$) is the discount factor from the normal yield curve we've constructed with our favourite methodology.

The second term ($e^{-r_{\text{credit}}t}$) is also a discount factor (in a sense). However, it represents *the risk of default*.

The table below shows how it breaks down:

Type	Rate (%)	Discount factor	Discounted premium
Risk-free rate	2.16	0.8977	$89.77
Credit spread alone	2.42	0.8862	$88.62
Credit-risky rate	4.57 (sum of above)	0.7955 (product of above)	$79.55

So what is the chance (according to the market, at least) that the risky company will default in 5 years? If the recovery value is zero (i.e. if default means everything is worthless) then the chance of default is (1 − 0.8862) = around 11 per cent.

We're saying two related things here. First: *the discount factor from the credit spread alone represents the chance of survival to a point in time without default*, and second: *the discount factor from the credit spread represents the riskiness of the investment*.

10.12   Recovery

Most of the time, after default, there *is* some value remaining in the company. Bonds that are sold at auction rarely go for zero – usually the credit event is (possibly) temporary – even a bankruptcy can result in administrators restructuring debt.

Credit derivatives involve, for this reason, the assumption of a *recovery rate*. This is a rate (typically chosen from actuarial tables based on credit ratings) which is plugged into the pricing models for CDS.

In the example above (where we calculated the default probability) – we can do a better job by assigning a recovery rate.

Typically, we can say:

$$\text{Value of a bond} = (\text{Probability of default} \times \text{Recovery value})$$
$$+ (\text{Probability of not defaulting}) \times 100$$

Subject to appropriate discounting, of course.

We've just said, however, that the probability of not defaulting (the probability of survival, that is) is measured by the discount factor on the credit-spread-alone curve (which we'll just call the spread curve, although it is a confusing name).

$$\text{Probability of not defaulting} = P_S = e^{-r_{credit}t}$$

Here we're calling this the probability of survival (P_s).

So if the credit spread is zero, then the term above becomes 1.0 exactly, which means there is a 100 per cent chance of survival, and a 0 per cent chance of default.

Obviously, the probability of default is $1 - P_s$. So the first equation becomes

$$\text{Value of a bond} = (1 - P_S) \times R + P_S \times 100$$

10.13   Probability analysis to value CDS

We can use this sort of analysis to get a value for the CDS. The approach is simply to value the protection leg on a periodic basis, say daily for instance.

- Calculate the probability of survival to the end of the prior period using the spread curve. (Call this PS_1)

- Calculate the probability of survival to the end of this period using the spread curve. (Call this PS_2)
- Calculate the probability, given that we've made it to this period, that we survive it (using the ratio of the above two results). (Call this $PS_a = PS_2/PS_1$)
- Use this to determine the probability that we default in this period (i.e. that we survive until the start of the period, then default) (This is $P_d = PS_1 \times (1 - PS_a)$)
- Multiply P_d by the payout (100 – Recovery, that is), then discount to the present.
- Sum for all periods to get an estimate of the value of the protection leg.

This approach, with more or less refinement, is the classic approach used by most institutions to value CDS. More advanced models are available, but this approach forms the basic reference point for CDS valuation.

The period used can be quite small (i.e. one business day), fairly large (one coupon period) or infinitesimally small even.

The same approach must be used to value the fee leg, of course. Even though there is no payout on default, the fee *is also not paid after default*, of course. So the above analysis must be repeated on the fee leg, but for each period, calculating simply the probability of surviving to the end.

It's also worth remembering that many CDS will require accrued fees on default – so the above calculations would be done, but substituting the accrued fee leg for the CDS payout, and adding the full fee at the end of the fee period, multiplied by the chance of survival to the end of that period. So for the fee leg with accrual:

- For each day: multiply the chance of default by the accrued fee and discount.
- At the end of each coupon period, multiply the chance of survival by the full fee.

10.14   Up-front fee versus conventional spread

Traditionally, credit default swaps were priced with a spread. That is to say, at the start of the contract (like in an interest rate swap), the buyer of protection would agree to pay a fee every 3 months in exchange for a payment on default. This fee was known as the *CDS spread*.

The spread was set so the initial price of the CDS was zero.

As mentioned earlier, the contract has changed (around 2009, in what was known as the 'CDS Big Bang'). Now there are two fixed coupons (usually 1% or 5%), and an up-front fee to make up for any market pricing differences.

This means there are two ways to price CDS contracts: a quoted up-front fee, or a spread. However, the spread used in quoting is now often what is called *conventional spread*, rather than 'the fee leg which would make the CDS value at par'.

What is conventional spread? Simply put, it is the single continuously compounded credit spread which explains the CDS value. Given a fixed coupon, the conventional spread will make the CDS value equal to the up-front fee.

Put another way: suppose we construct the credit spread curve with a single, flat credit spread across all time. If we use this credit spread to value both legs of the CDS, the total value will equal the up-front fee.

The conversion between the two measurement methods is not straightforward. The standard way to convert is:

- Build a CDS pricing model as outlined above – a method to price the protection leg and the fee leg, and find the difference between their present values.
- To convert from up-front fee to conventional spread:
  - Given the fixed coupon leg (1% or 5%) and a fixed up-front fee, search for a flat *credit spread* which would make the CDS legs equal in value to the up-front fee.
- To convert from conventional spread to up-front fee – reverse the process:
  - Find the credit spread which would make the conventional spread fee value a CDS to zero.

All of this functionality is available in the *standard CDS pricing model.*

10.15   The standard pricing model

In an effort to make CDS pricing more transparent, and more well understood by all parties, the market data and credit index firm Markit (www.markit.com) released the source code for JP Morgan's CDS pricing model (www.cdsmodel.com), and made a pricer based on the code available on their web site (www.markit.com/cds).

The main purpose of the standard model is to provide a standard way to convert between conventional spread and up-front price. The approach of the standard model is the same as the pricing approach outlined above, with a few variations.

The main features of the model are:

- It uses LIBOR as the risk-free interest rate curve. It builds a standard, single LIBOR curve for forward and discount purposes.

- It uses a continuous model for pricing defaults. That is, instead of finding the probability of default on each day (or in each week, or coupon period) and discounting it with the payoff, the model assumes a continuous default process. This is, actually, very simple to model. The assumption is (as stated above) that the credit spread curve represents the probability of default, so, for any period, for the protection leg, the value is:

$$PV_{period} = D_0 S_0 L \int_0^T (e^{-r_s t} r_s) e^{-r_L t} dt$$

Here, D_0 is the discount factor to the start of the period, S_0 is the chance of survival to the start of this period (i.e. the discount factor from the pure credit spread curve), L is the loss amount incurred on default (i.e. 1 − recovery), the first term in the integral represents the infinitesimal chance of survival to a moment in time, multiplied by the chance of default (i.e. the zero coupon rate from the spread curve) and the second term in the integral is just the discount on the LIBOR curve to the start of the period. In the standard model, the forward LIBOR rate is computed for each period (r_L) as the ratio of the discount factors to the start and end (i.e. $\ln(D_0/D_1)/(T_1 - T_0)$). The instantaneous chance of default (r_s) is computed in the same way: $\ln(S_0/S_1)/(T_1 - T_0)$.

When solved, the solution becomes:

$$PV_{period} = D_0 S_0 L \frac{r_s}{r_s + r_L} (1 - e^{-(r_s + r_L)t})$$

Which is easy to encode and evaluate for each period, and very quick as well.

- The fee leg approach is very similar, and the period-wise *PV* equation used is:

$$PV_{period} = FS_1 D_1 + D_0 S_0 r_s r_a \left(\frac{T_0 + \frac{1}{r_s + r_L}}{r_s + r_L} - \frac{T_1 + \frac{1}{r_s + r_L}}{r_s + r_L} \left(\frac{S_1 D_1}{S_0 D_0} \right) \right)$$

Not quite as concise, but still quite efficient to implement. Here *F* is the fee paid in that period. Note another new term here is r_a, which is the *accrual rate*. This assumes that on default, the fee payer pays accrued fees until the default time. The accrual rate is simply the annual fee (in %), multiplied by the day-count basis fraction for the period (e.g. 90 days/360), divided by the time in the period $(T_1 - T_0)$. (The final result must be multiplied by the notional of the trade, of course.)

- Note that if *no* accrued interest is paid on default, the formula is much simpler:

$$PV_{\text{period}} = FS_1D_1$$

- Since it assumes a continuous chance of default, the standard model does not truly model the actual financial process (whereby default can only happen on a business day), but goes one better by coming up with a simple, closed form solution.

10.16   Uses of the standard model

The standard model *could* be used for valuation, but it has a few drawbacks in the form in which it is supplied. The principal drawback is that it takes a LIBOR curve as its base curve over which the CDS is spread. This means that it assumes that LIBOR is truly 'risk-free', and assumption that, since 2007, it is dubious. (In addition, it discounts on LIBOR, which, given that most CDS are collateralized, is also dubious.)

That said, the standard model is quite useful in that it provides a *standard* way to find conventional spread given an up-front price (or vice versa).

CDS spread, therefore, is still quoted spread-over-LIBOR, even though we know that LIBOR is not a good proxy for a risk-free rate. The reason for this is simply convention.

11
Vanilla Options

11.1 A brief overview of calls and puts

The bulk of this book is not about derivatives – it's about the simple building blocks which are fundamental to working in a financial institution. We've been less concerned with esoteric deals which are much talked-about but little-traded. Vanilla options, however, are in a middle ground: while forming a small fraction of the total volume of a typical equities business, they are traded enough to justify proper discussion.

By 'vanilla', we mean simple options – either calls or puts.

The nature of a call or put option is very simple, as many people know. A call option is a trade where the purchaser of the option has the right (but not the obligation) to buy the stock in question, at the expiration date, at a given price. The 'given price' is the so-called strike price of the option. The buyer of course will *not* buy the stock if the market price is below the strike (they can buy it more cheaply on the market), but they *will* buy the stock if the market price is above the strike (they can resell immediately for a profit).

The put option is the opposite of a call – the option's buyer has the right to sell at a given price. The option buyer therefore will make money if the market price falls.

In both cases, the buyer of the option must pay a *premium*, which is the amount the seller deems the option to be worth. A couple of examples might help make this clearer.

Example 1: I buy a call option on XYZ Corporation, expiring in 1-month, with strike of $80. The current price of XYZ stock is $75. I pay a premium of $1.70.

Scenario 1: After 1-month, the stock price is $85. I exercise my option, and make a profit of $5 (the current price, minus the strike), less the $1.70 premium.

Scenario 2: After 1-month, the stock remains at $75. I don't exercise the option, and fail to make up the $1.70 premium.

Example 2: I sell a put option on XYZ Corporation, expiring in 1-month, with a strike of $70. The current price of the stock is, as above, $75. I collect $1.50 in premium for selling, or 'writing', this option.

Scenario 1: After 1-month, the stock price remains at $75. The option buyer will do nothing, and I keep $1.50 profit from the premium.

Scenario 2: After 1-month, the stock plunges to $65. The option's buyer exercises the option, and I must pay $5. My loss is $5, less the $1.50 premium, or £3.50.

For vanilla calls and puts, as with many option trades, there are two forms: cash settled and physically settled. In the cash settled version, the option buyer gets paid in cash (if the stock price is on the right side of the strike for them – i.e. 'in the money'). In the physically settled version, the option buyer must buy physical stock from the seller (usually via a clearing house).

In the case of the cash settled option, the documentation must (of course) mention where the market price will be sourced from. In the case of equities traded on exchanges, typically there will be a mechanism for determining the settlement price, usually by some end-of-day process designed to provide a closing price which is relatively immune to manipulation, and which represents the actual trading levels seen during the day.

Typically, options on single-stocks are physically settled, and options on stock indices (such as the FTSE 100, or S&P 500) are settled in cash.

Options can also be exercised in various ways.

In the example above, the person who bought the option could only exercise on the delivery date. This is a so-called *European* option. European options, because of their nature, are often cash settled, and are often on stock indices. The typical procedure on the day of expiration would be:

- The exchange publishes the closing price for the stock index.
- The buyer of the option notifies the seller of the intention to exercise (via one of several intermediaries, of course).
- The net cash settlement amount is credited to the buyer, being the difference between the strike and the closing price.

In the case of an American option, there is no publication of a closing price, and the notification of intention to exercise can happen at any time up to the exercise date. (The lack of requirement for a closing price being published means there is less pressure on the exchange to determine a fair level each day – which may be useful in the case of stocks where the volume may be lower than a stock index.) In American options, the buyer will notify the seller of the intention to exercise, and then the stock itself will change hands in exchange for the strike price.

We can enumerate, therefore, the parameters of a vanilla option quite simply:

- The underlying stock, or stock index, on which the trade is done.
- The strike price, on which the option buyer has the right to buy or sell at.
- The option type: physical or cash settled.
- The exercise type: is this an American- or European-style option?
- The exercise date: the date by which the option must be exercised.
- The settlement date: typically the date on which the cash or stock is settled after exercise.
- The premium: the amount which the buyer pays for the option.

There is one other parameter which comes into play, and is important with regard to how trades are managed: whether the trade is done on an exchange, or whether it is a bespoke 'over-the-counter' (OTC) transaction. Exchange-traded options form the bulk of the market by volume, but banks and financial institutions still make a good deal of money on OTC transactions. The advantage of OTC transactions is that they can be customized: they can be made on less common stocks, or they can be made on customized baskets of stocks, or stocks in different currencies, or with different exercise types and so on.

The dealing systems used to manage options portfolios differ as well. In the case of exchange-traded options, the specifications of each contract are exactly the same. So we can record the purchase or sale of thousands of options with just a few parameters for each: customer, strike, expiration and amount. In the case of OTC options, where the number of parameters is much greater, the systems used take a great many more inputs, and must report much more information as well.

11.2   An idiosyncratic introduction to option pricing

How much is an option worth? The pricing of options, using Black–Scholes and other approaches, has received a good deal of press, and there are thousands of books that go into great detail. It won't be worth our time, really, to provide a comprehensive guide to option pricing.

That said, it is important to provide some background as to why options have the price they do. A basic, intuitive explanation of how options are priced can be useful in practice.

Take as an example a call option on a stock:

Call option on XYZ corporation stock	
Expiration	1-month
Strike	105
Notional	$1000

If the price today is $100 per share, how much is the option worth?

The first thing to do is to realize that the easiest way to think about stocks is (of course) in price-per-share terms. So we must translate our dollar notional amount ($1000) into shares. In an OTC transaction, this is often done via a 'spot reference': a price-per-share used to translate the notional amount into shares.

With a spot reference of $100, the notional amount is 10 shares.

11.3 Volatility and price returns

The most important contributor to an option's value (especially one, like the example above, where the stock price is below the option's strike, out-of-the-money) is the volatility of the stock price. A stock whose value gyrates wildly is more likely to end up on the right side of the strike than one whose value plods along in a straight line.

In measuring volatility, we assume a few things. First, we assume that the *return* of the stock (not the price per se) is the thing which varies over time. That is to say, we assume that, in its gyrations, all other things being equal, a stock is just as likely to go up by 5 per cent as it is to go down by 5 per cent.

This assumption, that a stock is as likely to rise in value as it is to fall, is a direct result of the efficient market hypothesis. Briefly restated: if a stock were more likely to rise in value than to fall, everyone would buy it (of course). The fact that people are buying it would push the value up, eliminating any imbalance.

This is a theoretical assumption, of course, but it also makes sense practically. We know that the number of eager investors in the world is huge, and any asymmetry in expected returns would certainly be quickly pounced upon.

That said, of course, there is a caveat. Like all assets, stocks will rise in value over time. The efficient market hypothesis simply says that they cannot rise faster than other assets, such as the cash with which we finance them. Also, stock prices are subject to adjustments (such as dividend payments) which must be taken into account.

So, we can say that stocks jump up and down in value, by random amounts. If we assume that, each day (t), there is a random return X that affects a stock price, the price change will be:

$$\Delta S_t = S X_t + Srt$$

Here we have the change in the stock price being the sum of the random effect X and the effect of interest rates rt. Most people take this to the next level, and put it in continuous terms:

$$dS = S(\sigma\, dB + \mu dt)$$

Here μ is the replacement for the risk-free rate, B is a random return (a random variable with mean of 0 and standard deviation of 1) and σ is a measure of volatility.

Random effects are, by the nature of randomness, usually normally distributed processes. Any random effect, repeated over time long enough, will exhibit a normal distribution (thanks to the so-called Central Limit Theorem). If we assume our returns are random, then we can also assume that our returns are normally distributed.

The return on an investment, expressed as a continuously compounded rate, is e^{return}. In the case of our random variable, we assume that (thanks to the no-arbitrage assumption) the *mean* of the expected return is zero. That means, on average, we can't expect the random effect to have a preference of going up or down. In addition, we'll assume the standard deviation of our random variable is one. This is not true, of course, and to measure the size of the random effect, we re-introduce volatility.

The final result, if we wish to come up with an equation that satisfies the differential equation and describes how a stock price moves randomly over a given time period, is:

$$S = S_0 e^{X\sigma\sqrt{t}} e^{-\sigma^2 t/2} e^{\mu t}$$

The first part says: to get our random return, we take a normally distributed random variable (X), multiply it by our measure of volatility (σ) and the square root of the time over which we're measuring the process. Raise e to this power, multiply by the spot price of the stock and *voila*, we've randomized our stock price.

The final term $(e^{\mu t})$ is the interest rate return, which applies to every asset.

Of course, there is the other term as well: $e^{-\sigma^2 t/2}$. This is an 'adjustment', which falls out of the derivation of this solution via the application of *Itō's Lemma*, a classic of stochastic calculus. The key thing is that: we want it to be so that if we generate 10,000 random returns and take the *average*, we want it to closely equal the forward rate *without* volatility. This is a very important requirement: random simulation cannot introduce any bias upwards or downwards in a stock price. Without this adjustment, the mean of the distribution would be significantly too high.

This is all very well. What does this mean in terms of measuring the value of an option?

In the simple case, we could write a computer program or spreadsheet just to simulate the stock price changing. We generate some random numbers, assume a level for volatility and see what happens. This approach (called Monte Carlo simulation) is quite effective, and even surprisingly fast on modern computers. It's useful to see how such a simulation is done.

For our simulation, we'll simulate a call option on a stock. We'll make one further simplification first. Rather than simulating the so-called 'evolution' of the spot rate, with interest rate and dividend effects part of our equations, we'll simulate the random behaviour of the *forward* price of the stock.

Simulating the forward price is a very natural thing to do. The term in the equation above, $S_0 e^{\mu t}$, is another way of representing the forward price. Rather than having these terms in our simulation, we'll just simulate the forward price directly.

By simulating the forward price, it allows us to have one separate process for deriving the forward price, distinct from the process of simulating its random behaviour. This is very useful, since it's quite complex to derive the forward price of a stock at times, given the variety of dividend rules and funding rates which may apply. Once the forward price is derived, we can simply plug it into our simulation.

11.4 Random numbers

Doing Monte Carlo simulation requires first a source of random numbers. As mentioned above, these are not ordinary random numbers we're after: we require random numbers which are normally distributed.

Fortunately, most computer systems have mathematical libraries available with the necessary functions to do this. Using Excel, for instance, we can generate a random number between 0 and 1 using the RAND() function. We can turn this into a normally distributed random number by plugging it into the NORM.S.INV() function – the result is a random number with mean of zero, and standard deviation of one. (NORM.S.INV() is the so-called inverse cumulative normal function.)

In most financial computer systems which perform Monte Carlo simulation, the generation of random numbers is done by one of a number of sophisticated functions. There are, it turns out, two types of random numbers: pseudo-random numbers (which try to be truly random) and quasi-random numbers (which try to be evenly distributed). When pricing derivatives, it's often useful to use quasi-random numbers instead – in fact, simply using the numbers 0.001, 0.002, 0.003 and so on to get 999 'random' (and perfectly distributed) numbers is quite a good solution in many cases.

In Table 11.1, we'll assume the call option has forward price 100, and strike 110. The option expires in 1-month, and volatility is 40 per cent per year. We can now write out the terms of our stock price evolution.

If we continue this for, say, a few hundred rows, we will find that:

- The average of the random forward prices will converge on the actual forward price.
- The average of the payoffs will converge on the value of the option (without discounting).

This is interesting: *why* is this a representation of the value of the option? We can believe that if the prices evolve randomly, and the volatility is 40 per cent, then this has some validity, but why should we take the average price as the value? Surely there's no way to realize that value – there will, after all, be only one future path for the price.

If I sell a call option for $100, and in the end the stock price falls, I make $100 profit. If on the other hand the price rises, and the buyer makes $120, I suffer a $20 loss. How can I assure myself of a consistent level of profit no matter what happens to the stock price?

The answer lies in dynamic hedging.

Table 11.1   Example of using random numbers to simulate option payoffs

Random number 0...1	Inverse cum. normal (X)	$R = e^{X\sigma \sqrt{t} - \sigma^2 t/2}$	R times forward price	Payoff from call option
0.20636	−0.81912	0.903707	90.37071	0
0.323865	−0.45692	0.942304	94.23043	0
0.900736	1.285758	1.152346	115.2346	5.2346
0.920446	1.408077	1.168737	116.8737	6.87375
...	...	...	...	...

11.5 Dynamic hedging

Imagine that we've written a function to get the price for an option:

$$P = V(S, \sigma, r, t)$$

The function takes (at least) four parameters, an interest rate for discounting, the forward price S of the stock, the time-to-expiration of the option and the volatility of the stock price. We can measure the sensitivity of the price of the option to stock prices by taking its first derivative.

$$\frac{dP}{dS} = V'(S, \sigma, r, t)$$

This is called the delta of the option: the first derivative with respect to the underlying stock. (The first derivative with respect to the interest rate is called *rho*, with respect to the volatility is *vega*, with respect to time is *theta*.)

The delta is the most important number from a theoretical perspective. Suppose you sell an option: you may charge money for it. In order to try to ensure you don't lose any money, you hedge by purchasing (or selling) enough stock to make your entire position delta-neutral. In addition, each time the stock's price changes in the market, you re-compute the delta and re-hedge.

What happens if you pursue this strategy of continuously delta hedging?

One way to see is to look at the payoff profile for a European call option.

Figure 11.1 is a chart showing the value of an option (assuming 30% volatility) 1-month from expiration, and the same option at the time of expiration. The strike price is 100 and the price of the underlying stock is shown at various levels from 90 to 100.

We see that when the stock price is 90, the option has no value at expiration, but it has a slight value 1-month beforehand, based on the probability that it will rise over the next few weeks. When the stock price is 100, it also has no value at expiration, but the option value 1-month beforehand is even greater. As we go further and further to the right, the option value gets closer and closer to the value at expiration.

The first derivative of the option price with respect to the underlying stock price is simply the slope of this line. At expiration, if the stock price is over 100, we see the slope is 1. (This is the origin of the term *delta-one*:

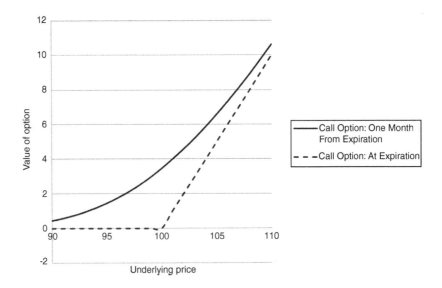

Figure 11.1   Payoff profiles for a call option

any financial product whose delta is always one. This means, also, that the delta-one financial products have no sensitivity to volatility.)

We can see that the delta changes with the stock price. When the underlying (forward) price is approximately equal to the strike, the delta is about 0.5 (or 50%, or just '50' as most people say). 50-Delta options are among the most actively traded. Higher strikes have lower deltas: 25-delta options are on the lower end, 10-delta even lower. Lower strikes (relative to spot) have higher deltas. In Figure 11.1, you see that when the spot is around 105 (higher than the lower strike of 100), the delta is around 75 per cent.

Delta hedging, then, simply means buying (or selling) as much stock as indicated by the delta to make your total position more-or-less neutral to price changes. If I sell a call option on 100 shares of XYZ Corporation, and the delta is 50, I should probably buy 50 shares today to make my position more-or-less neutral. Of course, if the price rises, the delta will go up, and I may be forced to buy more shares. If the price falls, the delta will go down, and I will be required to sell. (The change in delta with stock price is, of course, the *second* derivative of the value function, called *gamma*.)

Figure 11.2, the delta flattens out at the ends: going toward 100 at higher prices, and toward zero at lower prices.

Buying and selling delta over time will *theoretically* mean (if you've sold an option) you'll end up losing money – you will buy when the price is

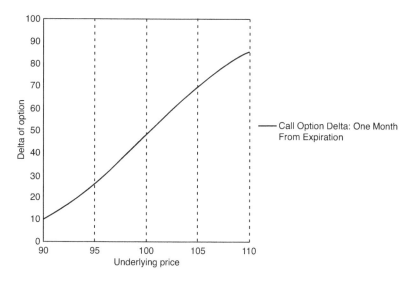

Figure 11.2   Delta profile of a call option

high, and sell when it's low. But if (and this is the crucial *if*) the stock's movements are an accurate reflection of the volatility you priced with, you'll end up losing exactly the premium charged for the option. That is to say, the theoretical option price is the same as the profit or loss on a stock portfolio used to hedge that same option.

The crucial thing to notice is that the so-called *realized volatility* must exactly match the volatility used to price the option. Realized volatility is, essentially, the *actual standard deviation* observed in the returns of the stock prices. If, for instance, you are looking at returns over a 1-month period, measured (say) daily, you would expect the daily returns to have standard deviation equal to:

$$\text{St. dev.} = \sigma \sqrt{t} \approx \sigma \sqrt{1/250}$$

(We're using 250-days-per year as a proxy. Most businesses will measure time in trading days per year, of which there are approximately 250. However, many will also allocate weekends credit for being 'partial days', depending on your point of view. Events occur over weekends which affect the price of stocks – just not as many events as happen on weekdays.)

How often does the realized volatility match the volatility used to sell an option? Not often, really, especially considering that trading does not happen continuously in the real-world. Fortunately, most dealers in options will trade hundreds of options (thus averaging out any error), and they hedge with other tools as well, such as buying and selling index options.

11.6 Direct integration

The Monte Carlo method described earlier would never be used in the real-world to price such a simple option – but these methods are used to price more complicated payoffs, when there's no simple formula. However, in cases where (as in a European option) we only care about the price at expiration, there's a simpler approach: direct integration.

The direct integration approach is essentially the same as Monte Carlo using quasi-random variables. The steps are:

- Decide on how many steps to use (say, 1,000): generate evenly spaced numbers from 0 to 1 in 1,000 steps.
- For each so-called random number, generate a final stock price and option payoff.
- The final value is the sum of the option payoffs, divided by 1,000.

This is essentially the same as drawing a graph of the payoff, and integrating the area under the graph by hand. By using this simple formula, we're essentially dividing the area under the graph into a number of very small rectangles. (To improve efficiency, we could make them into trapezoids.) (Doing this properly requires a bit of fiddling at the edges: the numbers chosen between 0 and 1 might not include zero itself, but should start at $1/2d$, where d is the spacing between the points.)

11.7 Black–Scholes

The famous Black–Scholes equation is really only used in a few situations: pricing European equity options. The equation is, in effect, a closed-form solution for the Monte Carlo simulation described earlier. Most option pricing systems will use the formula whenever possible, instead of using 'numerical solutions' such as Monte Carlo, or other solutions.

The Black–Scholes equation for the value of a European call option, which expires at time t in the future, is as follows:

$$\text{Let } d_1 = \frac{\ln\left(\frac{S}{K}\right) + \frac{\sigma^2}{2}t}{\sigma\sqrt{t}} \quad \text{and} \quad \text{let } d_2 = d_1 - \sigma\sqrt{t}$$

Then:

$$C(S,t,K) = (N(d_1)S - N(d_2)K)D_t$$

where S is the *forward* price of the stock in question, K is the strike of the option, σ is the volatility, t is the time (measured in year-fractions typically) until expiration and D_t is the discount factor from now until expiration. The function $N(.)$ is the *cumulative normal distribution function* with mean of zero and standard deviation of 1.0. (In Excel, $N()$ is NORM.S.DIST(), with second parameter *true*.)

(This is a slightly different notation than the classic formulation because we're using forward prices. As mentioned, most implementations will separate the forward price calculation from the option calculation, so this makes sense.)

The value of a put option is similar:

$$P(S,t,K) = (-N(-d_1)S + N(-d_2)K)D_t$$

11.8   Put-call parity

Another way to write the value of a put option is:

$$P(S,t,K) = C(S,t,K) + (K - S)D_t$$

This is based on the relationship:

$$(S - K)D_t = C(S,t,K) - P(S,t,K)$$

This says basically: imagine you have purchased a call option at strike K, and *sold* a put option at the same strike. If the price of the stock ends above the strike, you make money $(S - K)$. If it ends below the strike, you lose $(S - K)$. So you can replace the whole thing with the value of a simple forward contract at strike K: $(S \ K)D_t$.

11.9   Black–Scholes and delta

Having the Black–Scholes equation available gives us a handy way to compute delta (if, that is, we know the volatility). Suppose we wish to find the delta of a call option, Δ_{call} – all we must do is find the first derivative with respect to the forward stock price (for forward delta). If we ignore the terms inside the $N()$ function, this turns out to be:

$$\frac{dC(S,t,K)}{dS} = \Delta_{\text{call}} = N(d_1)D_t$$

And similarly:

$$\frac{dP(S,t,K)}{dS} = \Delta_{\text{put}} = -N(-d_1)D_t$$

What appears to be a rather naïve approach to differentiation does, in fact, achieve the correct result, since the terms inside the $N()$ will cancel out eventually when the full chain-rule method is applied.

If we write out the formula in full for the call delta, we can also derive a (very handy) formula for deriving the *strike* from a given delta. We'll see later on that often options are quoted in terms of delta, and finding the strike is very important.

Since:

$$\Delta_{\text{call}} = N\left(\frac{\ln\left(\frac{S}{K}\right) + \frac{\sigma^2}{2}t}{\sigma\sqrt{t}}\right)D_t$$

We can say (just by re-arranging):

$$K = Se^{\left(-N^{-1}\left(\frac{\Delta_{\text{call}}}{D_t}\right)\sigma\sqrt{t} + \frac{\sigma^2}{2}t\right)}$$

This formula for strike (given delta) relies on the *inverse* cumulative normal distribution – here called N^{-1} – which is also readily available in many math libraries (and of course Excel, where it is NORM.S.INV).

11.10   American options

As mentioned earlier, Black–Scholes is useful for European options, which generally are written on stock indices, or available OTC from brokers and banks. Options on individual stocks are usually American flavoured: that is to say, the holder of the option has the right to exercise any time from purchase until expiration.

When is early exercise of the option advantageous? Well, there aren't very many situations, in reality, where early exercise makes sense, unless you have some prior knowledge of the stock price's movements in the future. In most cases, since the general assumed trend of the stock price is upwards (due to the assumption that the forward price rises at the risk-free rate), holding on to an option is preferable to exercising it. This means, that in most cases, the price of an American option will be the same as that of a European option.

One exception to the rule against early exercise is when a dividend is anticipated. In this case, if the option is in-the-money, early exercise just prior to the dividend will allow you to purchase the stock at a price which is cheaper on a relative basis than it would be after the dividend. Imagine the following scenario (which removes all volatility – to make it easy to see what's happening).

Time	Stock price (no volatility)	Option value if exercised (Strike = 100)
Purchase	105	5
Week 1	105.01	5.01
Week 2 (pre-dividend)	105.02	5.02
Week 3 (dividend of 2.0 paid)	103.03	3.03
Week 4 (expiration)	103.04	3.04

This makes it pretty clear that the best time to exercise is Week 2: just prior to dividend payment.

11.11 An introduction to volatility

We mentioned volatility earlier – basically as an *annualized* measure of the standard deviation of the returns. Like an annualized interest rate, you must first multiply by some measure of time to get the actual standard deviation.

Also interesting is the *variance* of returns. In statistical terms, variance is simply the square of the standard deviation. In finance we have the following relations:

Volatility (annualized)	σ
Standard deviations of returns over time t (measured in years)	$\sigma\sqrt{t}$
Variance	$\sigma^2 t$

Volatility, it should be mentioned, is mostly used as both an *input to and output from pricing equations.* It is rarely directly measured to price options. (That said, it can be directly measured on a historic basis, which is useful to benchmark hedge effectiveness, for instance.)

In the market, options on, say, a stock index are very liquid. At a given strike level, it will be possible to view an accurate bid and offer price for a European option. Generally, practitioners use this strike to infer a volatility for the option: *if the option costs this much – volatility must be x per cent.* As mentioned in previous chapters, it is quite simple to reverse the volatility out of the option pricing equation by using Newton–Raphson or some similar technique.

Typically, derivatives trading desks will not deal in prices at all. Rather, they will simply quote bid and offer volatilities – it will be up to the system (or account representative) at the final point of sale to fill in all the exact strike levels and prices.

How does this process work? The first thing to understand is the concept of 'at-the-money'.

An at-the-money (ATM) option can be one of several things:

- An option whose strike is the forward price.
- An option whose delta is 50 per cent.
- An option whose strike is such that the price of a call = the price of a put

The first and last definitions are the same – because of put-call parity, when the price of a call matches the price of a put, then the strike is the forward price. The definition in terms of delta is slightly different sometimes, given differences in how delta is measured.

Delta, as mentioned before, is the first derivative of price with respect to the underlying. But what is the underlying in this case? Is it the forward price of the stock? If so, then we are measuring *forward delta.* Is it the cash price of the stock? If so, we are measuring *spot delta.* The measurement we use is not important, but whatever one it is, we should be careful to be consistent across systems. (Forward and spot delta differ, obviously, by the ratio of the forward to spot price.) In equity options, delta is almost always spot delta. As we will see, FX options vary depending on market and time-to-expiration.

Volatility will also vary, in the market, based on a number of things. (Notice how, for clarity, we're switching from talking about the price of an option, to talking about the volatility.)

Options with different expirations will typically have different volatilities. Options with expirations of 1-week, 2-weeks, 1-month, 2-months or 3-months will all have different volatilities quoted.

Options with different strikes will also have different volatilities. (The reason for this is the subject of much debate, but comes down in the end to supply and demand, as most things do.) Generally speaking, volatilities far from the ATM point are higher than those with close to 50 per cent volatility – this effect is called the *smile*, due to the fact that the volatility curve has an upward smile-shape. In addition, the volatility curve will often be higher at higher strikes, falling off for lower strikes. This is called *skew*.

Options traded on exchanges will typically be quoted with fixed strikes. For instance, Table 11.2 shows three expiration dates for options on the FTSE 100. For each expiration date, there are a wide range of strikes for both call and put options, of which we're only showing a few.

It's pretty easy to see the evidence of both smile and skew in these volatilities: the ones at the more extreme strikes are higher than in the middle – yet even so, the higher strikes are generally higher than the lower strikes (see Table 11.3).

We can see that the shape of the curve changes, as well, as the time until expiration lengthens. The longer dated options above seem to have a differently shaped curve – but it is hard to tell for several reasons.

One reason it is hard to make sense of these curves is that we don't have an idea where the ATM point is. While the forward value of the

Table 11.2   FTSE 100 call options (example as quoted on NYSE Euronext)

Strike	Price	Implied volatility (%)
5350	399.5	29.69
5650	159.5	14.68
5700	127.5	14.12
5750	99.5	13.65
5800	76	13.29
5850	56	12.92
6200	4	18.01

Table 11.3   Call options: 84 days to expiration (forward value = 5702)

Strike	Price	Implied volatility (%)
4700	1027	52.70
5300	470.5	20.05
5400	386.5	18.83
5500	308	17.71
5600	236	16.66
5700	172.5	15.70
6100	27	17.15

index is 'known' (as printed in Table 11.3), in fact the forward is just an assumption.

The level of the forward in this case is based on two assumptions, in fact: the level of the risk-free rate, and the level of dividends received from the index. While the risk-free rate is most likely based on OIS, which is the most common linkage to funding costs, the level of dividends is a matter of some speculation. On a large index like the FTSE, dividends are published well in advance, but even then practitioners often have their own views as to what levels will be realized.

In the case of Tables 11.2 and 11.3, we've simply assumed a dividend level for the index to make the example work. Calculating the forward level in a real-world situation would involve:

- Finding the spot level of the index (or stock).
- In the case of discrete dividends, grow the spot level to each dividend date (using a zero-coupon rate derived from the yield curve), subtract the dividend amount and repeat until expiration.
- In the case of a continuous dividend yield, simply subtract the yield from the zero-coupon rate derived from the yield curve to get a net rate to apply to maturity. The net rate may be negative in some cases, meaning the stock or index forward price will get smaller over time.

These approaches are typical, and can be used to find a forward price which can then be plugged in to the Black–Scholes equation to get an option value. The volatilities in Table 11.3 were found by iteration – finding the volatility which gave the correct price. (In Excel, this is the 'goal seek' function and, along with Black–Scholes, can be implemented in just a few cells. Unfortunately, goal-seek is not a proper Excel function, so some macro programming is needed to automate spreadsheet cell population.)

The fact that both volatility and dividends are, to some extent, 'unknown' makes option pricing tricky. It becomes easier if we pretend to be certain about dividends, but this is not always a realistic assumption.

11.12   Quoting in delta terms

One other problem with Table 11.3 is that it is statically linked to strikes. This is a feature of exchange-traded options: since each option is a contract which persists over many days, and can be bought and sold at any time, it would be impossible to have an option be quoted in terms of delta. A 50 per cent delta call would have a strike that varied every second! This would not do for a static options contract.

Dealers in options, however, will quote OTC trades in delta terms by preference. When the option is sold, the strike will be decided, but up until that point it can be referred to as simply a '50-delta call' or '25-delta put' or whatever is appropriate.

Quoting in delta terms makes the data-management part of trading options much simpler. A 50-delta option will usually have a stable volatility, and not change too much as the level of the index changes.

Table 11.4 fills in the delta for the longer dated call options.[1] We can then graph volatility against strike in two ways (see Figures 11.3 and 11.4).

These figures are not only pretty – they serve a useful purpose. They can help us visualize how we might price an option. The key thing to recognize is that when the spot price of the stock changes, ALL the option prices will change too. If the spot price is 100, and moves to 105, the price of a call option with strike 100 will change drastically – it will move from being more-or-less ATM, to being very far in-the-money.

Table 11.4   Call options: 84 days to expiration

Strike	Price	Implied volatility (%)	Delta (%)
5000	740.5	23.86	86
5300	470.5	20.05	76
5400	386.5	18.83	71
5500	308	17.71	65
5600	236	16.66	57
5700	172.5	15.70	49
6100	27	17.15	11

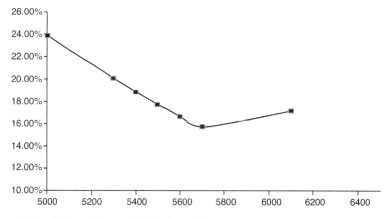

Figure 11.3   Call option, volatility-by-strike

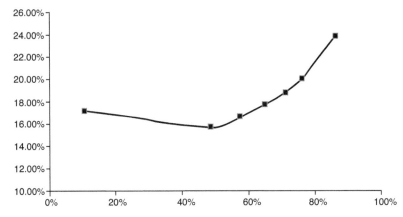

Figure 11.4 Call option, volatility-by-delta

However, no matter how the spot price moves, many practitioners assume that the volatility of an ATM option doesn't necessarily change very much. Under this formulation, the volatility-by-delta chart would be a far more stable representation of delta.

11.13   Sticky strike versus sticky delta

The difference between these two charts represents the difference between two views of volatility: the sticky strike view and the sticky delta view.

Sticky strike means that, as the underlying stock price changes, we should still be able to look up the appropriate volatility for an option on the 'Volatility-by-Strike' chart. The volatility for an option with strike 5600 should be around 16.66 per cent, regardless of the level of spot price (within reason).

Sticky delta means that, as the underlying stock price changes, we should be able to look up the appropriate volatility for an option on the 'Volatility-by-Delta' chart. The volatility for an option with delta 49 per cent should be 15.7 per cent. This means, of course, that as the spot changes, the volatility of an option with a fixed strike will change.

Which view one takes may well be dictated by the risk-management philosophy, but in a banking setting the sticky strike approach seems to be the most common, since it makes no assumptions about the past or future evolution of stock or index prices.

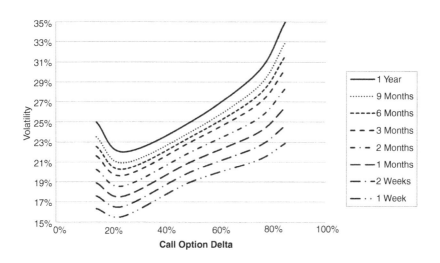

Figure 11.5 Volatility-by-delta for a variety of maturities

11.14 Interpolating volatilities

If we fill in the volatility-by-delta chart for a range of different option maturities, we might get something like this.

Figure 11.5 shows how, using a 'sticky delta' approach, we can interpolate a volatility for any option, at any maturity (under 1 year) and at any reasonable strike.

Interpolating a volatility is not completely straightforward, however. Once we have a chart like the one above (arrived at, perhaps, by using market prices for options, and finding their implied volatilities) we must still somehow be able to use it.

Suppose we want to price an option with strike 110, on an index with spot price level 100. The most straightforward procedure would be:

- Compute the delta of the option using ATM volatilities (assuming 50-delta, that is).
- Use this delta to find a new volatility, using the delta-to-volatility graph.
- Re-compute delta with the new volatility.
- Repeat until the volatility stabilizes to a required degree (e.g. no change beyond 0.001%).

This may seem a bit ad hoc, but given the shape of most volatility surfaces stability is usually achieved very quickly.

11.15 Smoothing the volatility surface

That said, the procedure above means that we really should use a smooth interpolation function for our volatility curve. One could use any number of smoothing techniques, such as splines, or more complex parameterizations. Many methods of smoothing volatility curves are found in practice. (For a description of how to fit with splines, see Chapter 4 on splines in yield curves. The approach is very general, and can be used in any case where fitting is required.)

One method (of medium complexity) that's caught on a bit is the so-called *kernel interpolation*. This is really a simple approach that allows us to fit to the data points, which gives us a smooth curve between points, no discontinuities, and allows us to extrapolate a bit beyond the end data points.

A simple formulation of this method can be written by defining a few functions. These functions suppose that we have a set of (say 5) volatilities, each measured for a given delta. So σ_2, in this case, would be the volatility corresponding to δ_2, the second delta in our series. We can define:

$$K(x) = e^{\frac{-x^2}{2\lambda^2}}$$

Here λ represents a *smoothing parameter*. (A typical value will range between 25% and 75%.) We can also set:

$$P(x) = \sum_{i=1}^{5} K(x - \delta_i)$$

We can say that the volatility at a given delta can be represented by:

$$\text{Vol}(\delta) = \frac{a_1 K(\delta - \delta_1)}{P(\delta)} + \frac{a_2 K(\delta - \delta_2)}{P(\delta)} + \frac{a_3 K(\delta - \delta_3)}{P(\delta)}$$
$$+ \frac{a_4 K(\delta - \delta_4)}{P(\delta)} + \frac{a_5 K(\delta - \delta_5)}{P(\delta)}$$

Since we can set:

$$\text{Vol}(\delta_1) = \sigma_1, \ \text{Vol}(\delta_2) = \sigma_2, \text{ etc.}$$

This leaves us with five equations in five unknowns: the weighting parameters a. Solving for these gives us a function which fits all the points, is

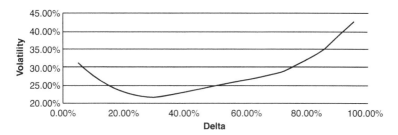

Figure 11.6   Option volatility smoothed with Kernel interpolation (λ = 25%)

smooth and allows us to extrapolate. Figure 11.6 shows volatilities extending below the lowest delta (15%) and above the highest (85%).

Solving systems of equations

Most of us have solved systems of linear equations, but it's worth reviewing some simple tools that are out there.

If we have n equations with n unknowns, we can usually write them as:

$$a_1 X_{1,1} + a_2 X_{1,2} + \cdots + a_n X_{1,n} = b_1$$
$$a_1 X_{2,1} + a_2 X_{2,2} + \cdots + a_n X_{2,n} = b_2$$

$$\vdots$$

$$a_1 X_{n,1} + a_2 X_{n,2} + \cdots + a_n X_{n,n} = b_n$$

Here, the X's are the coefficients for the equations (which we know) and the a's are the unknown parameters we're trying to solve for. The b's represent the solutions to each equation. (In the example in the text (with Kernel interpolation), each $X_{i,j}$ would be $\dfrac{K\left(\delta_j - \delta_i\right)}{P(\delta)}$.)

The first step in solving this is to make the X's into a n by n matrix, and the b's into a vector. The equation then becomes:

$$Xa = b$$

where X is a matrix, and a and b are both vectors. If we know how to take the *inverse* of a matrix (not a completely simple task by hand, but easy with a computer), we can say:

$$a = X^{-1}b$$

All we must do is invert matrix X, multiply by vector b and our solution falls out. In Excel, the matrix inversion function is *MINVERSE*, and the function to multiply a matrix by a vector (or other matrix) is *MMULT*. So, one simply writes out the matrix (as a square range of cells, say a1:e5), the vector (as a column of cells, say f1:f5) and then one creates a column of cells with the formula '=mmult (minverse(a1:e5),f1:f5)' (being sure to highlight the range, and hit Ctrl-Shift-Enter after typing the formula).

11.16 Interpolating in the time dimension

Once we have chosen a suitable volatility based on delta (or strike), we may also need to adjust it based on time-to-expiration. If we wish to value an option which expires in 3 weeks, for instance, but the market only quotes options expiring in 2-weeks or 1-month, what do we do?

The answer, typically, is to do *linear interpolation of variance*. This means, in simple terms:

- Determine the time-to-expiration (T) of the quoted options on each side of your option (with lesser maturity, and greater maturity) expressed in years.
- Compute the variance, equal to $\sigma^2 T$ for each quoted option.
- Compute the volatility to time t (between times T_1 and T_2) as

$$\sqrt{\frac{\sigma_1^2 T_1 + ((t - T_1)/(T_2 - T_1))(\sigma_2^2 T_2 - \sigma_1^2 T_1)}{t}}$$

which is just the formula for linear interpolation, applied to the formula for variance.

One issue with interpolating volatility in time is due to the fact that time is not really uniform. What that means is simply that some time periods (like weekends) have little volatility (because no trading is occurring) while other time periods (like days on which major economic announcements are made) may have *extra* volatility.

The way around this problem is to give each day a certain weight.

So, for instance, we could give each day on which the stock exchange is open a weight of 1.0, and each day it is closed a weight of 0.25. Days on which important announcements are made could get extra weight (1.5, for instance, for non-farm payrolls day). The actual weightings used vary among practitioners, but are usually of a similar order of magnitude.

If this approach is taken, we can replace the T terms in the equation above with the 'business day weighted time':

$$T \text{ goes form } \frac{\text{Calendar days}}{365} \text{ to } \frac{\sum(\text{Day} - \text{Weights in period})}{\sum(\text{Day} - \text{Weights in typical year})}$$

The denominator in these formulas is arbitrary (it can be anything), but choosing the day-weights in a typical year makes it easy to see at a glance how long a given period is. We'll know that 0.25 is about 3 months in both normal and day-weighted terms.

Does this day-weighting make a difference? Indeed, in options of maturity less than 1 year it can make a difference in the second order. For instance, if volatility between two listed options 1-month apart jumps by 10 per cent, interpolation differences between different dates can be up to 0.1 per cent.

11.17 Problems with volatility surfaces

Volatility surfaces can exhibit a number of problems, if the interpolation methods are not working as expected, or if the input volatilities are not right.

The first, and largest, problem is if the options priced with the volatility function you've put together don't behave in a sensible way. For instance, we know that:

- A call option with a lower strike is worth more than one with a higher strike.
- A put option with a lower strike is worth less than one with a higher strike.
- Future levels of volatility implied by the surface should be more than zero.

It's good practice to validate volatility surfaces after construction. This can be done simply by checking volatilities at different strikes to ensure they meet the first two criteria.

The third criteria is more tricky. We have not touched (yet) upon the concept of forward volatility explicitly. The idea can be expressed thus: if we know (for instance) the volatility of a 3-month option, and the volatility of a 6-month option, we should be able to find the expected volatility of an option, 3 months long, which starts in 3 months.

11.18 Forward volatility – the standard approach

Forward volatility is a useful concept in the valuation of more exotic options, and even some not so exotic ones. For instance, American options are often valued using models that depend on a way of calculating forward volatility. Calculation of forward volatility is quite simple, when using the standard approach.

If we know the volatility to time T_1 in the future, and also to later time T_1, and we wish to find the expected level of volatility at time T_1 up to time T_2, we can remember the simple equation:

$$\sigma_1^2 T_1 + \sigma_f^2 (T_2 - T_1) = \sigma_2^2 T_2$$

This says, basically, that the variances all add together: the variance to time T_1 plus the variance between T_1 and T_2 equals the variance to time T_2.

So this gives us another simple check on our volatility surface as well: the variance to time T_1 should never be greater than the variance to a later time – otherwise the intermediate variance will be negative, and the volatility will be imaginary. Not a realistic outcome!

We can thus simply compute the forward volatility as:

$$\sigma_f = \sqrt{\frac{\sigma_2^2 T_2 - \sigma_1^2 T_1}{T_2 - T_1}}$$

This formula is useful for two reasons. The first, as mentioned, is to check that the levels of volatility we've collected from the market are reasonable. The simplest and most useful check is to ensure that the levels of volatility for ATM options make sense: if we assume that the volatilities for these options are as recorded, will we be able to generate forward volatilities between each of them?

The second reason is that, in some cases, we will need to use the forward volatilities to calculate the price of options. (The simplest case where we use them is in pricing American options, as described in a later section.)

So far, we've built the volatility surface to deal with one type of option: European options. This means that we simply build the surface as a means to interpolate a single number for a single option. We don't care about using the surface for more complex options which may need more information from the surface.

11.19   More exotic options and the volatility surface

An example of a more exotic option is a so-called *knock-out* option. This is an option which automatically expires (or disappears) if the stock price goes above or below a given knock-out level. They come in many flavours, and with many features (such as having the knock-out provision only apply within a certain 'window' of time, or having it apply only at expiration). The simplest, however, is where the knock-out feature applies over the life of the option, and can happen at any time of day.

Exotic options such as this will depend on the movement of the stock during the life of the option. So modellers must simulate (using, for instance, a Monte Carlo technique broken down into daily steps) the movement of the stock price over the life of the option (Figure 11.7). If we do this, however, what volatility do we use?

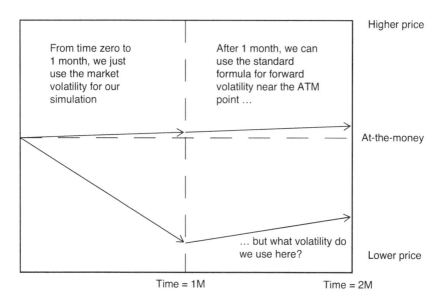

Figure 11.7 An example using two-step Monte Carlo

Note: Modelling a price using Monte Carlo in two steps. Each of the sets of arrows represents a single 'simulation' run of our model. We can simulate the stock price movement to 1-month quite simply (using the 1-month ATM volatility.) But what do we do between 1 and 2 months? We need a more complex model to guide us.

The easiest way to model an exotic option with Monte Carlo techniques is to simply choose the volatility at each point in time based on the ATM volatilities. If we are simulating the stock price moving from day 10 to day 11, we would calculate the forward volatility between days 10 and 11 based on the ATM volatilities. This is easy, and makes creating a model very straightforward. However, it's obviously wrong as well, since if we're simulating an option whose strike is not ATM, we're choosing the wrong levels of volatility.

That said, many practitioners still use ATM volatilities to model exotic options for the reason that any other approach is difficult to explain and implement. Typically, an adjustment will be made to the final price to account for the mismatch in volatilities used.

A second common approach is to come up with a model for getting volatilities at each point in the future that is consistent with the volatility surface as seen in the market. The models most often seen are the so-called *local-volatility* models. These models allow one to get forward volatilities which match exactly the volatility surface. If you price a knock-out option using a local-volatility model, you won't need to adjust the result to match the market volatilities.

Local-volatility models have drawbacks, however. They are complex to implement and force practitioners to make a great many assumptions about the shape of the interpolation between points before proceeding. Any mistakes are rewarded with unrealistic levels of local-volatility, resulting in poor hedging performance. The model may give a price which is consistent – but which does not reflect the real-world dynamics of prices. Nevertheless, because the approach is so general, and solves the problems neatly, local-volatility does have some adherents.

Another popular approach is embodied by the so-called *stochastic volatility* models. Stochastic volatility assumes that the forward volatility is in fact a random variable (usually the *instantaneous* forward volatility, between one instant and the next so to speak). By making this assumption, and making the volatility dependent on the price level as well as time, one can match a certain amount of the volatility surface. Stochastic volatility is, in fact, a way of coming up with a general model which will reproduce the volatility surface.

Stochastic volatility, however, doesn't reproduce the entire volatility surface very well. Since the model has only a few parameters, and the volatility surface is complex and large, it would be impossible to match the whole thing. A stochastic volatility model can't match prices in the market as well as a local-volatility model.

Also popular lately are the so-called *mixed models*, which model the asset price dynamics as a mixture of local and stochastic volatility. The underlying model is based on stochastic volatility, and then a local-volatility layer is 'mixed in' (usually with a parametric mixing weight of some sort). This helps the pricing and hedging performance, and allows the model to come much closer to matching the smile structure.

All of these approaches are interesting, and illustrate just how technical option pricing and hedging can become once one heads away from vanilla options. In fact, the pricing of even the simplest exotic, such as a knock-out call option, can be fraught with peril. Years ago, when option dealing was a new venture, this was not such a concern, because the profit on each option sold was great enough to paper over any cracks in the model structure. Today, however, exactitude is required in all things, and choosing the wrong model can lead to uncomfortable questions being asked by those examining the positions.

11.20 Pricing American options

One option type that's neither exotic nor completely vanilla is the *American* option. These are often sold on single-stocks: the default option flavour, in fact, for single-stock options is American. This allows the option buyer to exercise at any point before maturity (as opposed to the European option, which is exercisable only at maturity). If you, as the buyer, know that a dividend is about to be paid on the stock, for instance, then you have what amounts to prior knowledge that the stock price will soon decline, and you'll be wise to exercise if the option is in-the-money.

American options can be priced in a number of ways. One of the most widely used methods is the so-called *PDE* method, which explicitly solves the differential equations involved. PDE methods typically involve extensive development by specialized quant teams, but the end result can be a general framework, useful for pricing a wide variety of options from simple to more exotic. PDE methods however are expensive – they take quite a lot of computing power to come to a solution, and when thousands of positions are being revalued multiple times, this can be overkill.

Another related family of methods are the *tree* family of models. The classic model in this family is the *binomial tree*. The basic intuition behind the binomial tree pricing model is: if we can easily simulate all possible stock prices in the future – we can also see what decisions we would make under various scenarios. If we write out the scenarios and work *backwards*, we can figure out what the option value will be based on probabilities (just like we did with Monte Carlo).

There are many ways to generate the probability distribution we use. One of the conceptually simplest is as follows:

- Divide the time between today and the option expiration into a large number of time-steps (say 100 or more). For the binomial tree, the time-steps must be evenly spaced (although we'll see that other, related models don't have this restriction).
- We derive a *jump magnitude*, representing a multiplicative step upwards or downwards in the stock price which is equal to the *expected* jump size over each time-step given the level of volatility. Ignoring interest rates and dividends, the jump size for an upward jump would be $e^{\sigma\sqrt{t}-\sigma^2 t}$, where t is the time interval between one step and the next. The size of a downward jump is $e^{-\sigma\sqrt{t}-\sigma^2 t}$.
- We create, at the last time-step, a set of levels representing each combination of up and down-jumps. If there are n time-steps, there would be n possible final prices, representing (from biggest to smallest) n up-jumps, $(n - 1)$ up-jumps and one down-jump, $(n - 2)$ up-jumps and two down-jumps, etc. If we have the starting level set at 1.0, the ending levels might range from (say) 2.0 to 0.5.
- For each of the final levels, we multiply by the forward stock price at that point. We use this price to generate the payoff from the option at maturity (which may be zero if on the wrong side of the strike).

- Now, working backwards to the time-step beforehand: for each level at this new time-step:
  - We take the forward stock price at that point and multiply by the level from our tree.
  - We evaluate the option value if we were to exercise *at that time.*
  - We evaluate the average of the option values from the two next points in time (properly discounted, of course).
  - Comparing these two, we take whichever is the greatest and record it as the value at this point.
- We repeat the process, stepping back in time, until we reach the beginning. We can then estimate the value of the option as a whole as the value recorded at the starting price point, at the first time-step.

An example of how this works is shown in Figure 11.8, in a three-step example.

Here we see the process in action: from the volatility and the time-step size, we compute the size of the jumps. Then, step-by-step, we build the tree of jumps by compounding one jump upon the next.

To get the stock price levels for each leaf (or node) in our tree, we simply multiply the compounded jump levels by the forward stock price at each point. We then compute the value of exercising the option at each node, and the value of *not* exercising (equal to the average of the option value of each of the subsequent nodes, times a discount factor). The value of the option at each node is then equal to the greater of these two values: to exercise or not to exercise.

In Figure 11.8, the shaded box shows a case where it's optimal to exercise *early.* You can see this is caused by two things: the option is in-the-money in the shaded box (a stock price of 115.03, greater than the strike of 100), and the underlying forward stock price is *declining.*

It's worth noticing that this is not unusual. In an age of low interest rates, and reasonable levels of dividends, many stock indices will have

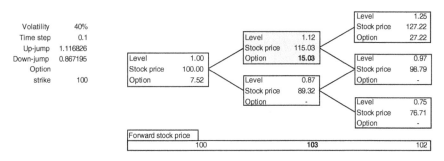

Figure 11.8   Using a binomial tree

forward values lower than today's settlement price. This means that from a traditional financial viewpoint, it will always be optimal to exercise American options as soon as they are in-the-money.

11.21 Trinomial trees

A simple extension to binomial trees can be added to account for differing levels of volatility over time (as well as variable time-steps). The same algorithm is used, with the following additions:

- Over each time-step, we compute the *forward volatility* for that time period (see previous section on how to do this). (Forward volatility is almost always computed from ATM volatilities, making this a contentious adjustment, perhaps not even a good idea!)
- We compute, over all time-steps, the maximum variance per time-step (call this V). That is to say, for each time-step we compute $\sigma^2 t$, and we find the maximum level for this value. Given that now we are allowing time-steps to be irregular (if desired), so t may vary, and that the forward volatility may vary, this value may also vary quite a bit.
- We compute the jump size based on V: up-jumps are $e^{\sqrt{V} - \sigma^2 t}$ and down-jumps are $e^{-\sqrt{V} - \sigma^2 t}$. Additionally, we add a *third* possibility : having no jump at all. This means that at each node, the value of the future option is now the *weighted average* of the up, middle and down jumps from the next time-step.
- We set the probability of an up-jump (or down-jump) to be level of the variance $\sigma^2 t$ between this time-step and the next, divided by 2*V. (Normally, in the binomial case, we see that this is just ½. Here, however, it can be less than that.) The probability of taking the middle route (having no jump at all) is then (1 – (up-jump probability + down-jump probability)).

Trinomial trees allow us more freedom in assigning a structure to the volatility curve, and having an irregular date structure. However, they are quite bad at representing any form of volatility surface. One can add adjustments, for instance, by using a trinomial tree to price a European option as well, then adjusting the final value by the difference between the European option with the correct strike-adjusted volatility. This is not a huge advantage over simply using the binomial model, however, with a single volatility number.

In the end, most practitioners are satisfied with a model (such as the binomial tree) which gives some reasonable performance, while perhaps lacking total awareness of the volatility surface. The problems with modelling the whole volatility surface remain: it's hard to have a solution which is simple, allows quick results on large portfolios and gives good hedging performance.

Further reading

Avellaneda, M. (n.d.) 'Trinomial Trees and Finite-Difference Schemes', http://www.math.nyu.edu/faculty/avellane/.

Homescu, C. (n.d.) *Implied Volatility Surface: Construction Methodologies and Characteristics*.

Wystup, U. (n.d.) 'FX Smile Modelling', *Wiley Encyclopedia of Quantitative Finance*.

12
More Vanilla Options

This chapter on options will delve a bit deeper into the subjects broached by the first chapter, and expand to cover foreign exchange (FX) options as well.

12.1   Notional units

One of the issues not discussed in the previous chapter is the obvious subject of *units*. For instance, if I have an option on a stock, what is the notional amount of that trade? A call option on a single stock, if the strike is 100, will pay 5 (dollars, for instance) if the price at expiration is 105. The notional on my trade is 1 stock.

This is an usual thing, having a 'notional amount' of a financial transaction being something other than an amount of money. Suppose, for instance, I have a stock position worth $10,000, and I want to protect myself against losses. I might buy an out-of-the-money put – ensuring that if the stock value falls too much, I'll be covered. I call my broker, and arrange to buy the option on a notional of $10,000. At some point, however, before arriving at a price for the option, we must convert the payment price into 'units' of stock.

The chain of events then results in:

- Value of stock we wish to cover: $10,000
- Current price per single stock: $100 (the reference price)
- Number of stocks notional = 100
- Cost of one option on one stock = $5
- Total cost of option = $500

At some point, the seller of the option must come up with a 'reference price' at which to convert the customer's investment into an option position. This reference price is almost always equal to the price at which the option seller buys their initial delta hedge.

So – if we're selling an option, what we must do is:

- Determine the delta of the option we're selling, and determine how much stock we must buy or sell to make ourselves *delta neutral.*
- When we buy or sell, use the price we get in the market as our reference price.
- Use this reference price as the spot price for the option.

This may seem circular (how can we price the option before buying the hedge?), but in reality a slight mismatch on the delta is inevitable.

This is simple enough in the case of stock options – FX options become a little more complex.

12.2   An introduction to FX options

When we looked at stocks, we noticed that the notional of a stock option is in 'stock units', and the value of the option is in currency units. In FX, both notional and option value are currency units – just different currencies.

Let's look at USD/JPY as an example, assuming that the quoted exchange rate is 100. This means 1 US Dollar buys 100 Japanese Yen (JPY). Now suppose that the value of a 1-month at-the-money (ATM) call option is 5. This means 'with a notional of $1, a 1-month call option with strike = forward costs 5 yen'.

Now, typically, the buyer of an option, at least half the time, will not be in a position to pay yen. So the option price must be converted to the currency of the option buyer as well. This conversion is simple, however, and can be done at the prevailing spot rate. In our example above, supposing the buyer is in the United States, the option cost would then be $0.05 – or 5 cents (using the dollar/yen rate of 100.0).

As in our example with stocks, however, much of the time option buyers will be looking to hedge a position they already have. That position may be in either or both of the two currencies.

Before we go further, however, we should clarify: just what *is* a FX option?

As mentioned, FX options are very much like equity options, with the difference being that rather than being based on a stock, they are based on a second currency. In all other respects, however, they are priced identically. One simplification over equity options is that FX does not have dividends, and so the forward value of FX is typically much simpler to arrive at. (Of course, as mentioned in the chapters on spot and forward FX

(Chapter 7), this does not mean *trivial*. Forward FX is a properly complex asset class.)

An FX option is, technically, an option to execute an FX *forward* transaction at a specified date in the future. (Most FX options are European – although American options are available, they are not as widespread as in the equity world.) This means, if we were to buy a 1-month put option on USD/JPY, with strike 100.0, and notional $10,000, it would mean:

- The option is to buy a forward FX contract in 1-month.
- The forward contract would be an option to *buy* 10,000 US dollars for 1 million JPY. This means that if the yen is weaker (so if the rate goes to 105, for instance) you'll be in a good position, since the US dollars you buy are cheaper than they would be on the open market.
- A typical formulation of this is 'Dollar call/Yen put'. Due to the symmetry of FX, a call on USD is the same as a put on JPY.
- One needs to be aware, of course, that a larger quoted FX rate means a stronger *base* currency (USD) and a weaker *term* currency (JPY). In this sense, FX is a bit confusing to those used to the stock market. If you watch the USD/JPY rate, you might think that buying a call option on 'the yen' would entail gains if the rate went up – when in fact it's quite the opposite.

The notional amounts in an FX option refer to the notional amounts on the forward rate transaction. The *spot* FX rate does not figure as greatly, since typically customers will not have cash positions they wish to hedge, but rather forward positions.

So how are FX options quoted? In a great many ways, it turns out.

Imagine an option on USD/JPY, in a time when the spot FX rate is 80, and the 1-month forward rate is 81. I want to buy dollar call/yen put, with notional of 1 million yen, *ATM*. This could mean:

- An ATM forward option, with strike 81, and notional of 1,000,000 JPY/12,345 USD.
- An ATM *spot* option, with strike 80, notional of 1,000,000 JPY/12,500 USD.

Suppose I choose ATM forward. The price of the option is 50,000 JPY. This could be expressed as:

- The option premium is 50,000 yen.
- The option premium is 625 dollars (the yen premium, converted at spot).
- The option premium is 5 per cent of the JPY notional.

- The option premium is 5.06 per cent of the USD notional.

Notice that the premium is not the same percentage of the USD or JPY notional. This is because the notionals of each currency have nothing to do with the spot rate – they are a function of the *option strike*. The option strike is in effect arbitrary – and so expressing the premium as a per cent of notional will be different in each currency.

   But now, what about the option delta? Many buyers of FX options will also want to *exchange delta* – they'll want to make themselves delta neutral after they buy the option. In addition, the option seller will probably want to do the same. This enables the buyer and the seller to agree to a spot rate at which to convert, without having to go to the market.

   A typical transaction, with all the bells and whistles, might look like the example below.

An example FX option: basic terms

- **Trade date:** 17 March
- **Spot date:** 19 March
- **FX rate:** USD/JPY
- **Spot reference price:** 80.00 yen per dollar
- **Expiration date:** 17 April
- **Final settlement date:** 19 April
- **Strike:** 81.00 yen per dollar

- **USD notional:** 12,345 US dollars
- **JPY notional:** 1,000,000 JPY
- **Option agreement:** the option buyer has the right to purchase USD notional in exchange for JPY notional on the option expiration date, with settlement on the final settlement date.
- **Premium amount:** 625 dollars
- **Premium payment date:** 19 March
- **Delta exchange date:** 19 March
- **Delta exchange:** The option buyer will buy 500,000 JPY in exchange for 6,172 USD, for settlement on the spot date.

12.3   Delta in FX transactions

In the example above, we neutralized our delta with a spot transaction. However, in many cases, we're pricing our FX option using *forward FX* rates. That is to say, the option is expressed as a forward FX transaction, and the input to our pricing formula is quite likely to be a forward FX rate.

   When we compute the delta of our option, we're most likely to calculate the sensitivity to the forward FX rate as well. Since the delta is expressed in terms of the forward rate, we need to convert from this to the spot rate.

As mentioned, the value of an option is expressed most naturally in units of the *term* currency. So in a USD/JPY option, the value is naturally expressed in JPY.

$$\text{Option value} = F(\text{Forward FX}, \text{Volatility}, \text{Interest rates}) = V(\text{term})$$

Now, the delta is of course the first derivative with respect to the FX rate. This will also be some amount in the term currency. How do we convert this into a spot transaction?

There are a few methods. The simplest is to imagine a spot transaction:

Buy in 2-days:	1,000,000 JPY	Sell in 2-days:	12,500 USD

Now, using an FX swap (where we cancel the spot transaction, and do a new forward transaction) move this trade forward 1-month, to the option expiration:

Buy in 2-days:	1,000,000 JPY	Sell in 2-days:	12,500 USD
Sell in 2-days:	1,000,000 JPY	Buy in 2-days:	12,500 USD
Buy in 1-month:	1,000,000 JPY	Sell in 1-month:	12,345 USD

Because these trades are all done at the market rate, we can imagine that their net value is exactly zero.

What is their value if we slightly vary the forward FX rate? In the example above, changing the forward rate by 1 loses 12,345 yen – not surprisingly. The delta is simply the notional of the base currency in the forward transaction (in term currency!) We can see this if we write down the formula for the value of a forward:

$$\text{Forward value in term currency} = \text{Term amount} \\ -(\text{Base amount} \times \text{Fwd FX rate})$$

So:

$$\text{Delta of forward} = \frac{d}{d(\text{Fwd FX rate})}(\text{Term amount} - (\text{Base} \times \text{Fwd FX}))$$
$$= \text{Base amount}$$

To compute the amount of our *delta hedge* – we simply compute the delta of the option (as an amount in term currency) and use this as the *base* amount of a hypothetical forward transaction. Quite easy, if somewhat confusing.

Suppose we sell an option on USD/JPY, which is a dollar put/yen call. In this case, since we're selling, we are essentially short yen and long dollars. If the yen goes up (and the FX rate as quoted goes down) we lose money.

Now suppose the delta is 5,000 yen. This means, to hedge ourselves, we should buy a forward with notional amount –5,000 USD and +405,000 JPY – essentially selling USD in the future in exchange for yen.

We can convert this to a spot transaction then by using a reversed FX swap: computing the ratio, essentially of the forward to the spot rate to compute the equivalent amounts of spot to transact. In this case, the ratio of forward to spot rate, multiplied by 5,000, gives a USD amount of 5,062.

12.4   Delta in percentage terms

Much like in the equities world, FX delta is often quoted in per cent. A 50-delta option is one which has exactly half the delta sensitivity of an equivalent forward (or spot) transaction. (Again, it's important to know whether to quote forward or spot delta.) How do you know when you have a 50-delta option though?

Here is where it is useful to think solely in numerical terms. If a variation of 0.01 in the value of the FX rate results in a change in the value of the option of 0.005 – then the delta is 50 per cent. This is true, however, only when the *base currency notional* is 1. In many FX applications, notional amounts are included at an early stage, so it may be necessary to divide by the notional amount to determine the delta.

More generally, the term '50-delta' may be confused with 'at-the-money' – which it is, in fact, if that's what we define 'at-the-money' as being. The strike, however, of a 50-delta option is not quite equal to the forward rate:

$$K_{\text{50-delta}} = Fe^{(\frac{1}{2}\sigma^2 T)}$$

Here F is the forward FX rate at time T, and K is the strike of the 50-delta option. Mostly the term 'at-the-money' refers to options where the strike is equal to the forward FX rate, or (in the case of 'at-the-money spot') when the strike is equal to the spot.

50-Delta options, however, are an important ATM indicator for the *straddle* market, discussed in the section below on options strategies.

12.5   Forward delta or spot delta?

We can quote delta in forward terms or spot terms. If we compute the delta with respect to the forward, then the delta is naturally in forward terms. We can then, as explained above, convert it to spot terms by multiplying by the ratio of spot to forward rates. But which does the market prefer?

The general rule is that, for options up to and including 1 year, spot deltas are quoted, with forward deltas after that. (Unless of course the currency pair contains an emerging market currency, in which case forward deltas are used throughout.) This is essential knowledge, of course, when using the quoted volatilities in any pricing model, since they must be handled appropriately to ensure that their meaning is properly understood. (And, as always, confirming the meaning of any source of quotations or data is essential before relying on it for doing business!)

12.6   Premium, premium currency and delta

When you buy or sell an option, you will pay or receive the cost of the option – the premium – in the premium currency. This means, of course, that the *delta* of the option can be seen as really being the delta of the 'option plus premium' portfolio.

The first question to ask, of course, is: what currency is the premium paid in? While one can negotiate anything one wishes, typically the premium currency for liquid options is determined by the currency pair. Any currency pair, for instance, with USD in it will have the premium paid in USD. If it does not involve USD, EUR is a good alternative. After EUR, in terms of importance, are GBP, AUD, CAD, CHF – although the most liquid pairs typically involve either USD or EUR. (Note that JPY is not on the list, generally settlement being easier in other currencies.)

Once we've determined the premium amount and currency, we can adjust the delta. Briefly put, if premium is in the base currency, we subtract the premium from the delta. If premium is in term currency, we subtract premium divided by the spot FX rate.

$$\text{delta}\left(\text{premium adjusted}\right) = \text{delta} - \text{premium}_{\text{base ccy}}$$

$$= \text{delta} - \text{premium}_{\text{term ccy}} \big/ \text{FX}$$

This is all very well – but what is the delta that is quoted in the market? Typically, the delta will be premium-adjusted *if the premium currency is the term currency*. So for instance, USD/JPY will be quoted with premium-adjusted deltas, whereas AUD/USD will be quoted with un-adjusted deltas.

12.7 Pricing FX options

In FX, we typically refer to the so-called 'Garman–Kohlhagen' model for European options. This is simply the Black–Scholes model (which, in its original formulation, refers to dividends) applied to FX rates. If we use Black–Scholes in the forward-price formulation (where the computation of the forwards is separated from the option calculation) then the two formulas are identical.

Like the classic Black–Scholes model, the Garman–Kohlhagen formulation starts with spot rates, and includes adjustments (based on interest rates) to convert to forward rates within the formula. Garman–Kohlhagen makes the classic assumption (which we cover in Chapter 7 on forward FX) that the forward FX rate can be determined by the ratio of discount factors between foreign and domestic currencies.

In forward FX, however, the market does not work this way. Forward FX is determined by looking at the market for forward FX points (typically) or, alternatively, at the cross-currency basis swap market. So, rather than using an approach like Garman–Kohlhagen, most practitioners will use a forward-price formulation of Black–Scholes with the forward FX rate as an explicit input, and then discount the result in the appropriate currency. Garman–Kohlhagen, written down, is as follows:

$$\text{Let } d_1 = \frac{\ln\left(\dfrac{S_0}{K}\right) + \left(r_d - r_f + \dfrac{\sigma^2}{2}\right)t}{\sigma\sqrt{t}} \quad \text{and} \quad \text{let } d_2 = d_1 - \sigma\sqrt{t}$$

Then:

$$C\left(S_0, t, K, r_d, r_f\right) = \left[N(d_1)S_0 \frac{e^{-r_b t}}{e^{-r_t t}} - N(d_2)K\right]e^{-r_t t}$$

The above formula is the formula for a call option, with strike K, time-to-expiration t, spot FX rate S_0, term currency interest rate r_t and base currency interest rate r_b. As we can see, the ratio of the discount factors multiplied by the spot FX rate is the classic formula for computing forward FX.

The more typical formula is simply, as in the previous chapter, the Black–Scholes formula with S being the forward FX rate.

12.8 FX volatility

As in equity options FX options are priced on a volatility surface. The main differences, from a practical standpoint, between FX and equity options, are around liquidity and contract types.

Very few FX options are done on exchanges. There are some exchanges which do deal in options (such as CME) but a large number are done over-the-counter, as customized trades between banks and their customers. Even so, the market is quite large, and extremely liquid.

Like equities, FX options are traded by delta. The options volatility surface will be parameterized by tenor (time until expiration, usually going forward several years) and delta (varying from 10% delta put options up to 10% delta call options, perhaps).

More than in equities, FX has a widely traded market in *strategies*. Strategies, which are combinations of options traded together, form the basis of building many volatility surfaces.

An introduction to options strategies

Option strategies are a staple of finance courses – only a few are commonly used, however. Since we're not talking about them from an investing perspective, we'll focus primarily on those used in institutional trading. The classic way to present strategies is with the payout profile: a simple chart of the payoff from the options at maturity, under different levels of underlying rates. Figures 12.1 and 12.2 are the payout profiles from simple call and put options:

The most basic strategy is the *straddle*. This is simply what we call buying a call option and a put option at the same time, with the same strike. The payoff of a straddle is simply the sum of Figures 12.1 and 12.2 (see Figure 12.3).

Of course, looking at the payoff profile, it is apparent that if you are *exactly* ATM (in delta-terms that is, with each option being 50-delta), the straddle as a whole has zero-delta. Put another way: with an ATM straddle, one is indifferent to whether the underlying rate goes up or down, since one makes money either way. For this reason, straddles are a convenient way to trade *volatility itself*. Since the buyer of a straddle makes more money the farther the rate goes from the strike – they are effectively a long buyer of volatility. For this reason, straddles are often purchased or sold by traders as part of their risk-management strategy.

Another close relative of the straddle is the *strangle*. Also a simple combination of a call and put option, the strangle's components have different strikes. The put option has a strike below the call option – making it similar in effect to the straddle. The strangle also functions as a long-volatility strategy, with somewhat less sensitivity (see Figure 12.4).

Similar to the strangle is the *risk-reversal*. A risk-reversal is a combination of a call and put, but with one bought and one sold (see Figure 12.5)

We can see that the risk-reversal is similar in payoff to actually owning the underlying asset – except with a flattening at the centre. Since in a risk-reversal one buys and sells options with strikes at similar

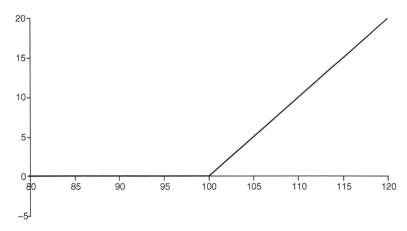

Figure 12.1   Call option payoff at maturity (Strike 100)

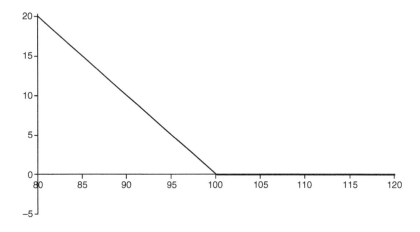

Figure 12.2   Put option payoff at maturity (Strike 100)

distances from the ATM point, in theory they can have zero cost to the purchaser. The amount gained by selling the put option can be used to purchase the call option (or vice versa, if one is buying a put and selling a call).

Combined with a position in the underlying asset, the risk-reversal can be a cheap form of insurance: selling potential profits in return for covering potential losses. For instance – if I have a long position in EUR/USD (long Euros, short Dollars), and the EUR/USD rate is 1.3 (dollars per Euro) – I might wish to sell a Euro call/dollar put struck at, say, 1.35, in exchange for a Euro put/dollar call struck at 1.25. This would allow profits and losses within a narrow range, but if the Euro went beyond the range, I would be totally unaffected.

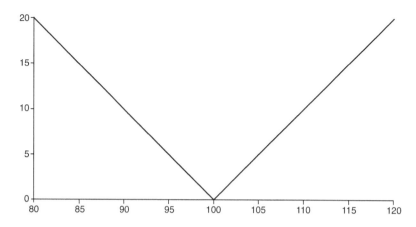

Figure 12.3 Straddle strategy payoff at maturity (Strike 100)

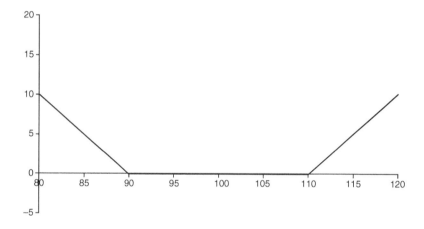

Figure 12.4 Strangle strategy payoff at maturity (Strikes 90, 110)

Risk-reversals are quite popular, and usually (as with many FX options) quoted in delta and volatility terms. A common form is the 25-delta risk-reversal: a strategy where the delta of both the call and put option is 25 per cent. These are often quoted in volatility terms: the volatility of the call option, minus the volatility of the put. A 1-month 25-delta risk-reversal quote of 0.1 means that the call option's volatility is 0.1 per cent higher than that of the put option. Dealers quoting risk-reversals will also agree.

The most complex of the simple strategies is the *butterfly*. Composed of a combination of a (short) straddle and a (long) strangle, the butterfly payoff looks like Figure 12.6.

Butterflies, in this formulation, are naturally a way to go short (or long) volatility without the unlimited up or downside of a straddle. This is simple enough. There are more common formulations in the inter-bank

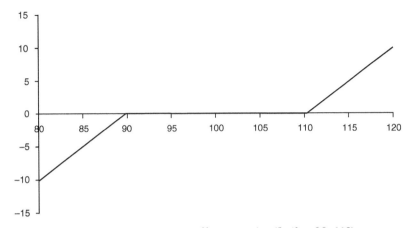

Figure 12.5 Risk-reversal strategy payoff at maturity (Strikes 90, 110)

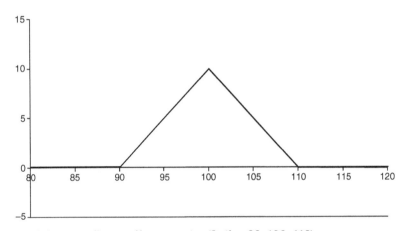

Figure 12.6 Butterfly payoff at maturity (Strikes 90, 100, 110)

market however, whereby the outside wings of the butterfly do not make the payoff flat at the edges (Figure 12.7).

The vega-neutral butterfly is a compound structure consisting of (typically) a long put option at the lower strike (with notional x), a short put option ATM, a short call option ATM and a long call option (with notional x) at the higher strike. Here x is adjusted so that the sensitivity of the entire structure to shifts in overall volatility is zero.

The vega-neutral butterfly is the opposite of the strangle, in a way. While both the butterfly and the strangle are delta neutral, the butterfly has significant *gamma*, with zero vega – while the strangle has low gamma with positive vega. In trader's language, gamma represents the trading risk to short-dated, soon-to-expire options, while vega is more affected by long-dated, long-term options. Butterflies and strangles can

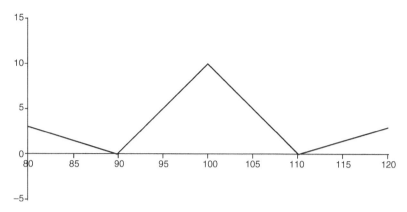

Figure 12.7 Vega-neutral butterfly payoff at maturity (Strikes 90, 100, 110)

be used to trade away risk to short- or long-dated parts of a trader's option portfolio.

From a practical perspective, to those away from the sales and trading desk, the true interest in these strategies is to divine the shape of the volatility surface. Looking at risk-reversals, strangles and butterflies will help to do this.

Risk-reversals are quoted in volatility terms, as the difference in volatility between the call (at the higher strike) and the put (at the lower strike). Strangles (and butterflies) are quoted as the difference in the average volatility of the wings (the options away-from-the-money) and the central ATM options.

Let's imagine a 25-delta strangle and a 25-delta risk-reversal.

Strangle quote: 1.5 per cent (25-delta, ATM volatility 15%)
Risk-reversal quote: 0.5 per cent

Using these quotes, we can derive the volatility for a 25-delta put (we'll call this σ_{put}) and a 25-delta call (σ_{call}).

$$\frac{\sigma_{\text{put}} + \sigma_{\text{call}}}{2} = \sigma_{\text{ATM}} + 1.5\%, \quad \sigma_{\text{call}} = \sigma_{\text{put}} + 0.5\%$$

A little substitution gives:

$$\sigma_{\text{put}} = \sigma_{\text{ATM}} + 1.25\%, \quad \sigma_{\text{call}} = \sigma_{\text{ATM}} + 1.75\%$$

Using this technique, it is possible to use risk-reversals, combined with strangles and butterflies, to build the entire volatility surface. This is quite useful, because it is these strategies which are most widely quoted in the market – unlike the equities market, it is often difficult to find matrices of options by strike and time-to-expiration.

The formulas, written out, are simply:

$$\sigma_{25 \text{ delta call}} = \sigma_{\text{ATM}} + \frac{\text{Risk-reversal}}{2} + \text{Strangle}$$

and

$$\sigma_{25 \text{ delta put}} = \sigma_{\text{ATM}} - \frac{\text{Risk-reversal}}{2} + \text{Strangle}$$

12.9 Interpolating FX volatility

The interesting thing about FX volatility surfaces is that while they are highly liquid, the heavily traded points are at the popular deltas – for the popular strategies.

ATM straddles (zero-delta) and 25-delta risk-reversals and butterflies are the instruments upon which most of the FX volatility surfaces are built. One can also add 10-delta risk-reversals and butterflies (or strangles), but many rely on simply the 25-delta points.

That said – this gives *only three points* on which to interpolate FX volatility. The obvious approach, then, is to rely on some method of interpolation which gives a smooth result but does not over-fit. Parabolic interpolation is one decent, simple choice which should give defensible results at least between the strikes set at 25-delta.

One approach that has gained popularity for interpolation is based on the actual *hedge cost* of an option. This approach – called Vega-Vanna-Volga (or VVV) interpolation – is based on the idea that we should base our estimate of volatility on the cost of a hedge portfolio of options which we would need to (more or less) neutralize our risk.

If we're selling an option, rather than simply engaging in zealous delta-hedging, it is far more profitable to hedge the higher-order risks associated with the option as well. This means far less buying and selling over the long-term – and far less overall risk.

If we hedge *vega* as well as delta, then we are protected against changes in volatility. As we saw in the sections above, the best vega hedge is a straddle or strangle. In addition, we'd like to insulate our vega hedge against changes in the ATM rate. As the FX rate changes, our vega may change as well (this second-order effect is called *vanna*). Risk-reversals have a decent amount of vanna, and enable us to 'trade away' this risk. Finally, we may worry about the change in vega with volatility itself – if vols go up, will our vega increase as well? This 'vega gamma' is called *volga*, and can also be traded by using strategies – especially strangles.

Traders may not actually neutralize their vega, vanna and volga risks in practice, but the theory is that, on the whole, they engage in hedging practices which approximate exact VVV hedging to a large degree.

When a trader sells an option, they will want to not only charge the 'theoretical value' but also charge a premium for the cost of the hedge they have to put on. In the VVV view of the world, the shape of the volatility smile is determined by these costs. We know exactly what the volatility is at certain points (25-delta puts, ATM and 25-delta calls, for instance) but outside these points we must rely on some theory to guide us.

There are excellent sources explaining (in quant mathematical terms) how to derive the VVV-based volatility surface (see the notes on this chapter for guidance). The goal of this text is merely to point out that this approach exists – and that it's pretty popular. We can also give the simplified version of the results, which are quite easy to implement. These simplified equations work well between the delta points, but may over-estimate the volatility at the edges.

Put simply, the volatility for any strike K, given known volatilities for lower (25-delta put), ATM (zero-delta straddle) and upper (25-delta call) options would be (approximately):

$$\sigma(K) = \frac{\ln \frac{K_{ATM}}{K} \ln \frac{K_c}{K}}{\ln \frac{K_{ATM}}{K_p} \ln \frac{K_c}{K_p}} \sigma_p + \frac{\ln \frac{K}{K_p} \ln \frac{K_c}{K}}{\ln \frac{K_{ATM}}{K_p} \ln \frac{K_c}{K_{ATM}}} \sigma_{ATM} + \frac{\ln \frac{K}{K_p} \ln \frac{K}{K_{ATM}}}{\ln \frac{K_c}{K_p} \ln \frac{K_c}{K_{ATM}}} \sigma_c$$

Here K_p is the strike of the (lower) 25-delta put, and K_c is that of the (upper) 25-delta call.

As you can see from Figure 12.8 – the volatility looks very much parabolic – which is what one would expect from a three-point interpolation. It has been suggested that simply fitting a parabola is sufficient to approximate the volatility surface in the first order. On the other hand, it's also been suggested that a more complex approach to fitting the surface within the VVV method gives better results beyond the 25-delta wings.

12.10 A brief introduction to options risk measurement

Consider again a simple option on a single stock or FX rate. The pricing function can be written as a function, with parameters:

- The price of the underlying (stock price, for instance).
- The strike and time-to-expiration of the option.

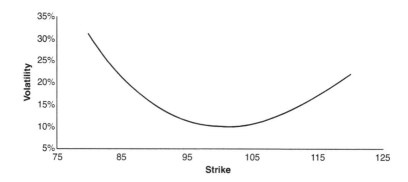

Figure 12.8   Option volatility smoothed by approximate VVV method

- The volatility of the underlying.
- The discount factor to expiration.

Each of these parameters has one or more risk measures attached to it. As we've seen, *delta* is the first derivative of price with respect to the price of the underlying. *Gamma*, similarly, is the second derivative.

Theta is the sensitivity to time, typically measured by finding the change in price after decreasing the time-to-expiration by one day.

Interest rate risk in the options world is due to the discount factor – and changes in the discount curve can be measured simply by the sensitivity to the zero-coupon rate to expiration. This risk (referred to as *rho*) can be measured with respect to the OIS or other discount curve as desired.

Finally, sensitivity to the volatility is known as *vega*. If we see the measured volatility of an option change by 1 per cent, the value of the option will change as well. Vega measures this change (typically as a dollar value per 1% change in volatility) and helps traders manage risk associated with changing volatilities.

All of these risk measures (delta, gamma, vega, theta and rho) are relatively simple to measure in the basic case.

The most import thing to know at any time is your *position*. If you hold 1,000 shares of stock, and the current market price is $50 per share, your position then is either 1,000 shares, or $50,000, depending on your preferred unit of measure.

When mixing options and cash positions, however, your overall position will change. The position becomes the cash position *plus* the delta of the options positions.

A typical position report would lay them out both separately and together:

Underlying	Cash position	Options delta	Total
XYZ	50,000	4,732	54,732
ABC	40,100	−12,730	27,370
...			

This is straightforward enough, and is a handy way to combine reporting. What happens, however, when the underlying price changes? The cash position will rise (or fall) in value in a linear manner, the options position will, however, be non-linear. In the first approximation, the options delta will change by the gamma: for every unit of change in the underlying price, the delta will increase by a given amount. If we measure delta first at price P_0, and then the price changes to P_1, the delta becomes $\Delta = \Delta_0 + \Gamma(P_1 - P_0)$. Here Γ is the gamma we've measured originally.

This is a good approximation if the spot does not travel far, but the best approximation is, of course, to recalculate everything. For a large portfolio (or for a portfolio that contains a lot of hard-to-compute positions) this is not always possible in real time. The next-best approach is to get a so-called *spot ladder*. This is a table showing spot, value and position (and other risks, if desired) for a series of hypothetical levels for the underlying price. This allows traders, as the price fluctuates during the day, to get a good approximation of their position without doing a complete recalculation.

Spot	PV	Delta (%)
95	14,410	26
96	17,537	30
97	21,102	35
98	25,119	39
99	29,597	44
100	34,539	48
101	39,940	53
102	45,791	57
103	52,078	62
104	58,779	66
105	65,872	70

The table above is an example of a spot ladder for a single call option struck at around 100 – the delta profile for a more complex portfolio would, of course, not be so predictable.

Vega

After delta and gamma comes vega. This is the sensitivity to changes in volatility – often represented by changes in the price of an option when the value of the underlying has not changed.

The simple representation of vega, for simple options, can be arrived at by simply bumping the input volatility, and normalizing the result to show the change in value per 1 per cent change in volatility. So, for instance, if you value your options with a volatility of 20 per cent (and get a value of 100), then 'bump' the volatility by 0.01 per cent and revalue (to get 101), your vega would be $\dfrac{\text{Value}_{\text{bumped}} - \text{Value}_{\text{original}}}{\text{Bump amount} * 100}$, or

$$\frac{101 - 100}{0.01\% * 100} = 100$$

Input volatility bumping is never quite so simple, however. In the world of equities and FX, we are usually dealing with volatility *surfaces*. A volatility surface will typically have its vega measured in buckets, with each bucket corresponding to an input tenor.

Because of smoothing and other volatility surface optimization algorithms which may or may not be in use, if we proceed with a bumping methodology external to the pricing model we'll need to insert the bumps after the smoothing has been completed, but before any time-interpolation has happened. Alternatively, we can insert the bump amount as a separate step.

In general, if our volatility function is some function of time, strike and spot level:

$$\sigma = V(t, T, S, K)$$

We will need to add a bump function which is purely a function of time, for each input tenor *i*:

$$K_{\text{50-delta}} = F e^{(\frac{1}{2}\sigma^2 T)}$$

The simplest form for the bump function is simply a linear function of variance – which we add (after the fact) to the variance we get from the volatility surface. Variance is simplest to use, since we usually linearly interpolate in variance rather than volatility when getting volatility to different times.

Figure 12.9 shows a simple linear function of variance, with the 3-month point corresponding to approximately a bump of 0.1 per cent in volatility. (Recall variance is vol-squared multiplied by time.)

What about the case where we have a trade which is in-between two tenors? It will receive small bumps from each of the surrounding tenors.

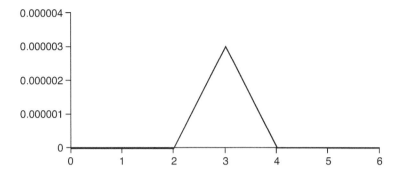

Figure 12.9 A variance bump

Will the sum of the contributions of each of these bumps to its value be correct? If we were to bump both surrounding tenors simultaneously, would it equal the sum of each tenor individually? The answer is yes: whether we bump in variance or volatility, the sum of the contributions for each bucket will add up to the total we would expect if we bumped all buckets at once.

One thing to be careful of is that the sum of all buckets will really only approach the total if we were to move all tenors at once – never equal exactly, even for simple options. As the size of the bump approaches zero, the approximation gets better and better, however. A good value for a vega bump is usually somewhere between 0.1 per cent and 0.001 per cent – depending on what sort of models are being used. Smaller numbers are sometimes not good if approximate valuation methods are employed (such as Monte Carlo simulation), larger numbers will give less exact results, however, especially when adding bucket contributions.

A simple vega-by-tenor report would look like:

Vega-by-tenor	
1M	1,499
3M	2,666
6M	5,210
1Y	1,200
...	
Total	15,740

Each bucket could then be hedged with an appropriate vega-hedging instrument if desired – or the overall vega could be hedged as one unit.

Further reading

Antonio Castagna, F. M. (n.d.) 'Consistent Pricing of FX Options', *www.fabiomercurio.it.*

Castagna, A. (2009) *FX Options and Smile Risk*, Wiley.

Dimitri Reiswich, U. W. (n.d.) 'FX Volatility Smile Construction', *No 20, CPQF Working Paper Series from Frankfurt School of Finance and Management, Centre for Practical Quantitative Finance (CPQF).*

13
Vanilla Interest Rate Options

13.1   Introduction

Interest rate options are perhaps the most complex type of options on which to do analysis without a rigorous quantitative backing. The danger in providing any sort of introduction is to make them appear simpler than they actually are. That said, the market conventions around basic interest rate options have been agreed for some time, and are not particularly complex. It is useful to understand the basic theory of simple interest rate options, and also have a look at the tools that are used in the analysis of more complex options.

Vanilla interest rate options can also be managed (with some care) using some rather simple tools. Complex models are used in more complex types of options (and most trading desks will do a few of these), but the vast majority of interest rate option products in circulation are of the plain vanilla type.

There are two main types of options we'll look at: caps and swaptions – with a later digression towards constant-maturity swap (CMS) products. These products make up the bulk of the interest rate option market. This market – if you measure it by notional amount outstanding – is the world's largest option market by far. (Of course, given the nature of interest rates, measuring notional amount can be misleading.)

An **interest rate cap** (or floor) is a simple trade, with settlements happening on a regular basis much like an interest rate swap. The agreement in an interest rate cap is exactly the same as the *floating* side of an interest rate swap – but in a cap the seller (who is paying the floating rate) pays the *difference* between the floating and a fixed-strike if the floating rate exceeds the fixed-strike. If the floating rate is less than the strike, no payments are made by anyone. This is, in effect, exactly like a vanilla call option on an interest rate, except paid on a regular schedule. Example

Table 13.1 An example schedule for an interest rate cap

Date	Rate (%)	Strike (%)	Day-count	Cap Payment (%)	Payment on 10MM Notional
16-Jun–14 Mon					
16-Dec–14 Tue	1.80	2	0.508333	*Excluded*	–
16-Jun–15 Tue	1.90	2	0.505556		–
16-Dec–15 Wed	1.97	2	0.508333		–
16-Jun–16 Thu	**2.12**	**2**	**0.508333**	**0.12**	**6,100**
16-Dec–16 Fri	**2.16**	**2**	**0.508333**	**0.16**	**8,133**
16-Jun–17 Fri	**2.25**	**2**	**0.505556**	**0.25**	**12,639**
18-Dec–17 Mon	**2.03**	**2**	**0.513889**	**0.03**	**1,542**
18-Jun–18 Mon	1.98	2	0.505556		–

schedule for an interest rate cap, with strike of 2 per cent, paying semi-annually. (This is presented supposing the trade has finished, and all the rates are known.)

Table 13.1 shows some fictitious payments made on a cap with strike of 2 per cent, settling semi-annually. As the rate goes above 2 per cent, payments are made, but as it falls below 2 per cent, they stop again. Caps are, not surprisingly, often used as insurance against rate fluctuations for those paying floating rates in other transactions.

Floors are simply the opposite – the seller of a floor will pay any amount by which the floating rate goes below a given floor rate. In Table 13.1, if the trade was a floor rather than a cap, floor payments would be made in the first three periods, and the last period, but not the four periods where cap payments are made (of course).

Caps and floors are typically quoted to a range of standard maturities – typically from 1 to 10 years in length. Quotations are either in basis-points of notional paid up-front or as a running basis-point cost paid each period, or (often) brokers will simply quote a volatility. Since the model used for pricing caps for quotation purposes is well understood and agreed, simply quoting the volatility gives the buyer a way to easily compute the cost, or include the cap price in another product.

A **swaption** is simply an option on a interest rate swap, starting in the future. Interest rate swaps are usually sold at the par rate – and so have (theoretically) a zero value. A swap which starts in the future at the future-expected swap rate will also have zero value. However, the option to enter into a swap will have some positive value, since the holder of the option may decide not to exercise unless the swap rates have moved in their favour.

Swaptions come in two flavours – *receivers* (where the option is to enter into a pay-floating, receive-fixed swap) or *payers* (options on pay-fixed, receive-floating swaps). The cost of the option, as with caps, is typically quoted in basis-points paid up-front, or (sometimes) in basis-points paid at the start of the swap period, and (as with caps) brokers will often quote simply a volatility.

13.2 Pricing interest rate caps

As mentioned, the model used in the public market for interest rate caps is well-understood. The so-called Black model is very much like the Black–Scholes model for equity options, applied to interest rates.

Caps are really not one single option – they are a series of options called *caplets*. Each caplet is an option on the interest rate payout for a single period of the cap. If, as in the example at the beginning of the chapter, we have a 4-year cap with semi-annual fixings, there are eight periods in the cap. The first period has already fixed, and so does not figure in the option calculation (indeed, it is typically excluded from the agreement, as mentioned in the table). So, the price of a cap is the sum of the price of its caplets.

$$P_{cap} = \sum_{i=2,\dots,n} P_{caplet\,i} D_i$$

Here, D_i is the discount factor for caplet I (calculated from the end, or payment date, of the caplet period).

As with Black–Scholes, let's define:

$$d_1(i,t) = \frac{\ln\left(\frac{F_i}{K}\right) + \frac{\sigma_i^2}{2}t}{\sigma_i\sqrt{t}} \quad \text{and} \quad d_2(i,t) = d_1(i,t) - \sigma_i\sqrt{t}$$

Here, F_i is the forward rate for caplet i and K is the strike, or cap rate. The volatility, σ_i, will often be the overall quoted *cap-volatility* for the entire cap trade.

The price of the caplet is then:

$$P_{caplet} = \left(F_i N(d_1) - KN(d_2)\right) b_i A$$

Here, b_i is the day-count fraction for the period (often the number of days divided by 360 or 365) and A is the notional. (Note that this is not discounted.) As in the case of Black–Scholes, $N()$ represents the cumulative normal distribution function. The price of the overall cap is then the sum of these caplet values, with the proper discounting on your favourite discount curve.

Just like a cap is constructed in the same manner as a call option, the floor has similar construction to a put:

$$P_{\text{floorlet}} = \left(- F_i N\left(-d_1\right) + K N\left(-d_2\right)\right) b_i A$$

This is all very straightforward, and allows us to build simple models (even in spreadsheets) to price caps and floors on a period-by-period basis.

Notice (as with swaps) that we are *not* assuming that the forward rate is related to the discount factors in these formulas (some older texts will give the forward rate as a function of discount factors). This is because we're no longer assuming that we can discount at LIBOR – indeed, we're making no assumption at all about which discount function we're using. The discounting is a step separate from, and done after, valuation.

13.3   Cap volatilities

Caps can be quoted at any number of strikes, or one can get quotations for *at-the-money* (ATM) caps and floors. ATM, in this case, simply means: the strike at which the price of a cap equals the price of a floor. The ATM cap strike will often be near the swap rate for a given period: indeed it should be very close to the 'money' swap rate, where the fixed-rate is quoted in the same basis as the floating.

As with equity or FX options, caps and floors have different volatilities for different strikes. This results in quotations in the form of a matrix of numbers: each row being quotations for a different length of cap, and each column a different strike. In addition, separate columns often give the ATM rate and volatility). Example of the form taken by a cap/floor volatility matrix (see Table 13.2). (See, e.g. Reuters VCAP, or ICAP pages on Bloomberg.)

Table 13.2   An example cap/floor volatility matrix

Term	ATM strike	ATM volatility (%)	0.5% (in %)	1.0% (in %)	1.5% (in %)	2.0% (in %)	2.5% (in %)	...	10% (in %)
1Y	0.90	49	49	52	53	53	54		60
18M	1.02	48	48	51	52	52	53		58
2Y	1.05	45	45	48	49	49	50		55
3Y	1.12	42	42	45	46	47	47		50
5Y	1.65	40	40	43	44	44	45		49
...									...
20Y	2.80	34	34	36	37	38	39	...	43

We can use the data in a cap-volatility matrix to derive the volatility needed to price any cap or floor. Caps whose strike falls between quoted rows can have their volatility linearly interpolated. Caps are, like swaps, available in a number of bases: 3- or 6-month being the most commonly quoted. Cap/floor markets are actively quoted on most of the major LIBOR-style markets (e.g. EURIBOR, USD-LIBOR and even more exotic indices such as CMS markets).

Often, caps will be quoted (like other interest rate products) in *basis-points*. This means that they are quoted as basis-points of 1 per cent of the notional amount of an example trade. The easiest way to find the basis-point value of a trade, given the volatility, is to price a trade with a notional of 10,000 (Euros, dollars or whatever the notional currency).

To convert from basis-point value to volatility, we must naturally use a root finding method such as Newton–Raphson. Starting with a 'guess' volatility (10%, or any reasonable number), we iteratively search for a volatility which makes the value of our cap equal to the quoted number.

13.4 Using cap prices to infer volatility

When we build our own interest rate environment, we will come up with a yield curve which supplies forward rates – rates which allow us to compute prices for caps and floors.

However, our own 'environment' will always, necessarily, be slightly different from the environment quoted by brokers. The ATM strikes given by the broker will be somewhat different from our view of the ATM strikes. Also – if we use the volatilities given by the market to price, say, a 2 per cent cap, we'll get a slightly different price than the one quoted on the market.

The fact is, however, that the market quotes *both* price and volatility, and we can pick which ones we want to use. It may be best, for instance, to choose the ATM volatilities for evaluation of ATM caps – even if the quoted prices are slightly different from those we derive ourselves.

In the case of the 2 per cent cap – it may be best to use the quoted prices. The 2 per cent cap price is a fixed point in the market – and if we infer a new set of volatilities (based on these prices) then we at least know that our pricing matches the market.

13.5 Uses of caps and floors in structured products

One of the more common uses of caps is within structures. One can have, for instance, a common interest rate swap deal combined with a cap, to provide protection to the buyer against over-large swings in the floating rate. Within structures like this, caps can be sold with a variety of different features. For example, a cap could have a variable strike: the strike rate can move up and down during the course of the trade to match the level of protection needed at different points of time. The cap could have variable notional amounts – if the underlying swap, for instance, is on a trade whose notional is paid off over time, the cap notional can also decrease over time. Various features can be added such as a 'chooser' option: the cap can be structured so that the customer can choose to exercise at most, say, four caplets within the trade's 5-year lifespan. Such a chooser option (whose value is equal to the sum of the four greatest-valued caplets) is one way to reduce the cost of the overall trade.

Using any of these features (variable strikes, notionals or exercise conditions) means that we can no longer use the quoted broker volatilities, but must rather use the correct individual caplet volatilities.

Why is this? Suppose we have a 2-year semi-annual cap with variable strike. The first period is ignored (since it has fixed at the time of the trade), leaving us with three cap periods, with strikes (let's say) of 2 per cent, 2.5 per cent and 3 per cent. We can price the second (2%) period at the quoted volatility for a 2 per cent 1-year cap – this is quite straightforward. But what about the next two periods? The third (2.5%) period can't be priced at the 2.5 per cent 18-month cap rate, because this rate is the *overall* rate for an 18-month trade with two periods of optionality. What we need is the rate for a single caplet, not the overall rate for a cap trade. The same problem applies to the last period.

To put it simply: *quoted volatilities for caps and floors are single numbers which apply to all periods of the trade. As such, they are average, overall volatilities, and do not apply to single caplets.* When pricing structured products, we need to have different volatilities for each caplet. Example schedule for an interest rate cap, with variable strike (see Table 13.3). This is presented from a pricing perspective – as if today is the start of the trade.

This problem comes up consistently in pricing interest rate products. Generally speaking, it is far easier to price any portfolio of interest rate caps and floors if we have a source of *caplet* volatilities.

Table 13.3 An example of a variable strike cap

Date	Fwd rate (%)	Strike (%)	Volatility used	Caplet value
16-Jun–14 Mon				
16-Dec–14 Tue	1.80	n/a	n/a	*Excluded*
16-Jun–15 Tue	1.90	2	1Y vol	V
16-Dec–15 Wed	1.95	2.5	Unknown	Unknown
16-Jun–16 Thu	2.2	3	Unknown	Unknown

13.6   Deriving caplet volatilities

It is possible (and not too difficult) to get the implied caplet volatilities from the market quoted cap-volatility matrix. It is even possible (though difficult without extensive macro-writing) in a spreadsheet. The end goal will be to determine, for each of the fixed strikes in the cap-volatility matrix, what the caplet volatility is for each period.

The first problem we face is that there are not enough caps quoted to determine uniquely the volatility for each caplet. That is to say, if we look at the semi-annual caps, we see caps at 2, 3, 4 years (and so on), but not at, say, 3.5 years. Since there is a caplet every 6 months, we need to have *cap* quotations every 6 months.

We can fill in the missing cap quotations by linear interpolation (for lack of a better option). By linearly interpolating for each strike, we can then (in the semi-annual case) fill in two cap volatilities for each year. The 3.5-year cap-volatility, then, will be the average of the 3- and 4-year cap volatilities.

Our goal is to fill in the 'caplet volatility' column of Table 13.4.

The key component we need to determine the caplet volatilities is a robust cap-pricing function. The procedure becomes:

1. Fill in the interpolated cap volatilities for each cap maturity.
2. For each cap, find the cap price using the appropriate overall cap-volatility.
3. For the first caplet volatility, use the first cap-volatility.
4. For each subsequent cap, price the cap using the caplet volatilities found so far. For the last caplet volatility, find the volatility level which makes the cap price match the price we found in step 2.

Using this method, it's easy to 'bootstrap' the caplet volatility curves. Doing this should fill in appropriate caplet volatilities for each of the fixed strikes presented in the cap-volatility matrix – giving us a corresponding caplet volatility matrix.

Table 13.4   Cap volatilities versus caplet volatilities – semi-annual case

Term	Cap-volatility (%)	Caplet vol
1Y	45	45%
1.5Y	44	TBD
2Y	42	TBD
2.5Y	(Interpolated) 41	TBD
3Y	40	TBD

But what about the ATM volatilities? In reality, these are the most liquid quotations available in the cap-volatility matrix, and should, ideally, play a role. These can be factored in to the end result, by computing a 'special' point in each row of our caplet volatility matrix. Since the strike of the ATM caps varies, we must amend step 4 to use *interpolated* caplet volatilities from the previous rows of the matrix. The end result should be a general mechanism to extract caplet volatilities for any strike, interpolating between strikes as desired, and where strikes may include an arbitrary ATM strike.

We should also be able to interpolate between dates. One of the common tasks financial institutions must do is to revalue (and re-compute risk on) a multitude of trades which have been done over the course of months or years. These books of trades may have dates that fall anywhere between the fixed 6-month points we can infer from the market.

The simplest solution (as before) is linear interpolation. If we have a 6-month caplet starting in 9 months time, we must interpolate the caplet volatilities between the caplet starting in 6 months time and the caplet starting in 1-year. To be accurate, we should of course interpolate *variance* – the square of volatility times time – rather than pure volatility numbers.

13.7   How does it add up?

The end result is that we have an extra step in pricing a cap or floor: the bootstrapping of the caplet volatilities. Admittedly, this is not necessary if the cap has constant strike and notional, and no special features. However, when pricing a portfolio which contains caps and floors, it is wise to adopt a consistent pricing approach. Pricing using caplet volatilities is a more flexible approach than using pure aggregate cap volatilities. Not only will having a caplet volatility curve allow one to price more complex trades, these caplet volatilities can also be used as inputs for the pricing of more exotic trades, using advanced pricing models.

Once the caplet volatility curve is constructed, for instance, one can compute risk (vega) in terms of the caplet volatilities. If we used the cap volatilities directly to price our cap portfolio, then we would only see our 5-year caps hedged by other 5-year caps. If we use caplet volatilities, this shows us that a 4-year cap could, conceivably, be used to hedge the majority of the vega risk in a 5-year cap.

What this means is that the pricing of a cap (from market data) is a 2 (or 3)-step process. First, of course, one must construct the interest rate environment: build all the necessary yield curves, so that forward rates and discount factors can be easily computed for each cap period. Then one must bootstrap the caplet volatilities. Finally, one can price a variety of caps and floors with these building blocks.

The first two steps in building the environment are not expensive to do – if one is pricing a variety of trades. However, when computing risk it can become more expensive if one has to re-build the curves and caplets each time a deal is priced. As a result, it is wise to ensure, whenever building systems around interest rate products like this, that curves and volatilities are built as few times as possible!

13.8 What about more sophisticated models?

The literature is replete with complex and sophisticated pricing models for interest rate products. The most commonly used in finance are models based around the Libor Market Model (LMM). These models typically will be based on simulations (or enumerations) of each forward rate within the trade being priced, with some assumptions made about correlations between the forward rates and the evolution of rates over time.

While these models will help price more exotic structures, they make little difference in the pricing of vanilla, unsophisticated caps and floors. This is because the market inputs they use are the same as we're using for pricing caps using the Black model. Since the price of a 10-year cap is quoted in the market, we can use whatever model we like – as long as we agree with the market. The Black model is usually sufficient to price and risk-manage large numbers of vanilla caps.

That said, one can ask: what is the boundary between a vanilla trade (where we can use a simple model) and an exotic trade? Clearly, trades which are directly quoted in the market, and for which there are simple, agreed models, can be termed vanilla. We've seen, also, that we can extend the concept of vanilla-ness, in the world of caps and floors at least, to extend to trades with variable strikes and notionals. There are a wide variety of more exotic variants of caps and floors for which these vanilla models are not suitable, however, including:

- Digital caps. These are trades where a fixed amount is paid each period if the rate exceeds the strike (or goes below it, in the case of a floor). Digital trades are tricky to both price and hedge, and require a good deal of expertise to trade.
- CMS/CMT caps. These are caps on the constant-maturity-swap (or constant-maturity-treasury) index, not a LIBOR-based index. The 10-year CMS rate, for instance, corresponds to the quoted rate for a 10-year swap. As such, a CMS cap will pay the different between the referenced CMS rate and the strike, if it's positive. Modelling CMS is tricky, to say the least.

- Accruals. There are a wide variety of trades in the 'accrual' family, such as range accruals (where a fixed amount is paid for every day a rate is within a range between an upper and lower strike) and target accruals (where an amount is paid every period – until a 'target' limit on payoffs for the deal is reached).
- Cancellable trades. Any cap trade can have a cancellation feature – adding complexity to the modelling task.
- Rates paid at the wrong time, or in the wrong currency. A basic example of this is a so-called *arrears* trade, where the rate which is used to calculate the cap payment is the rate *at the time of payment*, not at the beginning of the payment period. Arrears payments must be put into a volatility adjustment, which is best done (though not always) within a robust modelling framework. Similarly, rates paid in the wrong currency (such as a USD cap on EURIBOR) need a *quanto* adjustment to be correct. Quanto corrections can be approximated (with some knowledge of FX volatility, correlation and a bit of self-confidence) but are typically best managed in a multi-currency modelling system.

Once we've started to use sophisticated models in a trading system, we'll usually want to engage in some sort of calibration procedure to ensure that we agree, in pricing, with the market.

13.9   Calibration of models and risk management of exotics

Whatever model we use, no matter how complex it is, it will require a certain amount of adjustment of inputs to agree with the market.

A complex pricing model can be thought of as simply a pricing formula with *extra inputs*. Realistically, if the pricing model had the same number of inputs as the Black model, it would *be* the Black model! This is because, to agree with the market, it would have very little choice of behaviour.

We could of course imagine a model which gives the same price, but different answers for delta, for instance. But even in this case, the level of difference would usually be set by a parameter. This parameter is an input – and must be set, calibrated and adjusted.

A calibration procedure, therefore, is simply *the adjusting of model parameters to ensure that a pricing model matches the market.*

Calibration can be performed either automatically (in the case of very stable procedures) or manually, on a schedule, perhaps. Manual calibration is useful if the model is complex and parameter estimation must be judged for correctness. Manual calibration has the disadvantage of becoming off-market over time, however. Auto-calibration allows models to easily track changing market conditions, at the expense of (possible) risk of destabilizing errors now and again.

Once we've calibrated our model, we should be able to use it to price (vanilla) caps and get the same answer as our Black model. We can then also use it to price more exotic options. One common approach for traders of portfolios of vanilla and exotic products is to keep all the models in each portfolio the same: keep all products in one portfolio on the exotic model and all options in another on the vanilla model.

This allows simpler risk management. Suppose I have two portfolios: one large portfolio of vanilla caps and floors, and one small portfolio of exotics. I can measure the (vega) risk of the small portfolio, and use a combination of caps and floors to neutralize that risk as much as possible. These vega hedges would all be booked on the exotic model in the exotic book.

I can then book the *same vega hedges* (but reversed, bought rather than sold, or vice versa) in the vanilla book. I have essentially sold myself the hedges, and put them in with all my other vanilla options. I can now continue trading the vanilla book (using whatever methods I used before) – and the exotic book can now be hedged more easily.

13.10   Swaptions

The other commonly traded interest rate product is the swaption. As mentioned at the start of the chapter, a swaption is an option to enter into an interest rate swap *in the future*. The swap can either be one where the buyer pays a fixed-rate in exchange for floating (a so-called *payer* swaption) or one in which the buyer receives fixed and pays floating (a *receiver*).

The swap entered into can be of a variety of tenors (durations): anywhere between 1 and 30 years, but most commonly between two and ten. Similarly, the expiration of the swaption can be anywhere between 1 month and 10 years. The start of the swap is equal to the trade date plus the expiration of the option plus the relevant spot day convention – the first period of the swap then starts accruing exactly when a swap traded on the expiration date would.

For any strike (or for ATM strikes) quotations for swaption volatility take the form of a matrix: along the top are the tenors of the underlying swap, and down the side the time to expiration of the option.

Table 13.5 shows examples of how a swaption volatility matrix is laid out typically (see, for instance, ICAP broker pages for good examples). The tenors, or swap durations, are laid out across the top, and the swaption expirations are along the left side. (The tenors can go out to 30 years (or more) and the expirations can go out to 20 years in some cases.)

But what is this the volatility *of*? Specifically, it was supposed to be the presumed volatility of the forward swap rate. As such, we need a variant

Table 13.5 An example of a swaption volatility matrix

	1Y swap (%)	2Y swap (%)	3Y swap (%)	...	5Y swap (%)	10Y swap (%)
1M expiration	52	49	45		25	23
2M	51	48	44		24	20
3M	49	46	43		24	19
6M	47	45	42		23	18
...						
5Y	40	38	36		17	15
10Y	23	21	20		15	14

of the Black model to price a swaption in this model – which looks pretty much like the other Black models we've seen. Here S_0 is the observed *forward* break-even swap rate at the time of pricing, and T is the time to expiration of the swaption (in years):

$$d_1(S_0, T) = \frac{\ln\left(\frac{S_0}{K}\right) + \frac{\sigma^2}{2}T}{\sigma\sqrt{T}} \quad \text{and} \quad d_2(S_0, T) = d_1(S_0, T) - \sigma\sqrt{T}$$

The price of the swaption is then:

$$P_{\text{payer-swaption}} = \left(S_0 N(d_1) - K N(d_2)\right) AL$$

$$P_{\text{receiver-swaption}} = \left(-S_0 N(-d_1) + K N(-d_2)\right) AL$$

Here, A is the notional, and L is the *swap level* (or basis-point value, or annuity value) of the swap:

$$L = \sum_{i=0}^{n} b_i D_i$$

where b is the basis-factor (day-count fraction) for each period, and D is the discount factor (using the appropriate discount curve).

This is the classic formula. It is, interestingly, often wrong, even within its own limited context (see next section). However, using this formula for quoted volatilities should recover quoted prices, and allow a simple interpolation method between points on the swaption matrix.

One small note: often the volatility is quoted as a so-called **basis-point volatility**, or 'BP vol'. Basis-point volatility is the standard Black volatility multiplied by the forward swap rate. So, if the volatility is 40 per cent, and the forward swap rate is 2 per cent, the basis-point volatility quoted would be 80.

13.11 The normal model

The reason basis-point volatility is quoted is that it is a good approximation for volatility in another pricing model: the normal model.

The normal model assumes that swap rates move according to a normal distribution – in a familiar *additive* manner. Log-normal prices move geometrically, a log-normally distributed variable has about the same chance of rising by a given factor as it does of falling by the reciprocal. A normally distributed variable would have the same chance of rising by a given amount – or falling by exactly the same amount. So, log-normally, if I start at 100, I would be (approximately) equally likely to reach 50 or 200 (multiplying or dividing by 2). Normally speaking, I would be equally likely to reach 50 or 150 (adding or subtracting 50).

Log-normally distributed variables can never go below zero, whereas normally distributed ones can. This was always seen as a problem for interest rates, but there have been historical examples of rates falling below zero.

The formula for the value of a payer swaption under the normal model is:

$$P_{\text{payer-swaption}} = AL\sigma_N\sqrt{T}\left(\frac{e^{\left(\frac{-d^2}{2}\right)}}{\sqrt{2\pi}} + dN(d)\right)$$

Here, d is defined as

$$d = \frac{S_0 - K}{\sigma_N\sqrt{T}}$$

Similarly, a receiver swaptions formula is:

$$P_{\text{receiver-swaption}} = AL\sigma_N\sqrt{T}\left(\frac{e^{\left(\frac{-d^2}{2}\right)}}{\sqrt{2\pi}} - dN(-d)\right)$$

The important thing to notice is that the volatility, σ_N, is *not* the same as the log-normal quoted volatility. This is the *normal* volatility – a completely different number. (Some other names for it include Gaussian volatility, or absolute volatility.) We can derive the normal volatility, if we wish, by finding the value of a swaption using quoted Black volatility and solving for the normal version – or we can use the formula:

$$
\sigma_N \approx \left(\frac{S_0 - K}{\ln\left(S_0 \big/ k \right)} \right) \sigma \left(1 + \sigma^2 \left(\tfrac{T}{24} \right) \right)
$$

When looking at ATM volatilities (where the strike and forward are the same), we can approximate this even more with the formula:

$$
\sigma_N \approx S_0 \sigma \left(1 + \sigma^2 \left(\tfrac{T}{24} \right) \right)
$$

If we ignore the last term (which is fairly small), we get:

$$
\sigma_N \approx S_0 \sigma
$$

which is precisely what is quoted in the market as BP vol. (Note, of course, the scaling factor used: a quote of '80' for BP vol might represent 40% multiplied by 2% – or, in other words, 0.0080.)

13.12   Straddle prices

In addition to quoting volatility and BP vol, we often see ATM *straddle prices* quoted for swaptions. A swaption straddle is simply the combination of a payer and a receiver swaption:

$$
P_{\text{straddle}} = P_{\text{payer}} + P_{\text{receiver}}
$$

We can easily use these straddle prices to infer either the log-normal or normal volatility (if we agree the forward rate). In the case of the normal model, since the forward and strike are the same, the formula is especially simple:

$$
P_{\text{straddle}} = AL\,\sigma_N \sqrt{2T/\pi}
$$

13.13   Finding the forward swap rate

The forward swap rate is an important part of the pricing of a swaption, but it's not a directly traded product. The forward swap rate is usually computed by finding the break-even rate for a swap which starts at a date in the future (corresponding to the expiration of the swaption contract). Computing the forward swap rate requires a good yield curve model and computer system to manipulate it. Even in this case, however, there's no guarantee that the forward swap rate you compute will match that found on the market.

Fortunately, often brokers will also supply implied forward swap rates with swaption quotes. When building a system, it's important to be able to have one's own models match the market – but only if the forward rates you're using are also the same. For this reason, in the swaption market at least, straddle prices provide a more stable platform on which to provide pricing. As the formula in the previous section shows, straddle prices don't depend on the forward rate directly – merely on volatility.

13.14 Cash versus physical settlement

Most swaptions on the inter-bank market are *cash-settled* in one way or another. This means that when the option expires, the holder of the option does not enter into a swap, but rather receives a cash amount representing the payout, as agreed in the standard documentation for the swaption.

In the United States (and Canada), this means that the parties must agree the yield curve between them, and value the market value of the swap at expiration. Essentially, the cash payment is the mark-to-market of the swap itself, which means the Black model approximation (above) is essentially self-consistent at least.

In Euroland and Great Britain, cash settlement means that the formula used is:

$$P = (S - K) \sum_{i=1}^{n} \frac{1}{f\left(1 + \dfrac{S}{f}\right)^i}$$

This is the case of a receiver swaption – payer swaptions would of course include $(K - S)$ in front. What this is saying is that we're assuming the swap is using simple discounting *at the swap rate itself*. In addition, swap valuation is simplified to make the formula easy to use (no explicit day-counting is done). This makes the process of settlement quite straightforward (only one rate needs to be referenced), but from a mathematical perspective it makes the formulas used somewhat incorrect. The Black model, in particular, cannot be easily reconciled with this payout profile.

In effect, the cash-settled swaption is an exotic derivative. The payout is a complex formula depending on the swap rate, which is merely approximated by the value of the swap at expiration. The value of a cash-settled swaption is easy to come to (see the broker screens!), but a robust model which values swaptions which are *not* directly quoted is harder to come by.

Specifically, if the broker screens are showing the values of cash-settled swaptions in EUR, what is the value of a physically settled swaption? Many will use the same model for both, which is not exactly correct.

13.15   Premium payment: at trade date or at option-expiration?

Swaption premia were, prior to 2007 or so, paid when the trade was agreed. Now, due to collateral effects and other difficulties, it has become popular to settle the premium at the expiration of the swaption. This means that essentially the value of the trade is zero at inception (like a swap) – and the collateralization will only accrue after the trade date as the variation margin requirements change.

This does make a difference in quotation. The swaption prices seen from brokers must be interpreted as prices *at expiration* or *at trade date* – depending. The screens should usually be clear as to which is indicated. When a forward premium is quoted, it is not discounted. This means that for the same swaption, forward premiums will be slightly larger for the same underlying trade.

13.16   Using swaptions in structured products

Swaptions are often used in conjunction with swaps. For instance, suppose you hold a 10-year vanilla interest rate swap in which you receive a fixed-rate. If you also then buy a 5-/5-year payer swaption (i.e. an option in 5 years to enter into a 5-year *payer* swap), then you've essentially given yourself the option to cancel your original swap.

Original swap: Pay LIBOR every 6 months for 10 years.
Original swap: Receive X per cent every 6 months for 10 years.
Swaption: Option in 5 years to Receive Libor every 6 months for 5 years.
Swaption: Option in 5 years to Pay X per cent every 6 months for 5 years.

If we exercise the swaption... then we essentially cancel out the swap.

The use of swaptions in this manner is very common as a way to provide insurance to swap counterparties. If someone enters into a swap, but is nervous about the interest rate market turning against them in the future, a swaption can provide some insurance (of a different sort than a cap).

What if we want to provide the option to cancel the swap at any time, however, not just once in the lifetime of the swap? The most common flavour of swaption used to do this is the so-called **Bermudan swaption**. Bermudans are so-called because Bermuda lies between Europe and America, and so is neither European (single-exercise) nor American (where one can exercise at any time). A Bermudan swaption can be exercised, typically, on a frequency that matches the swap payment frequency. So a Bermudan swaption on a swap that settles every 6 months, for instance, would allow the holder to exercise once every 6 months.

Bermudan swaptions exercise into a swap whose length keeps diminishing – the end date of the swap is *fixed*. So a 10-year Bermudan (with exercise dates every 6 months) would have the first exercise date allow one to enter into a 9.5-year swap, the second into a 9-year swap, the third into an 8.5-year swap and so on. The reason for this, of course, is that when combined with a swap, a Bermudan swaption allows the swap holder to cancel their swap at any coupon payment date.

Valuation of Bermudan swaptions (like other interest rate exotics) requires a calibrated model beyond the Black framework. There are a host of sources (and a host of disagreements) about the 'best' way to do this. Whatever model is used, however, the approach is the same: market prices for vanilla options are collected from the market, the model is then used to value these options and model parameters are adjusted until the model matches the market. The 'calibrated' model is then used to value both exotics and hedges.

13.17 Using caplet volatilities with swaptions

Can you mix cap and swaption volatilities? In general, no – they are different products, and different markets. However, in the previous section, we derived the volatilities for the individual caplets which comprise a cap. Each of these caplets is, in effect, a swap with a single period. We can then add these caplets as the first column in our swaption volatility (or swaption price) matrix.

Suppose each caplet is 6 months in duration. This represents a 6-month swap with one period. If the caplet expires in 2 years – then we can add the caplet volatility to the swaption matrix as that of a swaption, expiring in 2 years, with a 6-month duration.

13.18 What about smile and skew?

Swaptions, like caps, trade at many strikes, not just ATM.

There are broker screens which will provide quotations for swaptions at various strikes, often at popular expirations and tenors. The strikes for these swaptions, however, are fewer and farther between than the ATM strikes which we've used, for instance, in the cap-pricing world. There are many data sources, both broker pages (such as ICAP) available on Bloomberg and Reuters and less frequently updated sources, such as the inter-bank revaluation service called Totem, available from Markit.com.

In addition, we have (as mentioned in the previous section) the caplet volatilities, which are readily available in a selection of strikes. We can quickly expand the swaption matrix into a 'cube' of prices or volatilities by adding the caplet volatilities as a first column in each strike. We can then fill a (perhaps sparse) selection of prices-by-strike for a selection of expirations and tenors.

Interpolation to missing expirations and tenors (or missing strikes) is more difficult. We'll see in the next section that most interpolation is usually done with complex formulas.

The swaption volatility profile is a *cube* of numbers. If we are quoting ten different expirations, with ten possible swap tenors and ten different strikes, that means we must keep track of 1,000 different prices or volatilities. In practice, not all of these points in the cube will be very much traded. This means that the points themselves were probably interpolated or extrapolated by banks or brokerages at some point. The liquid points in the cube will usually correspond to the most common pairings of option-expiration and tenor: 1y/5y, 2y/5y, 1y/10y, 5y/10y and a few others. In Euros, for instance, swap tenors of 2, 10 and 30 years are quite

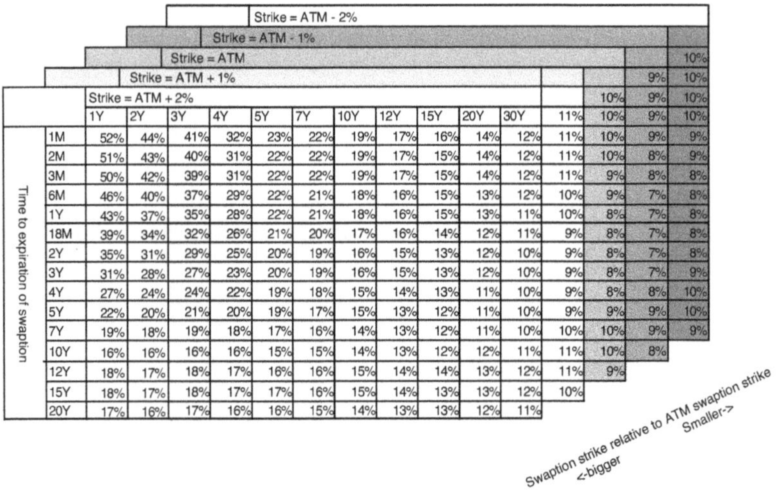

Strike = ATM - 2%
Strike = ATM - 1%
Strike = ATM
Strike = ATM + 1%
Strike = ATM + 2%

	1Y	2Y	3Y	4Y	5Y	7Y	10Y	12Y	15Y	20Y	30Y
1M	52%	44%	41%	32%	23%	22%	19%	17%	16%	14%	12%
2M	51%	43%	40%	31%	22%	22%	19%	17%	15%	14%	12%
3M	50%	42%	39%	31%	22%	22%	19%	17%	15%	14%	12%
6M	46%	40%	37%	29%	22%	21%	18%	16%	15%	13%	12%
1Y	43%	37%	35%	28%	22%	21%	18%	16%	15%	13%	11%
18M	39%	34%	32%	26%	21%	20%	17%	16%	14%	12%	11%
2Y	35%	31%	29%	25%	20%	19%	16%	15%	13%	12%	10%
3Y	31%	28%	27%	23%	20%	19%	16%	15%	13%	12%	10%
4Y	27%	24%	24%	22%	19%	18%	15%	14%	13%	11%	10%
5Y	22%	20%	21%	20%	19%	17%	15%	13%	12%	11%	10%
7Y	19%	18%	19%	18%	17%	16%	14%	13%	12%	11%	10%
10Y	16%	16%	16%	16%	15%	15%	14%	13%	12%	12%	11%
12Y	18%	17%	18%	17%	16%	16%	15%	14%	14%	13%	12%
15Y	18%	17%	18%	17%	17%	16%	15%	14%	13%	13%	12%
20Y	17%	16%	17%	16%	16%	15%	14%	13%	13%	12%	11%

Time to expiration of swaption

Swaption strike relative to ATM swaption strike
<-bigger   Smaller->

Figure 13.1   A visualization of the three dimensions of swaption volatility

liquid, paired with most expirations, provided the combination (tenor + expiration) is not ridiculous.

Figure 13.1 shows a small portion of the swaption cube. In reality, we might quote strikes (in a liquid currency such as USD or EUR) at ±4 per cent, ±3 per cent, ±2 per cent, ±1.5 per cent, ±1 per cent, ±0.5 per cent, ±0.25 per cent and ATM, giving 15 different levels of 'moneyness'.

The swaption market differs from the cap market in that the skews are measured in relation to the ATM levels. In the cap market, the ATM caps are a separate quotation – the ATM levels for caps vary daily, and the cap volatility 'matrix' is a fixed-strike table. In the world of swaptions, the swaption quotations are all done with respect to the ATM levels, making the ATM quotes part of the cube itself.

13.19   Choosing between normal and log-normal

In the prior sections we introduced the log-normal, Black model and the normal, Gaussian model for pricing swaptions. Neither model is perfect – and both are very unsophisticated. Most trading desks will use sophisticated models to price their complex trades (such as LMM or other parameterized, calibrated models) and a simple approach for the books of vanilla trades.

It should be obvious that, from a pricing perspective, it does not matter whether we use the Black model or the Gaussian model: with the correct parameters both will give the same price. The problem comes (as we will see) when computing risk – values for delta, gamma and vega will differ significantly.

One issue that arises is the sensitivity of volatility to movements in the forward rate. If the swaption market is behaving in a Gaussian (normal) way, then as the forward rate goes down the log-normal volatility would go up. This is simple to imagine: since the log-normal volatility is related to a percentage change in the rate, if the expected change remains constant as the rate goes down, the percentage change will increase. In other words:

$$\text{Since } \sigma_N \approx S_0\,\sigma, \text{ then if } \sigma_N \text{ is constant, } \sigma \text{ is proportional to } \frac{1}{S_0}$$

This means that if rates are behaving in a Gaussian way, then lower rates induce higher volatilities – a so-called skew effect. Similarly, if the log-normal volatility is constant – the Gaussian volatilities would decrease for lower rates.

We do notice, in the market, a real skew effect. In addition, we can measure the correlation (historically) between forward rates and volatilities to see if there is any 'normal' component to their movement. Usually the answer seems to be that the real world expects us to use something in between.

13.20 SABR in a nutshell

The most accepted model in the markets today for evaluating swaption portfolios is the SABR model. This model was developed around 2002 by Patrick Hagan (and collaborators) as a type of so-called *stochastic volatility* model – a model where the volatility itself is volatile. While complex in formulation, using the model is actually quite simple.

The important thing to know about SABR is that it does not require us to stop using the Black model, or even the normal model. The SABR model's primary purpose, when applied to vanilla options, is to supply a volatility for any level of forward swap rate or strike.

In other words: SABR is a way to calibrate the volatility smile. Given four parameters (*alpha, beta, rho* and *nu*), we can use SABR to produce an estimated volatility for a wide range of strikes. Used this way, SABR allows us to use any model we wish for pricing – the SABR model will give us a way to produce log-normal volatilities as a function of strike and forward rate:

$$\sigma_{SABR}(S,K) = F(\alpha, \beta, \rho, v, S, K)$$

The function F is the SABR function, which appears in full in Hagan's paper[1], and can be approximated by the formula:

$$\sigma_{SABR}(S,K) = \frac{\alpha}{S^{1-\beta}}\left(1 - \frac{1}{2}(1-\beta-\rho\lambda)\ln\left(\frac{K}{S}\right) + \frac{1}{12}\left((1-\beta)^2 + (2-3\rho^2)\lambda^2\right)\ln^2\left(\frac{K}{S}\right)\right)$$

Here

$$\lambda = \frac{v}{\alpha}S^{1-\beta}$$

It's not recommended to use this formula as a replacement for full SABR, but it gives an idea of the dynamics of the model.

The first thing to notice is the parameters: alpha, beta, rho and nu. (SABR itself is short for 'stochastic alpha-beta-rho', curiously one parameter too few.) Alpha, the first parameter, represents (broadly speaking, not exactly) the level of ATM volatility. Beta is the *mixing* parameter – it tells us what mixture of normal and log-normal dynamics we wish to use. A beta of zero implies a pure normal model, while a beta of 1 is pure log-normal. Rho is the correlation parameter, giving the correlation between the two random processes we're representing (i.e. the random movement of the rate, and the random movement of the rate's volatility itself). The final parameter, nu, is the *volatility of volatility*, the randomness of the volatility process itself.

The parameters for SABR are fitted from market data – so we need to have access to some swaption volatility quotations for different strikes: both at-the-money and away-from-the-money. The parameters can be fitted separately for different combinations of swaption expiration and tenor.

The exception to this is the *beta* parameter. Beta is usually picked before-hand, by choosing the 'best' value. As we mentioned, beta is a stand-in for the mixture between Gaussian (normal) and log-normal dynamics. A beta of zero means a pure Gaussian model, and a beta of one means a pure log-normal model. Beta can be picked in several ways, either by 'feel' (using a value such as 0.5, for instance) or by historical estimation (by looking at the correlation between volatility and forward rates) or by more complex methods (e.g. looking at the market for constant-maturity-swap swaps).

Once we've chosen a value for beta, and then used some approach to fit values for alpha, rho and nu, we can see how the SABR model performs. Not surprisingly, it fits market data quite well when given only a few points, in a sort of skewed-parabola way.

Perhaps the most interesting thing about SABR (and one of the reasons we don't just fit our volatilities with a simple parabola, or kernel inter-polation) is that it depends on both strike and forward rate. In a vanilla interpolation scheme (such as we might use with FX volatilities) we would simply look at the strike of our option relative to the ATM point, and choose the appropriate volatility from the curve. Under SABR, the curve itself moves with movements of the ATM point – making it somewhat more interesting.

Figure 13.2 shows a sample SABR calibration (using a low value of β – 0.1) for three different levels of the forward rate. The middle curve is the original – it's the curve we used to arrive at the calibration param-eters. The other curves show what happens when we move the forward rate up and down by ½ per cent: under this almost-purely Gaussian regime, the volatilities also increase as the forward goes down. (We've used a large smile in this example for effect: real curves may look a bit different.)

If we change the beta parameter to 1 (which assumes a purely log-normal world) the SABR results change dramatically (see Figure 13.3).

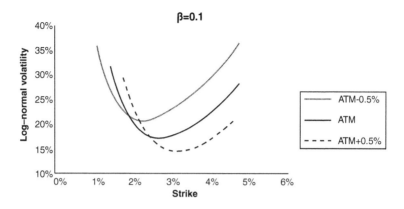

Figure 13.2   Swaption volatility by strike using SABR calibration with low beta

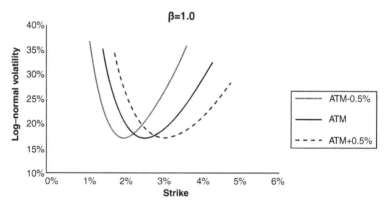

Figure 13.3   Swaption volatility by strike for beta of 1.0 – a log-normal world

We can see that the actual ATM curve is largely the same under both regimes, but the curves where the forward is shifted are quite different.

The key thing to notice is that, unsurprisingly, when beta is 1, the ATM volatility is a constant: the lowest part of each curve is at the same point. When beta is near zero, the at-the-money point increases as rates decrease.

13.21   Estimating parameters: fitting SABR

For each point in the ATM swaption matrix, we may have available quotations for away-from-the-money strikes as well. (If not available for a given point, we can also interpolate these values.) We can use these to estimate the levels for alpha, rho and nu using one of several fitting algorithms.

Since SABR is a complex function, we can't use any simple linear methods. We have to use what is called non-linear least-squares regression. This is one of the most delicate procedures: since we're trying to basically poke around in the dark for parameter values, we need to have an algorithm that will somehow intelligently let us find them.

The parameter estimate will be chosen to minimize the least-squares error from the function when evaluating the specific 'input' points. Specifically, suppose we have five known volatilities at different strikes – we'll use these values as inputs to the calibration function. The calibrator will then find the parameter values such that SABR will match these five points to the lowest level of least-squares difference – minimizing the function:

$$\sum_{i=1}^{5}\left(\sigma_{\text{SABR}}(S,K_i)-\sigma_i\right)^2$$

There are a host of algorithms used for parameter estimation. One popular approach is the so-called *Levenberg–Marquardt* method. Levenberg–Marquardt is fairly involved, but it is a well-understood and fairly robust parameter estimation procedure. It's available as a built-in function in MATLAB, Mathematica, GNU Octave (a free MATLAB-like system), SciPy (the python language add-on) and free for download source code exists as well.[2]

Once the parameter estimation code is in place, all you need is the SABR model (packaged in some convenient form) to hand to it. The parameter estimator will have to invoke the SABR model thousands of times, until the parameters it has chosen allow it to match the market smile/skew volatilities as exactly as possible.

One thing we might want to do, especially, is match the ATM volatility exactly. We can do this in two ways: we can put a weighting factor in the error function above, to explicitly overweight the ATM point, or we can rewrite the SABR function to explicitly match the ATM volatility. Part of the SABR formula (in Hagan's paper) is a relationship showing the ATM volatility as a function of the parameters, which is a simpler formula than the full SABR expression. In searching for a minimum, then, one could rewrite SABR to not take alpha as a parameter, but rather to find alpha, given the ATM volatility. SABR then becomes a function of strike, forward and ATM volatility. (Needless to say, although not guaranteed to be as accurate, overweighting the ATM point is faster.)

Rewriting SABR in this way has the advantage of not requiring frequent recalibrations. If we replace alpha in the inputs with the ATM vol:

$$\sigma_{\text{SABR}}(S,K)=F(\sigma_{\text{ATM}},\beta,\rho,\nu,S,K)$$

SABR becomes a function which only needs recalibrating when the away-from-the-money points change. We may only wish to perform that particular recalibration once or twice per day. This makes using SABR much easier, and allow something closer to real-time evaluation of price and risk for portfolios of swaptions.

13.22   A brief introduction to CMS

One final set of semi-vanilla instruments are worth mentioning – products built around the so-called CMS rate. There are several of these, with the simplest being the CMS swap and the CMS cap or floor.

CMS is simply the swap rate as quoted at a particular time. Swap rates are collected by organizations involved in creating 'fixing' indices (such as, in this case, ISDA and the ISDAFIX product). Each day there will be an official swap fixing rate for a range of maturities, in a range of currencies. So one can see the 10-year EUR swap rate fixing, the 5-year JPY swap rate and so on.

A CMS swap is simply a swap in which this CMS rate replaces the *fixed* side of the swap (usually). So, for instance, a 5Y swap against 10Y CMS would have the following properties:

- Duration of swap: 5-years.
- Floating leg pays every: 3-months (unless otherwise specified).
- Quoted spread paid against floating leg.
- CMS leg pays every 3-months the 10Y swap rate, on the same basis as the floating leg.

So if a 5-year EUR swap on 10-year CMS is quoted as '20', this means the receiver of CMS will get (CMS – (LIBOR+20)) paid to them (or paid by them, if negative) every 3-months, on the LIBOR basis.

However CMS is used, it is not a simple instrument. The main reason for this is convexity. If we imagine that the LIBOR rate we're using for the swap is volatile, it's natural to see that in the future, if LIBOR goes up, the value of swap payments (in a plain, fixed-rate swap) would go down. (This is assuming that we're discounting on a curve which is perfectly correlated with LIBOR, of course.)

Continuing this exercise, if we imagine that LIBOR goes up, we can see that the CMS swap rate in the future would go up as well. If we were to pay the CMS swap payments at the time they were meant to be paid, this would be fine, but we're instead simply using the CMS rate as an index. We have no reason to expect that the effect of volatility will be negligible, rather we should expect that as volatility increases, we'll have to adjust any expected forward swap rate by some formula.

Without volatility, pricing a CMS swap would be straightforward: for each period (using an appropriate yield curve model) generate a break-even swap rate based on the start of the period, and use it as an index for payment.

With volatility, we need to include a convexity adjustment in order to 'fix' the problem. The problem is that to compute the convexity adjustment properly, you really need some quite advanced techniques. That doesn't stop people from using the old approaches, however. The standard 'conventional' adjustment still can be considered to offer at least a step in the right direction.

$$CMS = CMS_0 - \frac{CMS_0^2}{2}\sigma^2 T\left(\frac{\frac{d^2}{dS^2}f(S_0)}{\frac{d}{dS}f(S_0)}\right)$$

Here S_0 is the CMS rate (as plucked from the yield curve), T is the time to payment of the CMS rate (from today) and σ is the volatility of the swap rate itself, as observed today. (The volatility of the swap rate is, of course, the swaption volatility – a readily available number.) The function f is defined as:

$$f(S) = \sum_{i=1}^{n} \frac{DS_0 d}{(1+S)^{\tau_i}}$$

In this formula, d is the day-count fraction for one period, τ is the day-count from the start to the end of period i and D is the discount factor to the payment time.

What does this assume? Well, firstly it assumes that the swap is discounted at its own swap rate (a dubious assumption). Secondly, it assumes pure log-normal dynamics for the swap rate (also, as we have seen, not something that's universally agreed). Nonetheless, we can use this adjustment as a first-order approximation, and compare it with what we see in the market. There are numerous sources of more sophisticated modelling techniques for CMS (it's one of the most written about fields in the quant literature).

13.23 Risk measurement for interest rate options: vega risk

In Chapter 5 we looked at measuring simple delta and gamma in interest rate portfolios. This approach to risk measurement, while quite simple, works for most vanilla options portfolios as well. There are some caveats (see the section on SABR delta), but the overall approach of measuring delta and gamma by externally perturbing the yield curve is quite valid.

Vega for interest rate option portfolios can also follow this approach. As with vega for equities and FX, interest rate vega can (if desired) be calculated by a bumping methodology.

Caps and floors can use input-rate bumping, if the interpolation scheme is simple. If using SABR, however, there are other concerns.

One issue is that, under SABR, the volatility is closely bound to strike and forward levels, and making assumptions about the level with which to 'bump' would be inappropriate. Hagan[3] in his paper on SABR recommends instead bumping the *alpha* parameter to the SABR model directly to get an estimate of vega. Since vega is usually measured with respect to a 1 per cent change in the ATM volatility, the result would then be scaled by the ratio of the sensitivity of the volatility at a given strike to alpha, over the sensitivity of the ATM volatility to alpha. Perhaps it makes more sense written out:

$$\text{Vega} \equiv \frac{dV}{d\alpha} = \frac{dV}{d\sigma_B} \left(\frac{\dfrac{d\sigma_B}{d\alpha}}{\dfrac{d\sigma_{\text{ATM}}}{d\alpha}} \right)$$

Here σ_B represents the Black model volatility at a given strike, whereas σ_{ATM} represents the ATM volatility as computed via the SABR model.

To the first-order, this can be approximated by simply bumping the 'output' volatility from the SABR model, and scaling the vega result by the ratio of the strike-adjusted SABR volatility to the ATM SABR volatility. As Hagan says, we are using proportional, not parallel, shifts of the volatility surface to compute vega.

13.24   SABR delta

Since volatility is a function of spot, the delta and vega become compounded when computing risk in a SABR world. In a totally Black world, this would be irrelevant, since a change in spot would mean no change due to the model to the ATM volatility. If the SABR model has a normal component, however, things change.

There are two formulas for SABR-adjusted delta: one for use when alpha is parameter we fit directly, and one for use when alpha is computed as a function of the ATM volatility. The first is straightforward (in abbreviated form):

$$\text{delta} = \frac{\delta V}{\delta f} + \frac{\delta V}{\delta \sigma} \left(\frac{\delta \sigma}{\delta f} \right)$$

Here σ is the SABR volatility, and as such is a function of the underlying rate (*f*). The first term is simply the delta as computed normally (by shifting the forward in the pricing function), the second term is the 'SABR delta-vega effect', which gives the vega impact of a change in spot. In this equation, we're looking at partial derivatives, of course, which makes the estimation simpler. To estimate $\delta\sigma / \delta f$ for instance, we need only revalue the SABR volatility function for a small shift in the forward rate, *f*.

As mentioned in the section on SABR, some practitioners prefer to explicitly use the ATM volatility instead of the alpha parameter in the SABR model, to avoid over-frequent recalibration, among other things. In this case, another term appears:

$$\text{delta} = \frac{\delta V}{\delta f} + \frac{\delta V}{\delta \sigma}\left(\frac{\delta \sigma}{\delta f} + \frac{\delta \sigma}{\delta \alpha}\left(\frac{\delta \alpha}{\delta f}\right)\right)$$

Hagan mentions in his paper in which he introduces SABR that this delta representation may be superior in some markets – suffice to say that trader experience is required to understand the best representation.

13.25 Profit and loss (P&L)

One report most traders see every day is the 'profit and loss attribution report'. This report should, in theory, explain the change in value of the trading book from one day to the next.

For a book of delta-one, cash instruments, this is straightforward. The components of P&L are, basically:

- P&L due to new trades, consisting of, for each trade (closing price – purchase price) × Position.
- P&L due to existing positions, consisting of (closing price – opening price) × Position.
- Any cash-flow adjustments. If a trade (such as a swap) pays cash out or in, then this must be accounted for. Maturing trades have their final cash-flow to account for.
- Any adjustments due to carry (i.e. funding costs).

When we combine options into a portfolio, the list expands:

- Delta effect – like P&L due to existing positions – accounts for the delta position of options.
- Gamma effect. P&L due to gamma is the *integral* of the change in delta over the change in the underlying price (or rate) (see below).
- Vega effect. P&L due to the change in volatility.

- Theta. Theta and carry are often measured together for options port-folios.
- Un-accounted for P&L. And residual P&L must also be listed. A large residual P&L can indicate problems with options models, or with the level of detail in the P&L report itself! If the traders are on top of the position, they may demand a finer-grained P&L report which mirrors their management strategy – by, for instance

Delta effect is quite straightforward – simply the delta 'position' times the change in price. Gamma effect, as mentioned, is the integral over the change in price. Just as gamma is the second derivative – so now, to get the 'effect' we must integrate. So gamma P&L becomes:

$$\text{Gamma P\&L} = \frac{1}{2}\Gamma\Delta_p^{\,2}$$

where Δ_p is the change in the underlying price, and of course Γ is gamma.

Gamma P&L only makes sense for small variations away from the start-ing price, of course, since gamma is simply an approximation at one point. The P&L explained report at this level is quite basic, but sometimes useful nonetheless.

P&L reports are typically based on rate levels as observed at the start and end-of-day. They will often be the same thing.

- *End-of-day* rates will be the rates collected at a given time near the end of trading hours. In banks, a small department is usually responsible for this process, since the rates must be collected at the same time, and checked for consistency. If we collected FX rates and interest rates at different times, for instance, we could end up with discrepancies in prices for cross-currency trades.
- *Start-of-day* rates can often be the end-of-day rates from the day before, applied to a pricing environment one day forward.

One can then estimate the P&L effect of moving from the rate environ-ment of one day to the next. What this does not do is tell the story of *how* we got from one day to the next. If the difference in rates is large, it could result in P&L changes not entirely captured by the report.

What does a large residual P&L mean?

The problem of residual P&L is inherent in P&L reports for complex port-folios. Since the report will only (usually) estimate the cause of the P&L

shift based on the risk numbers at the start of the day, a large change in rates could lead to an incomplete story being told.

The traders, in fact, could hedge most of the risk during the day, but still the report may not capture it.

Position	Value (start-of-day – or at trade inception)	Value (end-of-day)	Delta effect	Gamma effect	Residual P&L
Trade 1	100	110	3	2	5
Trade 2	0	–10	–3	–2	–5
Total	100	100	0	0	0

Here, for instance, a trader has done a new trade (Trade 2) which hedges Trade 1 quite well. The recorded delta and gamma from the original, un-hedged trade interfere with the story of the successful hedge. If we record the delta effect, however, from when the hedge trade was done, it looks a little better

Position	Value (start-of-day)	Value (end-of-day)	Delta effect	Gamma effect	Residual P&L
Trade 1	100	110	3	2	5
Trade 2	(none – new)	–10	n/a	n/a	n/a
Total	100	100	3	2	–5

We still have residual, unexplained P&L, but this is neutralized by the fact that the portfolio is hedged. Reporting in this way is more complex, of course, since we must evaluate the rate environment at the inception of each new trade, and compute the delta/gamma effect differently for new trades.

In a derivatives portfolio, the largest sources of residual P&L tend to be in imperfectly hedged portfolios, where there are complex cross-effects between the input rates. For instance, if a trade is sensitive to the second derivative of volatility (called *volga* sensitivity), or if it is sensitive to changes in both underlying rate and volatility (more so than to either one individually – called *vanna* sensitivity). Volga and vanna can be reported separately, but if not, their effect will show up in the residual P&L for each trade, and if not hedged, their effect will show up in the overall P&L.

Further reading

Bartlett, B. (n.d.) 'Hedging under SABR Model', *Wilmott Magazine*.
Fabio Mercurio, D. B. (2006) *Interest Rate Models – Theory and Practice*, Springer Finance.

Graeme West, L. W. (n.d.) 'Introduction to Black's Model for Interest Rate Derivatives', *www.finmod.co.za*.

Hagan, P. S. (March/April 2003) 'Convexity Conundrums: Pricing CMS Swaps, Caps, and Floors', *Wilmott Magazine*.

Henrard, M. (2011) 'Swaptions: 1 Price, 10 Deltas, and...6 1/2 Gammas', *Wilmott Magazine*.

Henrard, M. (n.d.) 'Cash Settled Swaptions: How Wrong are We?', *Available at SSRN: http://ssrn.com/abstract=1703846*.

Obloj, J. (n.d.) 'Fine Tune your Smile', *arXiv:0708.0998 (http://arxiv.org/abs/0708.0998v3)*.

Patrick Hagan, D. K. (2002) 'Managing Smile Risk', *Wilmott Magazine*.

Notes

1 The Structure of an Investment Bank

1. The Basel II Accords are guidelines which individual governments use to set banking regulation. Basel II concentrates on, among other things, defining the amount of capital banks must hold. It has slowly come into force in most jurisdictions in the decade up to 2010.
2. Sell-side means, basically, those who sell investment products: banks, mostly. Buy-side means hedge funds, investment funds, corporations and everyone else.
3. *Silo* is management-speak for 'department or division which has limited communication with other departments or divisions within the organization'. Many banks, unfortunately, are made up almost entirely of silos.
4. *The International Swap Dealers Association, Inc. ISDA members are* major international swap dealers. ISDA defines the standard master swap agreements and confirmation templates, published as the *Code of Standard Wording, Assumptions and Provisions for Swaps.*

2 Interest Rate Swaps

1. From the Bank for International Settlements, '*OTC derivatives market activity in the first half of 2012*' – interest rate contracts represented $494 trillion dollars in notional value.
2. IMM stands for the International Monetary Market. IMM was created in the 1970s as a division of the Chicago Mercantile Exchange (CME), primarily for trading futures contracts and options on futures.

3 An Introduction to the Interest Rate Yield Curve

1. This is not easy, and enters the realm of 'exotic derivatives' in terms of valuation complexity.

4 The Mechanics of Simple Yield Curve Construction

1. Asset managers in Europe who manage ETFs or other UCITS funds, as of 2013, are required to return to investors any revenues gained from stock lending. This removes one of the 'hidden fees' that asset managers relied on for quite some time (see http://www.esma.europa.eu/news/ESMA-publishes-ETF-guidelines-and-consults-repo-arrangements).
2. Delivery versus payment – where securities and cash are exchanged as one transaction. Most major electronically supported markets have this feature; however, it is not global.
3. Generally payment of variation margin is governed by agreements on rounding (amounts are rounded to the nearest, say, $1000), thresholds (a de-minimus amount below which no adjustments are made) and MTA (minimum transfer amount, a de-minimus amount for transfers).

4. See www.isla.co.uk, the International Securities Lending Association, for the GMSLA in PDF form. It is surprisingly easy to read.

9 Government Bonds

1. TARGET, or more precisely TARGET2, is the main European central bank settlement system. Holidays are generally referenced to its minimal holiday calendar and include New Year's Day, Good Friday, Easter Monday, Labour Day (1 May), Christmas (25 December), and 'Christmas Holiday' (26 December).
2. US Federal Reserve FEDWIRE holidays are, as per Operating Circular 7, New Year's Day (1 January), Martin Luther King's Birthday (third Monday in January), President's Day (third Monday in February), Memorial Day (last Monday in May), Independence Day (4 July), Labor Day (first Monday in September), Columbus Day (second Monday in October), Veterans' Day (11 November), Thanksgiving Day (fourth Thursday in November), and Christmas Day (December 25). If 1 January, 4 July, 11 November, or 25 December fall on a Sunday, the next following Monday is a standard Reserve Bank holiday.
3. UK Bank Holidays are, in other words: New Years' Day (or first weekday thereafter), Good Friday, Easter Monday, the first and last Mondays in May, the last Monday in August, Christmas Day, and Boxing Day (or first weekdays thereafter), as well as various ad-hoc holidays such as royal celebrations.
4. See www.boj.or.jp for the complete list.
5. See 'Valid Calculation Types', available from Bloomberg.
6. See http://www.dmo.gov.uk/index.aspx?page=Gilts/formulae
7. It's useful to read all the variations on repo transaction embodied in the Global Master Repurchase Agreement (GMRA) which can be found at http://www.asifma.org/pdf/GMRA.pdf.
8. See GMRA Gilts Annex, available from bankofengland.co.uk
9. The GMRA states that transaction exposure is typically adjusted by any coupons paid, and any prior margin amount which may have been paid or received.
10. Expected price doesn't mean the price we might forecast for a bond – we can't see the future. It is, rather, the future price of the bond we can arrive at by entering into repo and other agreements – it is the price we can 'fix' for the bond in the future. We can use this future price to determine our current financial position, but not to forecast our future state.
11. UK Gilts have special accrued interest calculations for the 7 business days before a coupon date. During this period, they trade 'ex dividend', meaning that the seller of the bond retains the coupon. The seller, however, will recompense the buyer by an appropriate amount for lost interest during what remains of the 7 days. This results, effectively, in negative accrued interest during this period.
12. Japanese convention is to ignore leap days, assuming all years have 365 days.
13. Canadian convention is to assume all coupon periods are 182.5 days long.
14. All bonds with an unexpired term less than 3 years settle in 2 days; all other bonds settle in three.

10 Corporate Bonds, Credit Spreads and Credit Default Swaps

1. See http://ftalphaville.ft.com/blog/2012/03/09/916321/ok-guys-hands-up-who-booked-the-weird-greece-cds-trades/ for a real-world example worth reading about.

2. Notice that we said *risk-free rate*. Typically bonds are valued in spread over LIBOR, and many discussions will confute LIBOR with the risk-free rate. For purposes of this discussion, we can assume that they are the same if desired – it makes no difference. However, many will prefer to think of OIS as a better proxy for risk-free.

11   Vanilla Options

1. Computing the delta, if you've computed the option value using Black–Scholes, is extremely easy. One of the intermediate terms, one may recall, is $N(d_1)S$ (see equation earlier in this chapter). This term represents the *forward delta* (the sensitivity with respect to the forward price), or, if multiplied by the ratio of spot/forward, the *spot delta*.

13   Vanilla Interest Rate Options

1. 'Managing Smile Risk', Hagan et al., 2002, available at http://www.math.columbia.edu/~lrb/sabrAll.pdf
2. See, for instance, http://devernay.free.fr/hacks/cminpack/index.html
3. Managing Smile Risk, Hagan et al., see notes.

Index

Printed and bound in Great Britain by
CPI Group (UK) Ltd, Croydon, CR0 4YY